SIXTH EDITION

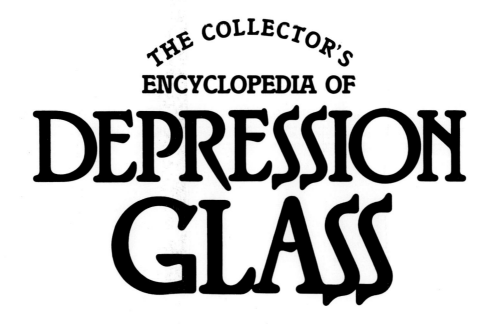

THE COLLECTOR'S ENCYCLOPEDIA OF DEPRESSION GLASS

By Gene Florence

COLLECTOR BOOKS
P.O. Box 3009
Paducah, KY 42001

The current values in this book should be used only as a guide. They are not intended to set prices, which vary from one section of the country to another. Auction prices as well as dealer prices vary greatly and are affected by condition as well as demand. Neither the Author nor the Publisher assumes responsibility for any losses that might be incurred as a result of consulting this guide.

Additional copies of this book may be ordered from:

COLLECTOR BOOKS
P.O. Box 3009
Paducah, Kentucky 42001

or

Gene Florence
P.O. Box 22186
Lexington, Kentucky 40522

@$17.95 Add $1.00 for postage and handling.

ACKNOWLEDGEMENTS

It was almost a pleasure to write this sixth edition book! The work involved makes that "almost" qualification necessary; but, you see, I almost wasn't here among the living to write it! After 41 shows and 51,000 miles of driving in 1982, I came to a nearly "dead" stop for the first 30 days of 1983, lying in a hospital room fighting to get "well enough" to be operated on for 18 gallstones I never knew I had, but which iritated my pancreas enough that it tried to eat me alive! Needless to say, I'm grateful to be alive through God's grace and the skills of a whole team of doctors (each of whom presented bills in accordance with his outstanding service); but I'm also running two and a half months behind schedule which is making for a horrendous upheaval in our lives to meet this book deadline!

I will be cutting back on some of my show travels in the future; and I've even scheduled a VACA-TION for myself and my family this year (between shows, of course); anyway, I hope you will understand my taking it easier for a while. Life becomes a whole new, shining discovery when you almost lose it! I intend to "smell some roses" from here on and to, hopefully, deal with my family and my fellowman as, if not a "better" man, a more "appreciative" one.

My wife, Cathy, has taken on more and more responsibilities, seeing we make deadlines, etc. She has always acted as editor, typist and translator for the hieroglyfics I inscribe as "notes"; but she's helped in a thousand more ways than that in getting this book together. We both owe our sons, Chad and Marc, thanks for the numerous tasks they performed in our stead and for the prodding, "When are you going to get that book done so we can . . .!" Thanks, too, to "Grannie Bear" who packed box after box of glass from the shop for the photography session, and who then had to unpack it all again when we came home! Also, there are Dad, Charles, Sib and Marie who hold things together here when we travel. I am indeed blessed!

Glass and information for this book were furnished by Earl and Beverly Hines (lovely, generous people who allowed us access to their collection); Kelly and Priscilla McBride; Tim and Bobbi Florence (who lent the glass for the cover); Kenn and Margaret Whitmyer; Nancy Maben; Benjamin Swann; Lou Ann Whitaker; Joe Reese; Lucille Kennedy formerly of Imperial Glass Corp.; Lloyd Thrush, Barbara Wolf and Philip Bee of Anchor Hocking Glass Corp.

Photographs for this book were made by Dana Curtis of Curtis and Mays Studio in Paducah, Ziegfried Kurz, and Janet Boyer of the Anchor Hocking photography lab. The drudgery of "on your knees work" at the photography session was performed by Steve Quertermous, Jane Fryberger, Bill Schroeder, Beverly Hines, Daisey Swanner and Cathy Florence. Only those who have engaged in these marathon photography sessions can truly appreciate the gigantic effort behind the quantity and quality of glass shown herein.

If I have inadvertently left someone out of the acknowledgements who helped, please know that I am not unappreciative of your aid. I keep saying that since my hospitalization, some of my memory cells seem to have died. My wife says I'm just getting forgetful!

As we go to press on this sixth edition, I sincerely wish to thank you, my readers, for making this the best selling glass book in America!

FOREWORD

There have been changes in the collecting of Depression glass since my first book was sold in '72, some 250,000 copies ago! Prices have soared; seemingly plentiful patterns have been secreted into vast collections and wiped from the market place; heretofore inconsequential Depression patterns and previously ignored crystal colors have picked up buyers; indeed, ANYTHING that is Depression glass, be it a particular pattern or not, suddenly has added value and collectibility. (Even that first book, I'm told, in its pristine condition, is bringing $80.00-$100.00; and no, I don't had any left)! Collectors have become vastly more knowledgeable and sophisticated in their collecting. They're quicker to spot and part with money for a good piece of glass; many are enhancing their collections of "A to W" (Adam to Windsor) with patterns chosen from kitchenwares and better glasswares of that same time frame. This broadening of interest on the part of collectors prompted me to research and write two more books on the field of Depression glass, one on the KITCHENWARE items to be found during that era, and one on the more ELEGANT glassware of the time. A few patterns, such as those made by Fostoria and Cambridge Glass Company, have been moved from this book into their rightful place as "Elegant" glassware. In their stead, I have placed some other glass patterns generally more suited to the overall make-up of this book.

Depression Glass as defined in this book is the colored glassware made primarily during the Depression years in the colors of amber, green, pink, red, blue, yellow, white and crystal. There are other colors and some glass made before, as well as after, this time frame; but primarily, the glass within this book was made from the 1920's through the 1930's. This book is mostly concerned with the inexpensively made glassware turned out by machine in quantity and sold through the five and dime stores or given away as promotional inducements to buy other products during that era known as The Depression.

Information for this book has come via research, experience, fellow dealers and collectors and over 425,000 miles of travel pursuant to glassware. Too, some of the more interesting information has come from readers who were kind enough to share their photographs and special knowledge with me. These gestures I particularly treasure.

PRICING

ALL PRICES IN THIS BOOK ARE RETAIL PRICES FOR MINT CONDITION GLASSWARE. THIS BOOK IS INTENDED TO BE ONLY A GUIDE TO PRICES AS THERE ARE SOME REGIONAL PRICE DIFFERENCES WHICH CANNOT REASONABLY BE DEALT WITH HEREIN.

You may expect dealers to pay from thirty to fifty percent less than the prices quoted. Glass that is in less than mint condition, i.e. chipped, cracked, scratched or poorly molded, will bring very small prices unless extremely rare; and then, it will bring only a small percentage of the price of glass that is in mint condition.

Prices have become pretty well nationally standardized due to national advertising carried on by dealers and due to the Depression Glass Shows which are held from coast to coast. However, **there are still some regional differences in prices due** partly **to glass being more readily available in some areas than in others.** Too, companies distributed certain pieces in some areas that they did not in others. Generally speaking, however, prices are about the same among dealers from coast to coast.

Prices tend to increase dramatically on rarer items and, in general, they have increased as a whole due to more and more collectors entering the field and people becoming more aware of the worth of Depression Glass.

One of the more important aspects of this book is the attempt made to illustrate as well as realistically price those items which are in demand. The desire was to give you the most accurate guide to collectible patterns of Depression Glass available.

MEASUREMENTS

To illustrate why there are discrepancies in measurements, I offer the following sample from just two years of Hocking's catalogue references:

Year	Pitcher Ounces	Flat Tumbler Ounces	Footed Tumbler Ounces
1935	37, 58, 80	5, 9, 13½	10, 13
1935	37, 60, 80	5, 9, 10, 15	10, 13
1936	37, 65, 90	5, 9, 13½	10, 15
1935	37, 60, 90	5, 9, 13½	10, 15

All measurements in this book are exact as to some manufacturer's listing or to actual measurement. You may expect variance of up to ½ inch or 1-5 ounces. This may be due to mold variation or changes made by the manufacturer.

Index

ADAM JEANNETTE GLASS COMPANY, 1932-1934

Colors: Pink, green, crystal, yellow, some delphite blue.   *(See Reproduction Section)*

We have speculated before that the inspiration for this "garden-like" pattern with its profusion of flowers, leaves and fern type scrolls may have been the Biblical story of Adam; and it may have been. However, I have since learned of some English architects named Adam who introduced a style of furniture under King George III which was characterized by simplicity of line but which depended on the use of garlands and medallions to enhance the appearance of their works. That, too, would fit as the inspiration of the artist who designed the Adam pattern for Jeannette. Unfortunately, little documentation is available on the artisans behind our beloved glassware; only the glass remains as testament of their skills.

Let me again state that the rarely found Adam/Sierra combination butter dish has BOTH patterns on the top. You can clearly see the Sierra striations which occur on the INSIDE of the butter top on the pink butter in the picture. The Adam pattern is found on the OUTSIDE of the same top. Speaking of butter dishes, the plain Adam butter has been reproduced. See details in the section on reproductions located in the back of this book.

You will notice some rarely found ROUND Adam luncheon items pictured in yellow and pink, i.e., plates and saucers. These are almost certainly experimental pieces as they were discovered in a house belonging to a former Jeannette employee. Even so, there were probably more pieces made than the 19 pieces of yellow and the few pieces of pink that have turned up. So, keep that in mind as you shop the markets.

The Adam lamps treasured by collectors were made from sherbets which were frosted and notched to accommodate a switch. The metal cover and bulb are difficult to locate separately though you can occasionally find a lamp base. You can see a similar lamp pictured under Floral.

Notice the style of the shaker tops. These differ from most Depression Glass shakers. I've even had people write me thinking these were the wrong tops!

An ash tray, pitcher, coaster, divided relish and grill plates have been found in crystal Adam which is rare. However, there is little demand for it; so these pieces don't command large prices. This is often the case when there are few pieces and few collectors in a pattern.

Adam pitchers come with both rounded and squared bases. The round base has concentric rings and most are a light pink color. Only the squared base carries the Adam motif.

Candy and sugar lids are interchangeable. Pink iced tea tumblers, vases, cereal bowls, green covered vegetable bowls and lamps are hard to find. Candy dishes and candlesticks are becoming more scarce as more and more disappear into collections. Newcomers can tell scarce or more desirable items in a pattern by noting the price variations in the listings below each pattern.

Check the inside rims of pieces in this pattern as they tend to chip. Don't pay "mint" prices for damaged pieces unless its a terribly rare, desirable and unusual piece of glass!

	Pink	Green		Pink	Green
Ash Tray, 4½"	19.50	16.50	**Cup	16.50	15.00
Bowl, 4¾" Dessert	10.00	9.50	Lamp	95.00	95.00
Bowl, 5¾" Cereal	22.50	20.00	Pitcher, 8", 32 oz.	23.50	32.50
Bowl, 7¾"	13.50	14.50	Pitcher, 32 oz. Round Base	35.00	
Bowl, 9", No Cover	17.50	30.00	Plate, 6" Sherbet	3.50	3.75
Bowl, Cover, 9"	15.00	27.50	***Plate, 7¾" Square Salad	7.00	8.00
Bowl, 9" Covered	37.50	57.50	Plate, 9" Square Dinner	15.00	14.00
Bowl, 10" Oval	15.00	17.50	Plate, 9" Grill	11.50	11.00
Butter Dish Bottom	20.00	50.00	Platter, 11¾"	10.50	12.00
Butter Dish Top	47.50	167.50	Relish Dish, 8" Divided	9.50	11.00
Butter Dish & Cover	67.50	217.50	Salt & Pepper, 4" Footed	42.50	75.00
Butter Dish Combination			****Saucer, 6" Square	3.00	3.00
with Sierra Pattern	457.50		Sherbet, 3"	15.50	19.50
Cake Plate, 10" Footed	12.50	16.50	Sugar	9.50	12.00
*Candlesticks, 4" Pair	49.50	69.50	Sugar/Candy Cover	15.00	20.00
Candy Jar & Cover, 2½"	52.50	57.50	Tumbler, 4½"	16.50	15.50
Coaster, 3¼"	14.00	12.00	Tumbler, 5½" Iced Tea	35.00	25.00
Creamer	11.50	12.50	Vase, 7½"	127.50	30.00

*Delphite $87.50
**Yellow $95.00
***Round Pink $57.50   Yellow $95.00
****Round Pink $67.50   Yellow $75.00

Please refer to Foreword for pricing information

AMERICAN PIONEER LIBERTY WORKS, 1931-1934

Colors: Pink, green, amber, crystal.

American Pioneer is a quietly elegant glassware that is slowly gathering more devotees. You don't find a great deal of this pattern readily available as it had a limited distribution. Most of the items have been found in the north eastern section of the country though I've now met collectors in several southern states who have managed to garner extensive collections.

What I first called a "rose" bowl is pictured in green in front of the candy. I am now convinced that the piece is an open mayonnaise, being footed and with a flared rim. I was entertained to see it recently listed as a rose bowl in another publication.

Liberty called their covered pitchers "urns". More and more they are being found with liner plates indicating they were probably intended as syrup or batter pitchers. One of these was featured in an August 4, 1975, issue of Newsweek magazine which contained an article on Depression Glass. The crystal urn is a rare piece.

Luncheon items (cup, saucer, plate, creamer, sugar) are more commonly found than other pieces shown here. Neither the 8¾", or the 9¼" covered bowls are easily found; the wine and water goblets are practically non-existent; and there's a little 2¼", 2 oz. shot glass (pictured in the 4th edition of this book) which is still lacking from several extensive collections. Don't pass these by even if you don't personally collect this pattern. A collector will be delighted to take these off your hands!

The ball shaped lamp (pictured in the 5th edition of this book) has only been found in pink and amber to date. Look for one in green or crystal!

Green is the color most in demand by collectors. Pink is, perhaps, their second choice. Crystal runs a poor third. Amber is possibly the color most rarely found but settings can be obtained in this with patience and searching.

	Crystal, Pink	Green		Crystal, Pink	Green
*Bowl, 5" Handled	8.00	8.50	Lamp, 5½" Round, Ball		
Bowl, 8¾" Covered	55.00	67.50	Shape (Amber $67.50)	57.50	
Bowl, 9" Handled	12.00	15.00	Lamp, 8½" Tall	57.50	67.50
Bowl, 9¼" Covered	72.50	87.50	Mayonnaise, 4¼"	37.50	55.00
Bowl, 10 3/8" Console	35.00	45.00	**Pitcher, 5" Covered Urn	97.50	127.50
Candlesticks, 6½" Pair	45.00	55.00	***Pitcher, 7" Covered Urn	115.00	147.50
Candy Jar and Cover, 1 lb.	57.50	72.50	Plate, 6"	4.00	6.00
Candy Jar and Cover, 1½ lb.	60.00	85.00	*Plate, 6" Handled	8.00	10.00
Cheese and Cracker Set			*Plate, 8"	5.50	6.00
(Indented Platter and Comport)	25.00	35.00	*Plate, 11½" Handled	9.50	12.50
Coaster, 3½"	13.50	14.50	*Saucer	3.00	4.00
Creamer, 2¾"	12.50	14.00	Sherbet, 3½"	10.00	12.50
*Creamer, 3½"	13.50	15.00	Sherbet, 4¾"	15.00	19.50
*Cup	6.00	7.50	Sugar, 2¾"	12.50	14.00
Dresser Set (2 Cologne,			*Sugar, 3½"	13.50	15.00
Powder Jar, on Indented			Tumbler, 5 oz. Juice	13.50	17.50
7½" Tray)	80.00		Tumbler, 4", 8 oz.	15.00	20.00
Goblet, 4", 3 oz. Wine	17.50	22.50	Tumbler, 5", 12 oz.	20.00	30.00
Goblet, 6", 8 oz. Water	22.50	27.50	Vase, 7", Four Styles	52.50	70.00
Ice Bucket, 6"	27.50	32.50	Whiskey, 2¼", 2 oz.	30.00	32.50

*Amber - Triple the price of green.
**Amber $200.00
***Amber $250.00

AMERICAN SWEETHEART   MACBETH-EVANS GLASS COMPANY, 1930-1936

Colors: Pink, monax, red, blue; some cremax and color rimmed monax.

American Sweetheart is one of the more popular patterns in Depression Glass and its an "interesting" pattern to collectors due to the rare and odd items that turn up from time to time having the American Sweetheart pattern. For example, there have been lamp shades found in this pattern (see picture). Sometimes they have orange, green, blue or brown panels in them; and at least one brass based floor lamp was found having the same grooved panels as the shade! Another MINIATURE version of the large console bowl with its large, flat rim (you can serve more off the rim than from the bowl) turned up in the east. It's a darling and RARE little bowl about 6½ " wide x 1¾ " tall. About five more of those tiny, hat shaped bowls have been found since the publication of the last book. On occasion, one of those rare ($150.00) monax sugar LIDS will surface. So, you can see that there's always something "happening" in this pattern that lends interest to the search.

No one has found another "vase" like the one pictured. It's generally thought to be some factory worker's "pet project" or simply a tumbler that failed to get cut properly. Whatever, it's unique.

Berry sets and lamp shades are found occasionally in the cremax color which is represented by the small berry bowl in the right of the picture. Even though these items are rarely found, they are in little demand; so the price remains low.

Prices for monax, particularly luncheon items, have softened somewhat due to a suddenly plentiful supply. Now might be the opportune time to collect a basic set of this since numerous dealers have indicated to me that they are almost overstocked with monax. I don't expect that condition to last forever; and it does set a superb table, particularly on colored table cloths.

Pink American Sweetheart shakers continue to be in shorter supply than Monax; neither are readily found. Five and ten ounce tumblers are also vanishing from the market place.

Novices to collecting can tell from the picture that the 80 oz. pitcher has the more bulbous shape.

	Pink	Monax		Pink	Monax
Bowl, 3¾ " Flat Berry	22.50		Plate, 15½ " Server		152.50
Bowl, 4½ " Cream Soup	25.00	35.00	Platter, 13" Oval	17.50	37.50
Bowl, 6" Cereal	9.50	9.50	Pitcher, 7½ ", 60 oz.	367.50	
Bowl, 9" Round Berry	16.50	32.50	Pitcher, 8", 80 oz.	347.50	
Bowl, 9½ " Flat Soup	27.50	35.00	Salt and Pepper, Footed	237.50	210.00
Bowl, 11" Oval Vegetable	27.50	38.00	Saucer	2.50	2.50
Bowl, 18" Console		277.50	Sherbet, 3¾ " Footed	11.50	
Creamer, Footed	7.50	7.00	Sherbet, 4¼ " Footed		
Cup	10.00	8.00	(Design Inside or Outside)	9.50	13.50
Lampshade		425.00	Sherbet in Metal Holder (Crystal		
Plate, 6" or 6½ " Bread & Butter	2.50	3.50	Only) 3.00		
Plate, 8" Salad	6.00	6.00	Sugar, Open, Footed	7.50	6.50
Plate, 9" Luncheon		7.50	Sugar Cover (Monax Only)*		150.00
Plate, 9¾ " Dinner	15.00	13.50	Tidbit, 3 Tier, 8", 12" & 15½ "		150.00
Plate, 10¼ " Dinner		13.50	Tumbler, 3½ ", 5 oz.	32.50	
Plate, 11" Chop Plate		11.00	Tumbler, 4", 9 oz.	30.00	
Plate, 12" Salver	9.00	11.00	Tumbler, 4½ ", 10 oz.	40.00	

*Two style knobs.

AMERICAN SWEETHEART (Con't.)

The stark white monax American Sweetheart can also be found rimmed with various colors such as gold, pink, green, or "smoke" which is a kind of blue-gray color that reaches a black trim at the extreme edges. Of all the "trims", the "smoke" is the most highly prized. However, when this luncheon set turned up with the pink trim, I couldn't resist picturing it here in place of the disappointing picture of the amberina console bowl shown in the 5th edition. (That was a beautiful piece to the naked eye; unfortunately, the camera didn't do it justice). Generally speaking, the pieces shown here are what is usually discovered in the trimmed monax American Sweetheart, relegating these sets to a basic luncheon or serving set. Its very attractive. It's a shame that not more of it was made.

Cups, saucers and plates appear with more regularity in red American Sweetheart than in blue. Other items in these colors appear with equal rarity. I have been privileged to see both red and blue tid-bit servers. Prices on the red have remained steady for the last few years; frankly, I wouldn't be surprised to see these start to rise soon.

Some blue and red sherbets and plates have appeared having the American Sweetheart SHAPE but not having the pattern. We can't call these anything but American Sweetheart BLANKS; and while they are novel, without the pattern they can command only a fraction of the price of the patterned pieces.

Newcomers will want to acquaint themselves with the console bowl prices so that if they run into one at a yard sale for $5.00 as one lucky lady did in New England, they'll know to buy it. The console bowl has huge rims on it making it an extremely hard piece to store in modern day cabinets. You need an old buffet cabinet for this piece. The MINIATURE console bowl in monax brings nearly as much as the red and blue! Don't overlook these pieces.

	Red	Blue	Cremax	Smoke & Other Trims
Bowl, 6″ Cereal			8.00	25.00
Bowl, 9″ Round Berry			33.00	62.50
Bowl, 18″ Console	625.00	700.00		
Creamer, Footed	77.50	87.50		57.50
Cup	77.50	87.50		52.50
Lampshade			400.00	
Lamp (Floor with Brass Base)			600.00	
Plate, 6″ Bread and Butter				13.50
Plate, 8″ Salad	60.00	82.50		25.00
Plate, 9″ Luncheon				30.00
Plate, 9¾″ Dinner				45.00
Plate, 12″ Salver	127.50	152.50		
Plate, 15½″ Server	225.00	285.00		
Platter, 13″ Oval				87.50
Saucer	30.00	35.00		13.50
Sherbet, 4¼″ Footed (Design Inside or Outside)				27.50
Sugar, Open Footed	77.50	87.50		57.50
Tidbit, 3 Tier, 8″, 12″ & 15½″	425.00	525.00		

ANNIVERSARY JEANNETTE GLASS COMPANY, 1947-1949

Colors: Pink, recently crystal and iridescent

Anniversary is a pleasing pattern to the eye as well as the purse! Naturally due to its short lived selling period, it isn't as readily available as some of the Depression patterns. However, a set of this can be obtained, a piece here, a piece there, with patience. Strictly speaking, this glass was made later than the Depression era glassware per se. However, as with some other later patterns, it's being collected by Depression enthusiasts.

A lot more iridized Anniversary is showing up at flea markets. Remember, this was made as late as the 1970's and shouldn't be priced more than crystal. It is NOT Carnival glass as some will say.

Some pieces of Anniversary (fruit bowl, candy dish, sandwich tray, butter dish, wine glass) are not easily found. It will help if you tell every dealer what you're looking for so they will help in the search. Most are glad to look for specific items they know they can sell immediately. This holds true for any pattern.

The bottom to the butter is harder to locate than the top; and there is almost no demand for later issued crystal Anniversary except for the butter dish and the pin-up vase. The supply of vases has recently dried up; so be on the lookout for these.

	Crystal	Pink		Crystal	Pink
Bowl, 4 7/8″ Berry	1.50	2.50	Pickle Dish, 9″	3.00	6.00
Bowl, 7 3/8″ Soup	3.00	6.00	Plate, 6¼″ Sherbet	1.25	2.00
Bowl, 9″ Fruit	7.00	11.00	Plate, 9″ Dinner	3.50	4.50
Butter Dish Bottom	10.00	18.00	Plate, 12½″ Sandwich Server	4.00	6.50
Butter Dish Top	12.50	22.00	Relish Dish, 8″	4.50	6.50
Butter Dish and Cover	22.50	40.00	Saucer	1.00	1.50
Candy Jar and Cover	17.50	25.00	Sherbet, Footed	2.50	4.50
*Comport, Open, 3 Legged	3.00	7.00	Sugar	2.00	4.50
Cake Plate, 12½″	5.50	8.50	Sugar Covers	3.00	4.50
Cake Plate and Cover	10.00	12.50	Vase, 6½″	6.00	9.00
Candlestick, 4 7/8″ Pair	12.50		Vase, Wall Pin-up	10.00	15.00
Creamer, Footed	3.00	6.50	Wine Glass, 2½ oz.	5.50	8.50
Cup	2.00	4.50			

*Old form; presently called compote.   Open compote or candy.

AUNT POLLY U.S. GLASS COMPANY, Late 1920's

Colors: Blue, green, iridescent.

Recently, at a show I attended, a dealer had a good supply of blue Aunt Polly on display. Seeing it all at once, I was struck anew by how very pretty this pattern is! Though there is some mold roughness to be found on the glassware routinely, its a very durable and attractive glass. Sears advertised it in one of their '20's catalogues which should attest to its dependability!

One of the drawbacks to the collecting of Aunt Polly is the absence of cups! Not being a coffee/tea person, that doesn't bother me; but the majority of people like cups and saucers in their sets of dishes.

Be advised that the oval vegetable bowl, covered sugar and shakers are difficult to find. Most of the pieces listed have surfaced in either green or iridescent, but not all have surfaced in both. The iridescent holds its own in price due to scarcity. The iridescent butter, in fact, is quite rare. However, there is little demand for either green or iridescent at present.

The blue butter top and bottom are equally hard to find. However, in green and iridescent only, the top is difficult as the bottom is the same as found in other U.S. Glass patterns such as Strawberry and Floral and Diamond.

	Green, Iridescent	Blue		Green, Iridescent	Blue
Bowl, 4 3/8″ Berry	4.50	6.00	Creamer	16.50	25.00
Bowl, 4¾″, 2″ High	8.50	11.00	Pitcher, 8″, 48 oz.		117.50
Bowl, 7¼″ Oval, Handled Pickle	9.00	12.50	Plate, 6″ Sherbet	3.00	4.50
Bowl, 7 7/8″ Large Berry	11.00	17.50	Plate, 8″ Luncheon		8.50
Bowl, 8 3/8″ Oval	19.50	32.50	Salt and Pepper		147.50
Butter Dish and Cover	187.50	147.50	Sherbet	7.50	8.50
Butter Dish Bottom	52.50	72.50	Sugar	11.50	16.50
Butter Dish Top	135.00	75.00	Sugar Cover	28.50	40.00
Candy, Cover, 2 Handled	35.00	47.50	Tumbler, 3 5/8″, 8 oz.		13.50
			Vase, 6½″ Footed	22.50	27.50

Please refer to Foreword for pricing information

"AURORA"   HAZEL ATLAS GLASS COMPANY, Late 1930's

Colors: Cobalt blue, pink.

This is a nice little set to collect! It comes in the highly prized cobalt blue color that has a mystique all its own with collectors; and it still falls within budget pricing!

My wife likes this. She collected what's here to use at "small meal" times when you just need a salad, sandwich and drink! She's derived a lot of pleasure from searching, buying, owning and using this set. I will have to tell you that she blends the cobalt petalware mustard bottom with this to serve fruit or custard desserts when she uses the "Aurora". I'll also have to admit the pattern has grown on me. I totally ignored it for years!

She found the small deep bowl on the right and the tumblers the most difficult pieces to get. Cereal bowls, cups, saucers and plates seem to be plentiful.

Not a great deal of the pink is seen. We've found bowls and cups and saucers.

I'm told that sherbets exist in this, but we've not seen them. Also, there's a tumbler without the clear rim at the top, just having the ribs, which will blend well with this pattern should you not be able to find these. They may even have the center plate motif in the bottom. There seems to be no sugar bowl for the creamer leading me to believe it may have been a promotional item for a dairy or a biscuit mix or something.

	Cobalt/ Pink
Bowl, 4½", Deep	7.50
Bowl, 5", Cereal	4.00
Creamer, 4½"	8.00
Cup	5.00
Plate, 6½"	3.50
Saucer	2.50
Tumbler, 4¾", 10 oz.	8.75

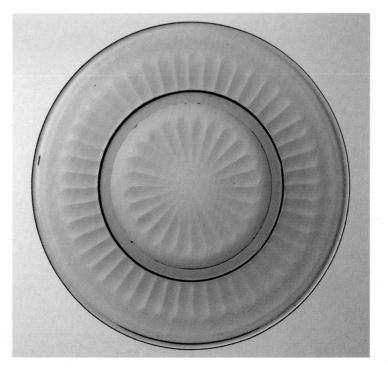

AVOCADO, No. 601   INDIANA GLASS COMPANY, 1923-1933

Colors: Pink, green, crystal.   *(See Reproduction Section)*

This is a beautiful pattern and it has numerous devotees. It was on its way to becoming one of the outstanding patterns in Depression Glass until Indiana Glass Company started remaking it for its Tiara Exclusive Home Products line. They first issued "collectible" pitcher and water sets in colors of red, peach, and frosted. Unfortunately, they made the mistake of remaking it in the older pink, too, thereby rather killing the goose that was laying their golden egg. Even though the newer pink was a more orange pink than the original, the price of the older glass stopped dead still and hasn't recovered in the ten years since. Since then, the company has marketed green sherbets, creamers and sugars and sherbet plates. Possibly, its only a matter of time until they market the rest of the pieces again. Thus, the prices for this glassware have come to a standstill. Traditionally, this is what happens in a pattern that is reproduced---at least until the "differences" between old and new become common knowledge. Unfortunately, when the original company remakes their own product, any differences are negligible! I'm not saying the glass is worthless as an investment, rather that it will take another forty or fifty years before it can be considered to be antique. Had the company had the foresight to remake the pattern in heretofore unknown colors, then they could have enhanced the collectibility of BOTH the older glass and the new. As it is, they've damaged the investment possibilities of their older product thereby souring everyone's taste for their glass. Indiana's Depression glass patterns are something of a pariah among the vast field of collectors at the moment. Agreed, there is much which is antique and which should be valuable as such. Unfortunately, the much that is new tarnishes the prospect of more immediate returns in the investor's eyes.

Green pitcher and tumbler sets have disappeared into collections. Saucers remain harder to find than cups. Milk white pieces of Avocado were probably a product of the 1950's Indiana milk glass push; and a few pieces have turned up with an apple design rather than the Avocado. These are considered more novel than collectible. They were remade in Amber for Tiara.

The insert below is from a 1930's catalogue. Notice the ad called the plates "eccentric" shaped!

	Pink	Green		Pink	Green
Bowl, 5¼", Two-Handled	20.00	22.50	*Pitcher, 64 ozs.	300.00	500.00
Bowl, 6" Footed Relish	14.00	18.50	***Plate, 6¼" Sherbet	9.50	11.50
Bowl, 7" One Handle Preserve	12.50	15.00	**Plate, 8¼" Luncheon	12.50	14.50
Bowl, 7½" Salad	23.50	37.50	Plate, 10¼" 2 Handled Cake	22.50	32.50
Bowl, 8" 2 Handled Oval	14.50	18.50	Saucer	20.00	22.50
Bowl, 9½", 3¼" Deep	57.50	77.50	***Sherbet	47.50	52.50
***Creamer, Footed	25.00	29.50	***Sugar, Footed	25.00	29.50
Cup, Footed	26.50	27.50	*Tumbler	69.50	99.50

Set of 6 Salad or Dessert Plates •
Made of good quality glass.   Attractive green pear and leaf design, making a strikingly novel plate in eccentric shape.   Diameter, 8½ inches. Weight, packed, 6 pounds.
35N1641—Set of 6..............98c

*Caution on pink. The orangeish-pink is new!
**Apple Design $10.00.   Amber has been newly made.
***Just remade in green.

Please refer to Foreword for pricing information

18

BEADED BLOCK IMPERIAL GLASS COMPANY, 1927-1930's

Colors: Pink, green, crystal, ice blue, vaseline, iridescent, amber, red, opalescent and milk white.

I recently saw the remains of a milk white pitcher in this pattern. It had been dropped and I was unable to tell from the remainders whether the pitcher had been stamped with an IG in the bottom of the pitcher. The "IG" symbol is something Imperial has been using since 1951 and that helps to date some pieces. If any of you have such a pitcher, I would appreciate knowing if it is stamped in the bottom or not.

Due to the colors that can be found in this pattern, it's often mistaken for "Carnival", "Vaseline" or "Pattern" glassware and unknowing dealers will price it along those lines. YOU ultimately decide what a piece is worth. If you feel a piece is exhorbitant, pass it by unless you can convince the dealer to moderate the price.

Imperial called the two-handled bowl a "jelly" rather than a soup and the tall, footed pieces were "footed jellies" rather than compotes. The opalescent blue piece at center is a "vase" rather than a parfait, also. Iridized pink items being seen at flea markets are of recent vintage.

	Crystal*, Pink, Green, Amber	Other Colors		Crystal*, Pink, Green, Amber	Other Colors
Bowl, 4½", 2 Handled Jelly	6.00	12.50	Bowl, 7½" Round, Plain Edge	7.50	14.00
**Bowl, 4½" Round Lily	8.50	15.00	Bowl, 8¼" Celery	9.50	15.00
Bowl, 5½" Square	6.00	8.50	Creamer	10.00	17.50
Bowl, 5½" Blue One Handle	6.50	8.50	Pitcher, 5¼", Pint Jug	120.00	
Bowl, 6" Deep Round	8.50	14.50	Plate, 7¾" Square	5.00	8.00
Bowl, 6¼" Round	6.50	13.50	Plate, 8¾" Round	6.00	10.00
Bowl, 6½" Round	6.50	13.50	Stemmed Jelly, 4½"	8.00	14.50
Bowl, 6½" 2 Handled Pickle	10.00	14.50	Stemmed Jelly, 4½", Flared		
Bowl, 6¾" Round, Unflared	8.50	12.50	Top	8.50	16.00
Bowl, 7¼" Round, Flared	8.00	14.50	Sugar	10.00	17.50
Bowl, 7½" Round, Fluted			Vase, 6" Bouquet	8.50	17.50
Edges	17.50	20.00			

*All pieces 25% to 40% lower.
**Red: $57.50.

"BOWKNOT" MANUFACTURER UNKNOWN, Probably late 1920's

Color: Green.

After nearly twelve years of intensive involvement with Depression Glass, there are still only seven pieces of this pattern known to exist! That's fine except that it defies all precedence for a company to make a cup without a saucer or a punch bowl to go with it. Surely we just haven't looked hard enough!

My wife is totally charmed with this pattern, liking the shapes and what she terms the pattern's "Depression era look". Maybe she equates its dearth of pieces to the lack of everything else during the Depression!

I get letters from people thinking they've found a creamer and sugar which so far have all turned out to be Fostoria's "June" pattern which also has a knotted bow design. However, green "June" would be a rare find!

	Green		Green
Bowl, 4½" Berry	8.00	Sherbet, Low Footed	8.00
Bowl, 5½" Cereal	10.50	Tumbler, 5", 10 oz.	10.00
Cup	4.50	Tumbler, 5", 10 oz. Footed	10.00
Plate, 7" Salad	6.50		

Please refer to Foreword for pricing information

BLOCK OPTIC, "BLOCK" HOCKING GLASS COMPANY, 1929-1933

Colors: Green, pink, yellow, crystal and some blue.

Block Optic continues to be one of the more popular patterns of Depression Glass! It never seems to attract the frenetic activity of some other patterns. Rather, it just quietly continues to attract new collectors and to steadily sell while other patterns go through "ups and downs". Were you to graph the activity generated by Block Optic, you'd just see a steady, gently rising line.

I was going to be extremely pleased to introduce three newly discovered pieces in Block, a BLUE butter dish, a one ounce shot glass and a yellow GRILL plate. I'm still very pleased to tell you about them and to show you the blue butter dish which many of you have seen featured on the cover of my new 2nd edition Kitchenware book! The smaller, crystal shot glass was shown to me at a show! The plate, however, was destroyed by a workman drilling through a wall in our home! If you find another yellow Block grill plate, please let me know. It was to have been the new pattern shot for this pattern!

New collectors should be aware that there are five styles of sugars and creamers, two short, tall, footed, and flat with each having handle variations. There are also four cup types plus one mug and three different saucers, two with a cup ring and one without. Finding cups to fit the ring in your saucers is sometimes tricky. It is permissible to use the sherbet plates as saucers as they were sometimes sold that way. Note the price increase on saucers with the cup ring which are scarce.

Cone shaped sherbets, luncheon and sherbet plates are readily available. The cone mayonnaise, candlesticks, squatty shakers, vases, tumble-ups (water jug in the back of the picture with the inverted glass), mugs, 4″ cocktail goblets and dinner plates are becoming quite scarce. Try to get these pieces first if you're just starting a collection. The jug to the tumble-up set is only worth about $10.00 by itself. Note the price jump on dinner plates! (There is a Block-like plate found in green with a snowflake design in the center which sells for around three to four dollars. Heretofore, they've been practically unsellable. With the supply of regular Block dinner plates drying up, I suppose that could change).

Yellow Block is gorgeous on a table, but it is in scant supply. If you choose this, be prepared to have extended patience.

Many Block Optic pieces have similar shapes to the very popular Cameo pattern which was also made by Hocking. Some Block Optic pieces have fired-on black feet. These are relatively scarce; but not everyone cares for them; so the price for these has remained relatively low.

Crystal Block Optic sells for about one half the prices of the pink.

	Green	Yellow	Pink		Green	Yellow	Pink
Bowl, 4¼″ Berry	4.50		4.00	Plate, 8″ Luncheon	3.00	3.75	2.50
Bowl, 5¼″ Cereal	7.00		5.00	Plate, 9″ Dinner	11.50	22.50	15.00
Bowl, 7″ Salad	10.00	12.50	8.00	Plate, 9″ Grill	6.50	12.50	9.50
Bowl, 8½″ Large Berry	12.50	17.50	9.50	Plate, 10¼″ Sandwich	12.50		12.50
*Butter Dish and Cover, 3″ x 5″	35.00			Salt and Pepper, Footed	22.50	55.00	42.50
Butter Dish Bottom	17.50			Salt and Pepper, Squatty	30.00		
Butter Dish Top	17.50			Sandwich Server, Center Handle	30.00		30.00
Candlesticks, 1¾″ Pr.	27.50		25.00	Saucer, 5¾″, With Cup Ring	7.00		5.00
Candy Jar & Cover, 2¼″ Tall	30.00	40.00	27.50	Saucer, 6 1/8″, With Cup Ring	7.00	7.50	4.50
Candy Jar & Cover, 6¼″ Tall	29.50		37.50	Sherbet, Non Stemmed (Cone)	3.00		
Comport, 4″ Wide Mayonnaise	17.50			Sherbet, 3¼″, 5½ oz.	4.50	7.50	4.00
Creamer, Three Styles: Cone				Sherbet, 4¾″, 6 oz.	9.50	10.50	7.50
Shaped, Round, Rayed Foot				Sugar, Three Styles: As			
and Flat (5 Kinds)	9.50	9.50	8.50	Creamer	8.50	9.50	8.00
Cup, Four Styles	4.50	6.00	4.00	Tumbler, 3″ & 3½″, 5 oz. Flat	12.50		11.00
Goblet, 4″ Cocktail	13.50		12.50	Tumbler, 4″, 5 oz. Footed	11.00		11.50
Goblet, 4½″ Wine	14.00		11.50	Tumbler, 9 oz. Flat	9.50		8.00
Goblet, 5¾″, 9 oz.	13.50		11.50	Tumbler, 9 oz. Footed	12.50	12.50	9.50
Goblet, 7¼″, 9 oz. Thin	18.50	17.50	12.50	Tumbler, 10 oz. Flat	11.50		9.50
Ice Bucket	27.50		22.50	Tumbler, 6″, 10 oz Footed	12.50	15.00	12.50
Ice Tub or Butter Tub, Open	22.50			Tumbler, 14 oz. Flat	15.00		
Mug, Flat Creamer, No Spout	25.00			Tumble-up Night Set: 3″			
Pitcher, 7 5/8″, 68 oz., Bulbous	30.00		40.00	Tumbler Bottle and Tumbler,			
Pitcher, 8½″, 54 oz.	27.50		27.50	6″ High	47.50		
Pitcher, 8″, 80 oz.	37.50		32.50	Vase, 5¾″, Blown	127.50		
Plate, 6″ Sherbet	2.00	2.50	1.50	Whiskey, 2½″	12.50		11.50

*Blue $125.00

Please refer to Foreword for pricing information

23

"BUBBLE", "BULLSEYE", "PROVINCIAL"

ANCHOR HOCKING GLASS COMPANY, 1934-1965

Colors: Pink, light blue, dark green, red, crystal.

This pattern was first introduced by Hocking as a pink 8¾" bowl called "Bullseye". You can find this bowl in almost any color Anchor Hocking made from jadite to fired-on pink. It was obviously a popular item. In one of my visits to the factory, I saw literally stacks of these pink bowls in storage. So, even though it was the first item, they are still around; so don't be duped into paying high prices for them.

In 1942, after the merger of Anchor and Hocking, the blue "Fire-King" line was introduced and touted with all its "heat proof" properties. It proved to be a popular line then and now with collectors. Blue grill plates and creamers are scarce. The scarcity of creamers has pulled the price of the sugar bowl up, too, due to some dealers refusing to separate the two items.

The green appeared in the 1950's and early '60's during the Forest Green production. Green Bubble is presently selling well. I've asked several buyers their reasons for buying it and gotten answers from "I'm using it for my Christmas table" to "The price is bound to go up on this, too!"

The ruby red was issued in the 1960's under the name "Provincial". Red "Bubble" is also enjoying a recent surge of interest on the part of collectors, I assume for as myriad reasons as expressed above. A red tid-bit server was pictured in the 5th edition book.

The flat rimmed bowl pictured in the pattern shot is rarely seen. Only two or three have turned up to date. Yet, with the numbers of collectors of "Bubble" increasing, surely more will be spotted. Other oddities to turn up have included an amber cup with no saucer and an opalescent "Bubble" bowl with a "Moonstone" label affixed. You can see that pictured with the Moonstone pattern. These items, though rare, are more intriguing than costly.

Notice the iridized green sugar bowl between the green creamer and sugar. Frankly, that process didn't enhance the piece in my estimation.

Crystal "Bubble" sells for about half the blue; yet crystal "Bubble" sets a very attractive table. I learned this first hand! My sister decided to collect that and I was served from it Thanksgiving. It really is eye pleasing!

Though they haven't yet, I would expect candleholders to rise in price soon as the numbers of collectors seem on the increase and they aren't that plentiful!

	Dark Green	Light Blue	Ruby Red		Dark Green	Light Blue	Ruby Red
Bowl, 4" Berry	4.00	7.50		Plate, 6¾" Bread and Butter	1.50	2.50	
Bowl, 4½" Fruit	5.00	6.00	4.00	Plate, 9 3/8" Grill		7.50	
Bowl, 5¼" Cereal	5.00	6.50		Plate, 9 3/8" Dinner	4.50	5.00	5.50
Bowl, 7¾" Flat Soup		8.00		Platter, 12" Oval		8.50	
Bowl, 8 3/8" Large Berry (Pink—$3.00)	7.50	8.50		***Saucer	1.00	1.50	1.50
Bowl, 9" Flanged		37.50		Sugar	5.00	12.50	
Candlesticks (Crystal - $10.00 Pr.)	17.50			Tidbit (2 Tier)			16.50
Creamer	6.00	17.50		Tumbler, 6 oz. Juice			6.00
*Cup	2.50	3.00	4.00	Tumbler, 9 oz. Water			5.50
Lamp, 2 Styles, Crystal Only - 22.50				Tumbler, 12 oz. Iced Tea			8.50
**Pitcher, 64 oz. Ice Lip			35.00	Tumbler, 16 oz. Lemonade			13.50

*Pink — $27.50
**Crystal — $32.50
***Pink — $17.50

CAMEO, "BALLERINA" or "DANCING GIRL" HOCKING GLASS COMPANY, 1930-1934

Colors: Green, yellow, pink and crystal with silver rim.   *(See Reproduction Section)*

I used to say that Cameo was one of the top five patterns in Depression Glass, but now I believe it to be in the top three! There are more unique and unusual pieces in this pattern, however, than in any other which makes owning a COMPLETE set virtually impossible as well as costly. Basic sets can still be easily put together and enjoyed; so don't let the prices of the "frill" items put you off collecting Cameo. I've had ladies tell me they've enjoyed using this glassware as no other they've ever owned!

Cameo saucers with the ring indent are probably the highest priced saucers in Depression glass--- but they are oh so hard to come by! One is pictured on the following page.

Other hard to find items pictured here are the crystal cocktail shaker, a decanter stopper, jam dish (between the cocktail shaker and decanter), cream soup, domino drip tray (sugar cubes in outer rim/creamer within center indent ring), the syrup pitcher and footed juice.

Collectors seldom notice grill plates, but take a look at the two handled one located behind the platter.

Those elusive Cameo shakers were reproduced as I warned in the 5th edition. They are easy to spot. The pattern proved to be so weak they are easily distinguished from the old. I've heard they're reworking the mold hoping to do better, however.

The odd lid pictured fits the "rope" top juice pitcher, but should it?

The little 3½" wine is turning out to be quite scarce.

Some 10 and 15 ounce flat tumblers have turned up in pink recently.

The small size children's dishes are new. (See Reproduction Section at back for details.)

More Cameo price listings are found on page 28.

	Green	Yellow	Pink	Crys/ Plat
Bowl, 4¼" Sauce				4.00
Bowl, 4¾" Cream Soup	43.50			
Bowl, 5½" Cereal	21.50	22.50		3.00
Bowl, 7¼" Salad	25.00			
Bowl, 8¼" Large Berry	24.50		100.00	
Bowl, 9" Rimmed Soup	30.00			
Bowl, 10" Oval Vegetable	13.50	20.00		
Bowl, 11", 3 Leg Console	40.00	52.50	17.50	
Butter Dish and Cover	130.00	625.00		
Butter Dish Bottom	67.50	300.00		
Butter Dish Top	62.50	325.00		
Cake Plate, 10", 3 Legs	14.00			
Cake Plate, 10½" Flat	57.50			
Candlesticks, 4" Pr.	72.50			
Candy Jar, 4" Low and Cover	40.00	50.00	350.00	
Candy Jar, 6½" Tall and Cover	90.00			
Cocktail Shaker (Metal Lid) Appears in Crystal Only				325.00
Comport, 5" Wide Mayonnaise	19.50			

CAMEO, "BALLERINA" or "DANCING GIRL" (Con't.)

	Green	Yellow	Pink	Crys/ Plat
Cookie Jar and Cover	36.50			
Creamer, 3¼"	16.50	12.00		
Creamer, 4¼"	16.00		50.00	
Cup, Two Styles	11.00	6.50	50.00	5.00
Decanter, 10" With Stopper	82.50			150.00
Decanter, 10" With Stopper, Frosted (Stopper Represents ½ Value of green Decanter)	23.50			
Domino Tray, 7" With 3" Indentation	67.50			
Domino Tray, 7" With No Indentation			147.50	87.50
Goblet, 3½" Wine	147.50			
Goblet, 4" Wine	47.50		175.00	
Goblet, 6" Water	35.00		110.00	
Ice Bowl or Open Butter, 3" Tall x 5½" Wide	97.50		400.00	175.00
Jam Jar, 2" and Cover	87.50			97.50
Pitcher, 5¾", 20 oz. Syrup or Milk	137.50	177.50		
Pitcher, 6", 36 oz. Juice	40.00			
Pitcher, 8½", 56 oz. Water	37.50			225.00
Plate, 6" Sherbet	3.00	2.00	45.00	1.75
Plate, 7" Salad				3.00
Plate, 8" Luncheon	7.00	2.50	23.00	3.50
Plate, 8½" Square	25.00	55.00		
Plate, 9½" Dinner	13.50	6.00	30.00	
Plate, 10" Sandwich	9.50		30.00	
Plate, 10½" Grill	7.00	6.00	32.50	
Plate, 10½" Grill With Closed Handles	47.50	5.75		
Plate, 11½" With Closed Handles	6.50	5.00		
Platter, 12", Closed Handles	13.50	13.50		
Relish, 7½" Footed, 3 Part	15.50	47.50		
*Salt and Pepper, Footed Pr.	50.00		500.00	
Sandwich Server, Center Handle	1,350.00			
Saucer With Cup Ring	75.00			
Saucer 6" (Sherbet Plate)	3.00	1.75	45.00	
Sherbet, 3 1/8"	11.00	15.00	25.00	
Sherbet, 4 7/8"	22.50	22.50	47.50	
Sugar, 3¼"	11.50	9.50		
Sugar, 4¼"	16.50		50.00	
Tumbler, 3¾", 5 oz. Juice	18.50		60.00	
Tumbler, 4", 9 oz. Water	18.50		60.00	7.50
Tumbler, 4¾", 10 oz. Flat	20.00		72.50	
Tumbler, 5", 11 oz. Flat	20.00	22.50	72.50	
Tumbler, 5¼", 15 oz.	37.50		85.00	
Tumbler, 3 oz. Footed Juice	45.00		80.00	
Tumbler, 5", 9 oz. Footed	20.00	11.50	75.00	
Tumbler, 5¾", 11 oz. Footed	35.00			
Tumbler, 6 3/8", 15 oz. Footed	150.00			
Vase, 5¾"	92.50			
Vase, 8"	18.50			
Water Bottle (Dark Green) Whitehouse Vinegar	18.50			

*Beware Reproductions

CHEROKEE ROSE   TIFFIN GLASS COMPANY, 1940's-1950's

This pattern belongs in the Elegant glassware book and I will eventually move it into that book as I have the Fostoria patterns previously introduced here. However, we're not scheduled to photograph another Elegant book for a couple of years, and I want the collecting public to be aware that this pattern is becoming collectible NOW, so they can buy at today's prices rather than those that will be asked two years from now!

Cherokee Rose rivaled Cambridge's "Rose Point" and Heisey's "Orchid" pattern as bridal giftware in the late 1940's. In fact, the lady who sold me the pieces you see here said she'd had it since 1948.

Notice the beading on the pieces which is reminiscent of Heisey's "Waverly" blank. If you think of the Cherokee Rose design as being THREE cameo's, you're less likely to confuse it with "Rose Point" which is a single cameo design with roses within. Or, you may prefer to remember this as the cameo with the urn inside. However, it's a beautiful pattern that is coming to the attention of collectors, particularly those who have moved from Depression Glass per se into collecting the better glasswares of the time. If you haven't pursued my *Elegant Glassware of the Depression Era* book, perhaps you should do so; buying just one piece of this can often pay for the price of the book!

Most Tiffin patterns seem to have a multitude of stems. Both the wine and the cocktail hold 3½ ounces. The wine is pictured behind the cocktail on the right side of the picture.

I doubt this listing is complete. Please let me hear of your finds in Cherokee Rose!

	Crystal		Crystal
Bowl, 5", Finger	8.00	Stem, 2 oz., Cocktail	12.50
Bowl, 6", Fruit or Mint	10.00	Stem, 3½ oz., Cocktail	12.50
Bowl, 7", Salad	10.00	Stem, 3½ oz., Wine	15.00
Bowl, 10", Deep Salad	17.50	Stem, 4 oz., Claret	13.50
Bowl, 10½", Celery, Oblong	17.50	Stem, 4½ oz., Parfait	12.50
Bowl, 12", Crimped	25.00	Stem, 5½ oz.	
Bowl, 12½", Centerpiece, Flared	22.50	Sherbet/Champagne	11.50
Bowl, 13", Centerpiece	25.00	Stem, 9 oz., Water	15.00
Cake Plate, 12½", Center Hdld.	20.00	Sugar	9.00
Candlesticks, Pr. Dble. Branch	32.50	Tumbler, 4½ oz., Oyster Cocktail	8.50
Comport, 6"	15.00	Tumbler, 5 oz., Ftd. Juice	8.50
Creamer	10.00	Tumbler, 8 oz., Ftd. Water	9.50
Mayonnaise, Liner & Ladle	22.50	Tumbler, 10½ oz., Ftd. Iced Tea	10.00
Pitcher	87.50	Vase, 6", Bud	10.00
Plate, 6", Sherbet	3.50	Vase, 8", Bud	12.50
Plate, 8", Luncheon	7.50	Vase, 10", Bud	15.00
Plate, 13½", Turned Up Edge	17.50	Vase, 11", Bud	15.00
Plate, 14", Sandwich	14.00	Vase, 11", Urn	25.00
Relish, 6½", 3 Part	17.50	Vase, 12", Flared	25.00
Stem, 1 oz., Cordial	25.00		

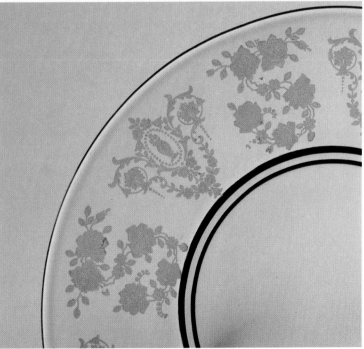

CHERRY BLOSSOM   JEANNETTE GLASS COMPANY, 1930-1939

Colors: Pink, green, delphite (opaque blue), crystal, jadite (opaque green), red, yellow.
(See Reproduction Section)

Cherry Blossom is one of the most popular patterns in Depression Glass. It's easily recognized, has a good selection of pieces, and has some intriguing odd colors and unusual pieces to titilate the collecting instinct of ardent collectors. Unfortunately, all this has made it a prime target for the copy artists. More reproductions have occured in this pattern than any other pattern of Depression glass. Naturally, prices on this glass at present have stagnated due to the reproduction blitzkreig. However, though shaken, collectors need not feel their pattern has been mortally wounded. All the reproductions I've seen have some tell-tale signs which shriek "reproduction" once you learn to read them. I will endeavor to pass what I know along to you in the back of this book. I would encourage everyone to "learn to read the signs" and pass the knowledge on to others. Indeed, write me of any better ways to tell new from old than those I've found so I can pass the information to everyone. Don't be alarmed. Old Cherry Blossom is still old and still valuable. It will help protect everyone if you try to refrain from buying the new. If there are no buyers, there will soon be no reproductions.

I get more inquiries about Cherry Blossom trays than anything in this pattern other than reproductions. The two handled green tray in the center of the top picture is the 10½ " sandwich tray. A similar tray has turned up without the handles. Also, another tray has been found which has a circular middle section with raised divisions raying from the center circle. These last TWO trays are considered to be real "finds"---not the commonly found sandwich tray.

I met a man at a show who "traced" the Cherry Blossom cookie jar through price. It ran thusly: $1.50; $65.00; $500.00; $2,500.00. Only one has been found to date. Wouldn't you have liked to buy it at that first price!

The crystal, two handled bowl in the lower picture sells in the $11.00 to $12.00 range and is not a rare piece.

That older, red Cherry Blossom pieces are an amberina red---firing to yellow tint in places.

The rare 9″ platter (pictured in pink) measures nine inches OUTSIDE edge to OUTSIDE edge. There are rumors that this extremely rare piece is a candidiate for reproduction. I have not confirmed this. Just carefully confirm the "age" of any you run into.

Notice the Cherry Blossom mugs pictured. These are still considered to be quite scarce and a very good find.

With the collecting of children's dishes coming into vogue, the Cherry Blossom children's dishes should be a very good set to own. As you can see, there are various amber child's dishes pictured; there had to be an entire set somewhere.

The letters AOP in the price listing refer to pieces having an "all over pattern"; PAT means "pattern at the top" only.

See page 34 for prices.

CHERRY BLOSSOM — CHILD'S JUNIOR DINNER SET

	Pink	Delphite
Creamer	25.00	25.00
Sugar	25.00	25.00
Plate, 6″	7.25	8.25 (design on bottom)
Cup	20.00	22.50
Saucer	4.00	4.50
14 Piece Set	165.00	177.50

Original box sells for $10.00 extra with these sets.

CHERRY BLOSSOM (Con't.)

	Pink	Green	Delphite	Jadite
Bowl, 4¾" Berry	8.50	11.50	10.00	
Bowl, 5¾" Cereal	21.00	21.50		
Bowl, 7¾" Flat Soup	35.00	36.50		
*Bowl, 8½" Round Berry	15.00	16.00	39.50	
Bowl, 9" Oval Vegetable	17.50	17.50	41.50	
Bowl, 9" 2 Handled	13.50	16.50	12.50	275.00
Bowl, 10½", 3 Leg Fruit	35.00	37.50		275.00
Butter Dish and Cover	65.00	75.00		
Butter Dish Bottom	20.00	22.50		
Butter Dish Top	45.00	52.50		
Cake Plate (3 Legs) 10¼"	15.00	16.00		
Coaster	11.50	9.50		
Creamer	11.00	13.00	16.00	
Cup	13.00	13.50	14.00	
Mug, 7 oz.	140.00	137.50		
Pitcher 6¾" AOP, 36 oz. Scalloped or Round Bottom	32.50	39.50		
Pitcher, 8" PAT, 42 oz. Flat	30.00	37.50		
Pitcher, 8" PAT, 36 oz. Footed	35.00	42.50	80.00	
Plate, 6" Sherbet	5.00	5.50	8.50 (design on top)	
Plate, 7" Salad	13.50	15.50		
**Plate, 9" Dinner	12.50	14.50	12.00	32.50
Plate, 9" Grill	16.00	17.50		
Plate, 10" Grill		40.00		
Platter, 9" Oval	627.50			
Platter, 11" Oval	20.00	22.50	30.00	
Platter, 13" and 13" Divided	35.00	37.50		
Salt and Pepper (Scalloped Bottom)	925.00	650.00		
Saucer	4.00	3.50	4.25	
Sherbet	11.00	13.50	11.00	
Sugar	9.00	10.50	16.00	
Sugar Cover	10.00	11.00		
Tray, 10½" Sandwich	12.50	15.00	13.00	
Tumbler, 3¾", 4 oz. Footed AOP, Round or Scalloped	11.50	15.50	16.00	
Tumbler, 4½", 9 oz. Round Foot AOP	23.50	27.50	16.50	
***Tumbler, 4½", 8 oz. Scalloped Foot AOP	23.50	27.50	16.50	
Tumbler, 3½", 4 oz. Flat PAT	13.50	16.00		
Tumbler, 4¼", 9 oz. Flat PAT	13.50	16.50		
Tumbler, 5", 12 oz. Flat PAT	30.00	40.00		

*Yellow — $350.00.   Red — $375.00.
**Translucent Green, Red — $175.00
***Red — $175.00

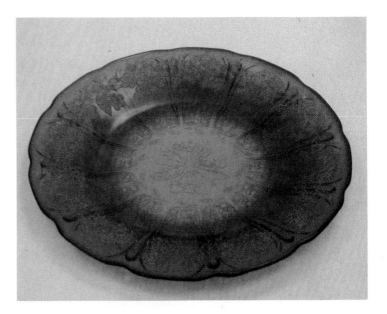

CHINEX CLASSIC
MACBETH-EVANS DIVISION OF CORNING GLASS WORKS, Late 1930's · Early 1940's

Colors: Ivory, ivory w/decal decorated.

People love the castle decorated Chinex Classic. Unfortunately, so little has been found, it's virtually ignored. If I had been aware of its scarcity ten years ago when I first put it in the book, I probably would not have included it. I assumed that over the years more of it would surface. Some has, but not enough to make this a viable collectible for most people.

Don't, however, ignore any butter dishes or sugar and creamers you run into in the pattern. Numerous collectors of these items will be glad to have them finally in their collections.

Chinex has an embossed, scroll-like design in the dishes which will distinguish them from the Cremax pattern with which it is often confused. The scrolling is found on the lid only of the butter dish. The base has only the pie crust type edging which leads people to believe they've discovered a Cremax butter bottom. The decaled butter has the same decal on the top and bottom.

	Browntone or Plain Ivory	Decal Decorated*
Bowl, 5¾" Cereal	3.50	4.50
Bowl, 7" Flat Soup	11.50	12.00
Bowl, 9" Vegetable	9.50	12.50
Butter Dish	50.00	62.50
Butter Dish Bottom	15.00	17.50
Butter Dish Top	35.00	45.00
Creamer	4.50	7.00
Cup	3.50	4.50
Plate, 6¼" Sherbet	2.00	2.50
Plate, 9¾" Dinner	3.50	5.00
Plate, 11½" Sandwich or Cake	6.50	8.00
Saucer	2.00	3.50
Sherbet, Low Footed	6.50	9.00
Sugar, Open	4.00	7.00

*Castle decal about 20% higher in most areas.

CIRCLE HOCKING GLASS COMPANY, 1930's

Colors: Green, pink.

In the last couple of years, Circle has gained buyers. You see it more and more at markets and you see people quietly making purchases from the pieces offered. It is a pretty pattern and there seemingly is more of it available than was first believed. Granted, it will probably take a while to gather a collection; but I now believe it could be done, something I was skeptical about for a time.

Circle has a lot going for it in that it has stemmed ware, two types of cups and saucers, attractive shapes and design and it's still very reasonably priced for a Depression ware pattern.

The rounded cup takes a saucer with a cup ring whereas the flat bottomed cup takes one without. The bi-colored stemmed ware has been found from coast to coast. I suspect there are more pieces to be found in this pattern than are listed here. Please let me know of any others you find!

	Green/Pink		Green/Pink
Bowl, 4½"	3.00	Plate, 9½" Dinner	6.00
Bowl, 8"	6.00	Saucer	1.00
Creamer	4.50	Sherbet, 3 1/8"	3.50
Cup (2 Styles)	2.50	Sherbet, 4¾"	4.50
Decanter, Handled	16.50	Sugar	4.50
Goblet, 4½" Wine	4.00	Tumbler, 4 oz. Juice	3.50
Goblet, 8 oz. Water	6.50	Tumbler, 8 oz. Water	4.50
Pitcher, 80 oz.	17.50	Vase, Hat Shape	17.50
Plate, 6" Sherbet	2.00		

Please refer to Foreword for pricing information

CLOVERLEAF HAZEL ATLAS GLASS COMPANY, 1930-1936

Colors: Pink, green, yellow, crystal, black.

I recently purchased a seven year accumulation of all colors of Cloverleaf! That collection was very revealing and I have had to revise my thinking on several items. For example, it would seem that the 8″ bowls are harder to find than the 7″ since this man had only located seven of the larger bowls but had managed to acquire seventeen of the smaller ones. (There appears to be no 8″ yellow Cloverleaf bowl). The green cereal bowl is harder to find than the yellow one; and the flat 9 oz. tumbler is even more difficult to locate than I had previously thought!

I was entertained when a lady with an utterly charming accent stopped by my table at a show where I'd set up tables of glass for sale and told me in a lilting Irish brogue that she just "loved the glass with the shamrock"!

We had enough glass to set out all the known pieces of pink and crystal for the picture, but the photographer cried, "Enough! Have a heart!"

The black Cloverleaf sherbet plate carries the design in the center. The saucer does not. Only plain ovide shaped candy dishes have surfaced in black, never one having the Cloverleaf design. Remember to check all black glass displays for the Cloverleaf ash trays! Not everybody knows Depression glass!

I can personally attest to the fact that Cloverleaf pattern is quite popular and sells very well!

	Pink	Green	Yellow	Black
Ash Tray 4″, Match Holder in Center				55.00
Ash Tray 5¾″, Match Holder in Center				70.00
Bowl, 4″ Dessert	8.00	12.50	16.00	
Bowl, 5″ Cereal		15.00	20.00	
Bowl, 7″ Deep Salad		22.50	37.50	
Bowl, 8″		42.50		
Candy Dish and Cover		37.50	95.00	
Creamer, 3 5/8″ Footed		7.50	12.50	12.50
Cup	5.00	5.50	11.50	9.50
Plate, 6″ Sherbet		3.50	5.00	20.00
Plate, 8″ Luncheon	5.00	5.00	10.00	10.50
Plate, 10¼″ Grill		15.00	17.50	
Salt and Pepper, Pair		22.50	82.50	52.50
Saucer	2.00	2.50	3.00	3.00
Sherbet, 3″ Footed	5.00	4.50	8.50	12.50
Sugar, Footed, 3 5/8″		7.50	12.50	12.50
Tumbler, 4″, 9 oz. Flat		27.50		
Tumbler, 3¾″, 10 oz. Flat Flared	13.50	22.50		
Tumbler, 5¾″, 10 oz. Footed		16.50	22.50	

COLONIAL, "KNIFE AND FORK" HOCKING GLASS COMPANY, 1934-1936

Colors: Pink, green, opaque white.

Colonial exudes a timeless elegance and grace. The longer you are around it, the better you like it. What better accolade for a design than that!

I am including a picture of one of the 15 known pink mugs as well as one of the 3 known green ones. There are bound to be more of them than that!

The rare, beaded edge pitcher (shown on the 4th edition cover photo repeated at the back of this book) has remained in hiding. There must be others of these.

Spooners, (one pictured in pink), are 5½ inches tall whereas a sugar bowl without its lid will measure only 4¼ inches tall. Often these are confused. Also, the lid of the butter will fit the wooden cheese dish. However, the cheese dish lid is ½ inch shorter than the butter lid.

Demand seems to be exceeding supply on some items in this pattern and prices are steadily rising. Dinner plates, 15 oz. flat tumblers, 5½" cereal bowls, 7" soup bowls, 3¾" berry bowls and the 3" sherbet in pink are all getting very hard to find. In fact, much of Colonial has already been swallowed up into collections and more is leaving the market place daily!

Crystal Colonial as listed by Hocking is priced here; however, I have yet to see all these items in my travels. There are few collectors for crystal at present.

A plate has turned up to match the white Colonial-like cup and saucer. From all indications, this may have been made by Corning, possibly in their Canadian plant.

	Pink	Green	Crystal		Pink	Green	Crystal
Bowl, 3¾" Berry	23.50			Plate, 6" Sherbet	3.50	3.50	2.00
Bowl, 4½" Berry	6.50	8.50	3.50	Plate, 8½" Luncheon	5.50	6.00	3.00
Bowl, 5½" Cereal	23.50	37.50	9.50	Plate, 10" Dinner	22.50	39.50	12.00
Bowl, 4½" Cream Soup	28.50	35.00		Plate, 10" Grill	15.00	17.50	7.50
Bowl, 7" Low Soup	25.00	35.00	9.00	Platter, 12" Oval	13.50	14.50	10.00
Bowl, 9" Large Berry	12.50	17.50	8.50	Salt and Pepper, Pair	100.00	107.50	45.00
Bowl, 10" Oval Vegetable	13.50	18.50	9.50	Saucer (White 3.00) (Same			
Butter Dish and Cover	450.00	42.50	32.50	as Sherbet Plate)	3.50	3.50	2.00
Butter Dish Bottom	300.00	25.00	20.00	Sherbet, 3"	9.00		
Butter Dish Top	150.00	17.50	12.50	Sherbet, 3 3/8"	5.50	10.00	4.00
Cheese Dish (As Shown)		77.50		Spoon Holder or Celery	77.50	85.00	35.00
Creamer, 5", 8 oz. (Milk				Sugar, 5"	10.00	11.00	6.00
Pitcher)	13.50	14.50	6.50	Sugar Cover	20.00	13.50	6.50
Cup (White 7.00)	6.00	8.50	5.00	Tumbler, 3", 5 oz. Juice	9.00	15.00	6.00
Goblet, 3¾", 1 oz. Cordial		23.00	10.00	**Tumbler, 4", 9 oz. Water	8.50	15.00	6.50
Goblet, 4", 3 oz. Cocktail		17.50		Tumbler, 10 oz.	13.50	17.50	7.50
Goblet, 4½", 2½ oz. Wine		18.50		Tumbler, 12 oz. Iced Tea	19.50	30.00	8.50
Goblet, 5¼", 4 oz. Claret		17.50		Tumbler, 15 oz. Lemonade	27.50	57.50	15.00
Goblet, 5¾", 8½ oz. Water	20.00	20.00	11.00	Tumbler, 3¼", 3 oz. Footed	10.00	15.00	7.00
Mug, 4½" 12 oz.	150.00	600.00		Tumbler, 4", 5 oz. Footed	12.50	18.50	8.00
Pitcher, 7", 54 oz. Ice Lip or				Tumbler, 5¼", 10 oz. Ftd.	15.00	20.00	10.00
None	32.50	35.00	20.00	Whiskey, 2½", 1½ oz.	7.00	9.00	4.00
*Pitcher, 7¾", 68 oz. Ice Lip							
or None	35.00	47.50	22.50				

*Beaded top in pink $500.00
**Royal Ruby $27.50

COLONIAL BLOCK HAZEL ATLAS GLASS COMPANY, Early 1930's

Colors: Green and pink; white in 1950's.

One of these pitchers has turned up in Alabama marked "HA". Thus, it could well be that Hazel Atlas did indeed manufacture these as Colonial Block pitchers. It was previously thought they were the product of U.S. Glass. So, people who bought them to "go with" Colonial Block did the right thing!

Notice the goblet. Often you see these labeled "Block" and so priced. They are NOT "Block Optic" and should only command a $7.00 or $8.00 price at best.

The Colonial Block butter dish is this pattern's chief claim to fame. Also, it is often mistaken for an exciting new find, a "round" Block Optic butter!

I have only seen the creamer and the sugar with lid in white. Let me know if you have or know of other pieces.

	Pink, Green	White		Pink, Green	White
Bowl, 4″	5.00		Creamer	7.50	5.50
Bowl, 7″	11.50		Goblet	8.00	
Butter Dish	27.50		Pitcher	22.50	
Butter Dish Bottom	7.50		Sugar	7.50	4.50
Butter Dish Top	20.00		Sugar Lid	5.50	3.00
Candy Jar w/Cover	25.00				

COLONIAL FLUTED, "ROPE" FEDERAL GLASS COMPANY, 1928-1933

Colors: Green, crystal.

That's a vegetable bowl to the right of the background lest you think at long last we had discovered a dinner plate to go with a "luncheon" plate. Most of the depth of the piece was lost by the camera. There are some dinner plates out there bearing the Federal mark. One has the panels but no roping; the other has the roping but no panels. Thus, neither quite fit this pattern although some people are blending them into their sets quite successfully.

This pattern is often badly scratched indicating it was widely used.

Looking closely, you should be able to see the "F" within a shield that was Federal's symbol.

Crystal has only been found as a bridge set having plates, cups and saucers with heart, spade, diamonds and clubs decals.

	Green		Green
Bowl, 4″ Berry	4.00	Plate, 6″ Sherbet	1.50
Bowl, 6″ Cereal	5.00	Plate, 8″ Luncheon	3.00
Bowl, 6½″ Deep Salad	9.00	Saucer	1.50
Bowl, 7½″ Large Berry	9.00	Sherbet	4.50
Creamer	4.50	Sugar	3.50
Cup	3.50	Sugar Cover	7.50

COLUMBIA   FEDERAL GLASS COMPANY, 1938-1942

Colors: Crystal, some pink.

Tumblers with plain, bulbous tops seated on inch high beaded bottoms have turned up in boxed sets of Columbia; so, it will have to be assumed they were meant to be Columbia tumblers though they weren't catalogued as such.

This is an extremely attractive pattern that for some unknown reason has attracted few collectors to date, perhaps because its crystal. It's dressy, inexpensive and fairly easy to locate except in cereal and soup bowls and the cup and tray snack set.

Butter dishes can come with various flashed-on colors (blue, iridescent, red, purple, amethyst, green) and with decal decorated tops.

Those luncheon pieces in pink are extremely hard to find!

	Crystal	Pink		Crystal	Pink
Bowl, 5" Cereal	7.50		Butter Dish Top	3.00	
Bowl, 8" Low Soup	8.50		Cup	3.50	7.50
Bowl, 8½" Salad	8.50		Plate, 6" Bread & Butter	1.50	3.50
Bowl, 10½" Ruffled Edge	12.50		Plate, 9½" Luncheon	3.50	12.50
Butter Dish and Cover	15.00		Plate, 11¾" Chop	5.50	
Ruby Flashed (17.50)			Saucer	1.00	5.50
Other Flashed (16.00)			Snack Plate	12.50	
Butter Dish Bottom	12.00		Tumbler	8.00	

CREMAX   MACBETH-EVANS DIVISION OF CORNING GLASS WORKS, Late 1930's · Early 1940's

Color: Cremax, cremax with fired-on color trim.

I have met a few hardy souls who have managed to put a set of this together! If you like challenges, this is the pattern to choose. Actually, this is rare glass; but because it's so hard to find, few people make the attempt.

There are various floral decals to be found other than those pictured here which further compounds the issue of gathering a set together. As I reported last time, one lady uses hers everyday and says she enjoys it a "thousand times more than Melamine"! The castle decal is most prized.

There is no butter dish in Cremax although the base to the Chinex butter is similar to the Cremax pattern.

This PATTERN is called Cremax. MacBeth-Evans also used cremax to describe the beige-like COLOR used in some of its patterns such as American Sweetheart, Dogwood, and Petalware. Be aware of this overlapping of meaning.

	Cremax	Decal Decorated		Cremax	Decal Decorated
Bowl, 5¾" Cereal	2.50	4.00	Plate, 9¾" Dinner	3.50	5.00
Bowl, 9" Vegetable	5.50	7.50	Plate, 11½" Sandwich	4.00	6.50
Creamer	3.00	5.50	Saucer	1.50	1.50
Cup	3.00	3.50	Sugar, Open	3.00	5.50
Plate, 6¼" Bread and Butter	1.50	2.50			

CORONATION, "BANDED RIB", "SAXON" HOCKING GLASS COMPANY, 1936-1940

Colors: Pink, green, crystal, royal ruby.

Imagine my surprise. I was being shown through Hocking's morgue in 1981 and when another section was rolled out for my viewing pleasure, there set a color of Coronation I'd never seen before---green! I could hardly believe my eyes. Since then, I've found three luncheon plates at a flea market in Indiana and that green bowl (without handles!) in northern Kentucky. The four pieces I saw in green at Hocking are shown in the smaller photograph at the bottom and were graciously photographed for all our pleasure by Anchor Hocking Glass for use in this book! The larger green tumbler (never seen before) is 5 7/16" tall and holds 14¼ ounces! I have no idea how plentiful the green actually is since I've been able to find four more pieces just this year! It's stumbling across "finds" like this that make collecting Depression glass so exciting. Keep your eyes open for other pieces in green and let me know what you find!

A couple of more Coronation pitchers have surfaced since people first saw the photograph in my last book. Exciting!

Notice that the handles on the pink bowls in Coronation are closed whereas the red bowls all have open handles. Why? All we know is they were made at different times. Hocking promoted a whole line of Royal Ruby products in the late '30's and early '40's; perhaps it was felt the open handles made the red bowls more attractive, less of a great red blob. It was interesting to learn that as recently as 1975 over 600 of the Coronation Royal Ruby berry sets were discovered in a warehouse still in the original Hocking packages!

You who are just learning Depression glass should pay careful attention to the tumbler shown here in Coronation because it's often confused with the more costly Lace Edge tumbler (one pictured with Lace Edge). You will notice that the rays are well up the sides of the Coronation tumbler but only up about a third of the glass in the Lace Edge tumbler. There is more plain glass to be seen in the Lace Edge.

You will also find no ruby saucer to match the Royal Ruby Coronation cup that you occasionally find simply because this cup was sold with a crystal saucer.

	Pink	Ruby Red	Green		Pink	Ruby Red	Green
Bowl, 4¼" Berry	3.00	5.00		Pitcher, 7¾", 68 oz.	125.00		
Bowl, 6½" Nappy	3.50	6.50		Plate, 6" Sherbet	1.50		
Bowl, 8" Large Berry, Handled	7.00	11.50		Plate, 8½" Luncheon	3.50	5.00	12.00
Bowl, 8", No Handles			20.00	Saucer (Same as 6" Plate)	1.50		
Cup	3.50	4.50		Sherbet	3.50	4.50	
				Tumbler, 5",10 oz. Footed	8.50		25.00

Please refer to Foreword for pricing information

CUBE, "CUBIST" JEANNETTE GLASS COMPANY, 1929-1933

Colors: Pink, green, crystal, ultramarine.

Since we showed you predominately green Cube in the last photograph, we decided to treat you to mostly pink this time. You can see from the picture that there are various hues of pink from extremely pale to very dark. This bothers some collectors. It's due merely to a lack of scientific and exacting controls under which the glassware was made back then.

Before I get letters, that is a dip in that pitcher rather than a chip. Either the mold didn't completely fill out or the glass "slipped" when it was taken from the mold all those years ago. This, too, happened. Now, a flawed piece would be immediately scrapped. Pitchers and tumblers in Cube are hard to find.

This pattern is often mistaken for Fostoria's "American" pattern. The design is similar but Fostoria's glass is better grade glassware. "American" pattern listings can be found in my book on *Elegant Glassware of the Depression Era*. The 2" creamer and sugar in crystal are abundant but seldom collected.

	Pink	Green		Pink	Green
Bowl, 4½" Dessert	4.50	5.00	Plate, 8" Luncheon	3.00	4.50
Bowl, 4½" Deep	4.50	5.00	Powder Jar and Cover,		
*Bowl, 6½" Salad	6.50	10.50	3 Legs	12.00	15.00
Butter Dish and Cover	45.00	50.00	Salt and Pepper, Pr.	25.00	27.50
Butter Dish Bottom	15.00	17.50	Saucer	1.50	2.00
Butter Dish Top	30.00	32.50	Sherbet, Footed	4.50	6.00
Candy Jar and Cover,			**Sugar, 2"	2.00	
6½"	21.00	25.00	Sugar, 3"	4.50	5.50
Coaster, 3¼"	3.50	4.50	Sugar/Candy Cover	6.00	8.00
**Creamer, 2"	2.00		Tray for 3" Creamer		
Creamer, 3"	4.50	6.00	and Sugar, 7½"		
Cup	4.50	7.00	(Crystal Only)	4.00	
Pitcher, 8¾", 45 oz.	130.00	147.50	Tumbler, 4", 9 oz.	21.50	30.00
Plate, 6" Sherbet	2.00	2.50			

*Ultramarine — $30.00
**Amber — $3.00

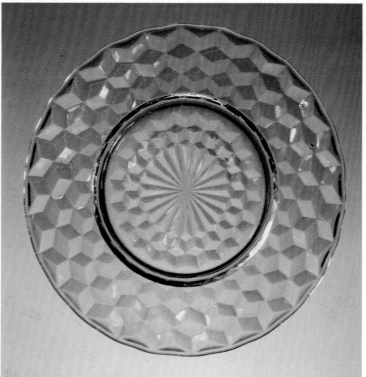

"CUPID"   PADEN CITY GLASS COMPANY, 1930's

Colors: Pink, green, light blue.

Everyone seems to like this pattern; the romanticists love it! It's gracefully shaped, artistically etched, and comes in pleasing colors. What more could anyone want from a pattern?

Most of the "Cupid" that has surfaced so far are serving pieces or dressy pieces for the table. Maybe that gives this pattern an "edge" so to speak with all collectors. Anyone can blend a piece or two into their table arrangement, be it antique or modern, and derive an aesthetic pleasure from owning a lovely piece of glassware. It isn't necessary to have a whole set of "Cupid", in other words, to derive an intense satisfaction from it.

Little by little as readers and collectors share their finds with me, we're adding to the list of what is available in this pattern. Two new candy dishes have been discovered, a 4¾" footed one with lid and a flat, three part candy with lid. Also, a 5" sugar and creamer have turned up. These items have been pink or green. Surely there are more of the lovely blue pieces than the plate shown!

Now that I have the computer, it will be very easy for me to store your information; so please don't hesitate to share it with me. I know that no matter how careful I have tried to be in the past that I have mislaid notes that were given to me at shows. Since there are two or three year intervals between books also, some of the things I thought I'd remember have fallen through the cracks of time. I want you to have every facet of information that's available; and I expect to be able to save every scrap you share with me from now on. So, thank you for your help both past and future!

The center handled trays were called sandwich trays by Paden City and those handled bowls were called candy trays. Every child would appreciate your owning (and filling) one of the latter!

	Pink, Green & Blue
Bowl, 8½" Oval Footed	32.50
Bowl, 9¼" Footed Fruit	30.00
Bowl, 9¼" Center Handled	35.00
Bowl, 11" Console	35.00
Cake Plate, 11¾"	35.00
Candlestick, 5" Wide, Pair	32.50
Candy w/Lid, Footed, 4¾" High	37.50
Candy w/Lid, 3 Part	47.50
Comport, 6¼"	22.50
Creamer, 4½" Footed	25.00
Creamer, 5", Footed	32.50
Ice Bucket, 6"	50.00
Ice Tub, 4¾"	37.50
Mayonnaise, 6" Diameter, Fits on 8" Plate	40.00
Plate, 10½"	22.50
Sugar, 4¼" Footed	25.00
Sugar, 5" Footed	32.50
Tray, 10½" Center Handled	27.50
Tray, 10 7/8" Oval, Footed	37.50
Vase, 8¼" Elliptical	60.00

"DAISY", NUMBER 620 INDIANA GLASS COMPANY

Colors: Crystal, 1933; amber, 1940; dark green and milk glass, 1960's, 1970's, & 1980's.

As some of you know, I was hospitalized the entire month of January. Flowers were delivered to me by a local florist in that green bowl! It's dated 1981 in the bottom; so, Indiana still makes these bowls. We're grateful for the date, of course; and I did tell you that Indiana had marketed these in green under the name of "Heritage" (not to be confused with Federal's "Heritage" pattern) as late as the '70's. A few collectors are beginning to consider the green which is fine; just know its newer glass and pay accordingly.

Few collectors even consider the antique crystal "Daisy"; most prefer the amber made during the war years. In this color, the 12 oz. tumblers and that 9 3/8" berry bowl shown standing at the back are the hardest pieces to find.

	Green, Crystal	Amber		Green, Crystal	Amber
Bowl, 4½" Berry	2.50	6.00	Plate, 9 3/8" Dinner	3.00	5.50
Bowl, 4½" Cream Soup	3.00	6.00	Plate, 10 3/8" Grill	4.00	9.00
Bowl, 6" Cereal	6.00	17.50	Plate, 11½" Cake or		
Bowl, 7 3/8" Deep Berry	4.50	10.00	Sandwich	5.00	8.50
Bowl, 9 3/8" Deep Berry	6.50	20.00	Platter, 10¾"	5.00	10.00
Bowl, 10" Oval Vegetable	6.00	12.50	Relish Dish, 3 Part, 8 3/8"	8.50	15.00
Creamer, Footed	4.50	6.50	Saucer	1.00	1.50
Cup	2.50	4.50	Sherbet, Footed	2.50	7.00
Plate, 6" Sherbet	1.00	2.00	Sugar, Footed	3.00	6.50
Plate, 7 3/8" Salad	2.00	5.50	Tumbler, 9 oz. Footed	5.00	12.50
Plate, 8 3/8" Luncheon	2.00	4.50	Tumbler, 12 oz. Footed	10.00	27.50

DIANA FEDERAL GLASS COMPANY, 1937-1941

Colors: Pink, amber, crystal.

Diana is often lumped into "one of those swirling patterns" of Depression Glass. As such, its potential has been overlooked in the past. As you can see from the picture, there are numerous pieces to be found and a quick glance at the price listing will show you that it's still inexpensive, something which can't be said of many Depression glass patterns.

Unfortunately, a pink demitasse set on the wire rack arrived too late to be photographed. One in crystal was pictured in the 5th edition.

Occasionally, frosted items turned up. In fact, one entire set showed up in pink. Frosted glass generally has little appeal for Depression glass people.

Newcomers take note that Diana pieces are swirled in the bottom as well as on the edges. This generally distinguishes Diana from other "swirled" patterns.

	Crystal	Pink	Amber		Crystal	Pink	Amber
*Ash Tray, 3½"	2.00	3.00		Plate, 5½" Child's	2.00	3.50	
Bowl, 5" Cereal	2.50	3.50		Plate, 6" Bread and Butter	1.00	1.50	1.50
Bowl, 5½" Cream Soup	2.50	5.00	6.00	Plate, 9½" Dinner	4.00	5.50	6.50
Bowl, 9" Salad	5.00	6.50	5.50	Plate, 11¾" Sandwich	4.50	5.50	6.50
Bowl, 11" Console Fruit	5.00	6.50	8.00	Platter, 12" Oval	5.00	6.50	7.50
Bowl, 12" Scalloped Edge	4.50	7.50	8.50	Salt and Pepper, Pr.	17.50	30.00	65.00
Candy Jar and Cover, Round	12.00	20.00	22.50	Saucer	1.00	1.50	1.50
Coaster, 3½"	2.00	3.50		Sherbet	2.50	5.00	5.00
Creamer, Oval	2.00	3.50	3.50	Sugar, Open Oval	2.50	3.50	3.50
Cup	2.50	3.50	3.50	Tumbler, 4 1/8", 9 oz.	5.00	8.50	9.50
Cup, 2 oz. Demitasse				Junior Set: 6 Cups,			
and 4½" Saucer Set	4.50	12.50		Saucers and Plates with			
*Green — $3.00				Round Rack	50.00	100.00	

DIAMOND QUILTED, "FLAT DIAMOND"
IMPERIAL GLASS COMPANY, Late 1920's · Early 1930's

Colors: Pink, blue, green, crystal, black; some red and amber.

This is one of the few patterns in Depression Glass that has a punch bowl. That fact alone should tell you something of the Depression itself and something of the quality of glass of this pattern. The blue is very attractive and never fails to "sell itself". Collectors keep hoping to discover a blue punch bowl! I will say that the green bowl shown is a much prettier green than this picture shows it to be.

Most of the blue and black Diamond Quilted pieces have the quilting effect on the inside of the dish. You have to turn the black plate over on its face to see the quilting, however.

Creamers, sugars, cups and saucers have shown up in amber and red leading one to believe it was probably sold as a luncheon set. All we need find now are the plates!

According to Imperial files, the candle holders were made in two styles. I've only ever seen the one shown. There should be one with a rolled edge somewhat on the order of the 10½" bowl featured below in the old catalogue ad.

Lest you confuse the pattern, Hazel Atlas also made a quilted patterned pitcher and tumblers in cobalt blue, pink and green. The quilting effect stops and becomes a straight line before it reaches the top of the dish. These are heavy glass, too.

	Pink, Green	Blue, Black		Pink, Green	Blue, Black
Bowl, 4¾" Cream Soup	6.50	12.50	Mayonnaise Set: Ladle, Plate, 3 Footed Dish	17.50	
Bowl, 5" Cereal	4.50	7.50	Pitcher, 64 oz.	27.50	
Bowl, 5½" One Handle	5.50	8.50	Plate, 6" Sherbet	2.50	3.50
Bowl, 7" Crimped Edge	5.50	10.00	Plate, 7" Salad	4.00	6.50
Bowl, Rolled Edge Console	13.50	25.00	Plate, 8" Luncheon	4.00	10.00
Cake Salver, Tall 10" Diameter	27.50		Punch Bowl and Stand	257.50	
Candlesticks (2 Styles), Pr.	9.50	22.50	Plate, 14" Sandwich	8.50	
Candy Jar and Cover, Footed	16.50	27.50	Sandwich Server, Center Handle	15.00	25.00
Compote and Cover, 11½"	37.50		Saucer	2.00	3.50
Creamer	6.00	9.50	Sherbet	4.00	8.50
Cup	4.00	6.00	Sugar	6.00	9.50
Goblet, 1 oz. Cordial	5.50		Tumbler, 9 oz. Water	6.50	
Goblet, 2 oz. Wine	5.50		Tumbler, 12 oz. Iced Tea	7.50	
Goblet, 3 oz. Wine	6.50		Tumbler, 6 oz. Footed	6.00	
Goblet, 6", 9 oz. Champagne	7.50		Tumbler, 9 oz. Footed	9.50	
Ice Bucket	37.50	55.00	Tumbler, 12 oz. Footed	12.50	
			Vase, Fan, Dolphin Handles	22.50	32.50
			Whiskey, 1½ oz.	6.50	

Covered Bowl—6¾ in. diam., deep round shape with 3 artistic feet, dome cover, fine quality brilliant finish **pot glass**, allover block diamond design, transparent Rose Marie and emerald green.
I C5603—Asstd. ½ doz. in carton, 20 lbs.
Doz $6.95

I C989—3 piece set, 2 transparent colors (rose and green), good quality, 10½ in. rolled rim bowl, TWO 3½ in. wide base candlesticks. Asstd. 6 sets in case, 30 lbs..............**SET (3 pcs) 65**c

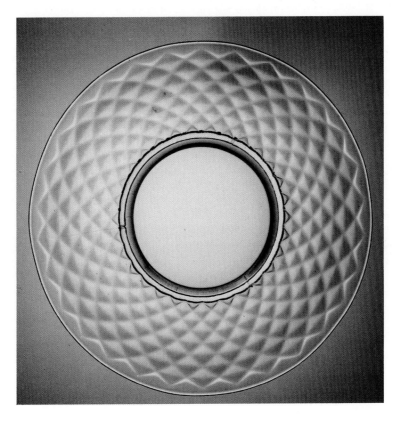

55

DOGWOOD, "APPLE BLOSSOM", "WILD ROSE"

MACBETH-EVANS GLASS COMPANY, 1929-1932

Colors: Pink, green, some crystal, monax, cremax and yellow.

Dogwood always attracts admiration, particularly the pitcher and tumblers which have the silk screened Dogwood design on them. Both pink and green are pictured here. There is also a more bulbous pitcher to be found having what collectors refer to as "an American Sweetheart shape". Remember, the pitchers MUST have the Dogwood design, not just SHAPE, to be considered to be Dogwood. These plain pitchers were simply made by the same company.

Pink grill plates come in both styles, all over design or design at the rim only. Green comes only with the rim design. Luncheon plates are plentiful; dinner plates, which occur only in pink, are becoming scarce.

The 10¼" fruit bowl which is so rarely seen any more unhappily is the one turning up frosted and drilled through to be used as a lamp shade!

New collectors should know that PINK cups, creamers and sugars come in both a thick and thin variety, the thin having a slightly rolled edge. See the pink cups pictured. The green comes only in the thin shape. Both styles of sugars and creamers are pictured.

The platter shown is a rarely seen piece. Only a few collections have these.

Only a yellow luncheon plate and a cereal bowl have surfaced in that color. The yellow bowl was pictured in a previous edition.

There is also a smaller, 11" cake plate in Dogwood like the one pictured in "S" pattern. It has to be considered a rare piece.

There is little demand for the monax items; they remain more interesting than desirable. We turned the bowl over in the picture so you could see the design. The monax salver is turning out to be more plentiful than first believed and makes an excellent decorated cake base, as I've been shown. It sort of "shows off" your cake.

The 4¾" stemmed wine goblet was not made by MacBeth-Evans; but it's so close to Dogwood pattern that I wanted collectors to be aware of it.

The ad shown below is from a '30's magazine; please, no more "orders" for sets!

	Pink	Green	Monax, Cremax
*Bowl, 5½" Cereal	14.00	17.50	15.00
Bowl, 8½" Berry	32.50	69.50	39.50
Bowl, 10¼" Fruit	177.50	97.50	
Cake Plate, 11" Heavy Solid Foot	152.50		
Cake Plate, 13" Heavy Solid Foot	62.50	52.50	125.00
Creamer, 2½" Thin	11.00	35.00	
Creamer, 3¼" Thick	13.50		
Cup, Thin or Thick	9.00	15.00	35.00
Pitcher, 8" 80 oz. Decorated	127.50	450.00	
Pitcher, 8" 80 oz. (American Sweetheart Style)	457.50		
Plate, 6" Bread and Butter	4.00	5.00	20.00
*Plate, 8" Luncheon	4.00	5.00	
Plate. 9¼" Dinner	17.50		
Plate, 10½" Grill AOP or Border Design Only	12.50	11.50	
Plate, 12" Salver	18.50		23.50
Platter, 12" Oval (Rare)	247.50		
Saucer	4.00	5.00	15.00
Sherbet, Low Footed	17.50	47.50	
Sugar, 2½" Thin	9.50	35.00	
Sugar, 3¼" Thick	10.50		
Tumbler, 3½", 5 oz. Decorated	117.50		
Tumbler, 4" 10 oz. Decorated	22.50	52.50	
Tumbler, 4¾", 11 oz. Decorated	30.00	62.50	
Tumbler, 5", 12 oz. Decorated	35.00	67.50	
Tumbler, Molded Band	9.00		

*Yellow — $45.00

Please refer to Foreword for pricing information

DORIC JEANNETTE GLASS COMPANY, 1935-1938

Colors: Pink, green, some delphite, yellow.

Take a good look at the pitchers shown here! That yellow footed and blue delphite pitcher are unique at this writing. There are bound to be others! Also, the footed green Doric pitcher is something of a wizard at hiding. Now, in the pink footed pitchers you will notice there are two styles due to a variation at the lip.

Hard to find items in Doric include the 4½", 9 oz. tumbler, both footed tumblers, (often have mold roughness when found), cereal bowls, cream soups and, of course, footed pitchers.

The square Doric dish shown in pink can be found on a metal tray having "two stories" so to speak. It was called a relish tray and comes in two sizes. One was pictured in previous editions.

Sugar dish and candy lids in this pattern do not interchange since the candy lid is taller and has a more traditional cone, candy lid shape.

Delphite Doric, though attractive, is hard to find except for sherbets and the three part candy dish. This is a bit of irony since sherbets in pink and green are "hen's teeth" hard to find!

The Doric cake plate is footed and not to be confused with the two handled serving tray pictured in pink.

The pink Doric shaker lids are original; the green lids are newly made. I point this out merely to let people know that new lids are now being made available for Depression glass shakers. Original lids are preferable unless they're corroded or caved in.

There is a three part, iridized candy dish that was made as recently as the '70's and was selling in my area at the local dish barn for about 79 cents. If there is a dish barn in your area, it would pay you to go through it from time to time and acquaint yourself with what and from where some flea market dealers are supplied.

	Pink	Green	Delphite
Bowl, 4½" Berry	5.00	5.50	27.50
Bowl, 5" Cream Soup		127.50	
Bowl, 5½" Cereal	16.00	18.50	
Bowl, 8¼" Large Berry	9.50	12.50	77.50
Bowl, 9" Two Handled	9.50	9.50	
Bowl, 9" Oval Vegetable	11.00	12.50	
Butter Dish and Cover	55.50	67.50	
Butter Dish Bottom	17.50	25.00	
Butter Dish Top	37.50	42.50	
Cake Plate, 10", Three Legs	12.00	11.50	
Candy Dish and Cover, 8"	25.00	25.00	
*Candy Dish, Three Part	4.50	5.50	4.50
Coaster, 3"	9.50	11.00	
Creamer, 4"	7.50	8.50	
Cup	5.50	6.50	
Pitcher, 6", 36 oz. Flat	25.00	27.50	377.50
Pitcher, 7½", 48 oz. Footed	257.50	457.50	
(Also in Yellow at $750.00)			
Plate, 6" Sherbet	2.50	3.00	
Plate, 7" Salad	12.50	11.50	
Plate, 9" Dinner (Serrated 35.00)	7.50	9.50	
Plate, 9" Grill	7.50	10.00	
Platter, 12" Oval	11.00	12.00	
Relish Tray, 4" x 4"	5.00	7.50	
**Relish Tray, 4" x 8"	6.50	9.50	
Salt and Pepper, Pr.	24.00	27.50	
Saucer	2.00	2.50	
Sherbet, Footed	7.50	8.50	5.00
Sugar	8.50	9.50	
Sugar Cover	9.00	15.00	
Tray, 10" Handled	7.50	9.50	
Tray, 8" x 8" Serving	7.50	8.50	
Tumbler, 4½", 9 oz.	27.50	40.00	
Tumbler, 4", 10 oz., Ftd.	18.00	30.00	
Tumbler, 5", 12 oz., Ftd.	35.00	37.50	

*Candy in metal holder — $37.50. Iridescent
    made recently.
**Trays in metal holder as shown — $27.50

Please refer to Foreword for pricing information

DORIC & PANSY JEANNETTE GLASS COMPANY, 1937-1938

Colors: Ultramarine; some crystal and pink.

For those of you with travel plans to England or Canada, keep a weather eye out for Doric and Pansy salt, peppers and butter dishes. It might help pay for your trip should you find some and I have reports of at least four sets coming out of England! Maybe that's why there are few to be found here; they were shipped out of the country.

Many Doric and Pansy shakers are weakly patterned; they need to have SOME pattern design to be called Doric and Pansy, however. I've seen a few that had the shape and color only.

Ultramarine Doric and Pansy is not easily found, but once found, it doesn't always "match". Due to the unstable ways of heating the glass back then, there are various shades of ultramarine from one batch to the next.

With the increased interest in the collecting field of children's toys and miniature dishes, owners of the "Pretty Polly Party Dishes" in Doric and Pansy should be feeling very smug. If you haven't completed your set, I suggest you do so quickly before the prices start climbing.

Only berry sets and the children's set have been found in pink.

	Green, Teal	Pink, Crystal		Green, Teal	Pink, Crystal
Bowl, 4½″ Berry	9.50	6.00	Plate, 6″ Sherbet	8.00	6.00
Bowl, 8″ Large Berry	57.50	17.50	Plate, 7″ Salad	27.50	
Bowl, 9″ Handled	25.00	9.50	Plate, 9″ Dinner	19.00	5.00
Butter Dish and Cover	625.00		Salt and Pepper, Pr.	400.00	
Butter Dish Bottom	150.00		Saucer	4.00	2.25
Butter Dish Top	475.00		Sugar, Open	162.50	57.50
Cup	15.00	7.50	Tray, 10″ Handled	17.50	
Creamer	167.50	57.50	Tumbler, 4½″, 9 oz.	35.00	

DORIC AND PANSY
"PRETTY POLLY PARTY DISHES"

	Teal	Pink		Teal	Pink
Cup	25.00	20.00	Creamer	27.50	22.50
Saucer	4.25	3.25	Sugar	27.00	22.50
Plate	8.00	6.00	14 Piece Set	192.50	160.00

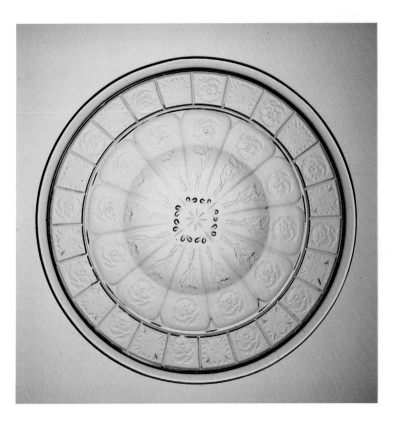

ENGLISH HOBNAIL   WESTMORELAND GLASS COMPANY, 1920's - 1970's

Colors: Crystal, pink, amber, turquoise, cobalt, green, blue, red.

This is a beautiful pattern which has had tremendous longevity, meaning there is much old to be found and much new! For instance, red English Hobnail was causing quite a stir in collecting circles until Westmoreland made 17 pieces, including the pitcher, for LeVay Distributing Company in the late '70's. Thus, though very attractive, this is a "collect at your own risk" pattern as far as collecting for investment goes.

Pink is about the only COLOR you can hope to collect an entire set of and there are at least two different shades of that. There are three distinct greens, two ambers (the lighter version being made in the 1960's), two turquoise, and a number of fired-on colors, plus round and squared shapes. NO, I'm not trying to put you off collecting this, just letting you know what you'd be in for once you decide to collect it. Actually, I like this pattern. My wife used the crystal goblets for several years at our table. I don't price crystal. It reappears too frequently. It's relatively inexpensive. Some of the crystal comes with black bases or trims.

This is another pattern that you can enjoy owning an occasional piece of without coveting an entire set. Many people buy the candy dishes or cologne bottles, a lamp or serving tray, a pitcher or shakers just to add color to a room or set of china. One man told me he enjoyed being served his egg in his fancy English Hobnail egg cup!

To help new collectors to distinguish English Hobnail from Miss America I offer the following observations. English Hobnail pieces have center rays of varying distance; the hob tips are more rounded giving it a smoother "feel"; and the goblets have rims that flair slightly plus moving directly from the hobs to the plain glass rim. Miss America rays flair equi-distant from the center; the hobs are sharp to touch and the goblets don't flair at the rim and have three sets of rings above the hobs before entering a plain glass rim.

	Cobalt, Amber, Turquoise*, Pink, Green		Cobalt, Amber, Turquoise*, Pink, Green
**Ash Tray, Several Shapes	18.50	Goblet, 5 oz. Claret	13.50
Bowls, 4½", 5" Square and Round	9.50	**Goblet, 6¼", 8 oz.	17.50
Bowl, Cream Soup	13.50	Grapefruit, 6½" Flange Rim	13.50
Bowls, 6" Several Styles	10.00	Lamp, 6¼" Electric	60.00
Bowls, 8" Several Styles	16.00	**Lamp, 9¼"	117.50
**Bowls, 8" Footed and Two Handled	37.50	Lampshade, 17" Diameter (Crystal)	117.50
**Bowls, 11" and 12" Nappies	35.00	Marmalade and Cover	32.50
Bowls, 8", 9" Oval Relish	15.00	Pitcher, 23 oz.	117.50
Bowl, 12" Oval Relish	17.50	Pitcher, 39 oz.	120.00
Candlesticks, 3½" Pair	30.00	Pitcher, 60 oz.	137.50
Candlesticks, 8½" Pair	45.00	Pitcher, ½ Gal. Straight Sides	155.00
Candy Dish, ½ lb. Cone Shaped	45.00	**Plate, 5½", 6½" Sherbet	3.50
Candy Dish and Cover, Three Feet	57.50	Plate, 7¼" Pie	4.00
Celery Dish, 9"	16.50	**Plate, 8" Round or Square	7.50
Celery Dish, 12"	20.00	Plate, 10" Dinner	17.50
**Cigarette Box	22.50	Salt and Pepper, Pair, Round or Square Bases	67.50
**Cologne Bottle	25.00	Salt Dip, 2" Footed and with Place Card Holder	16.50
Creamer, Footed or Flat	15.00	Saucer	3.50
Cup	12.00	**Sherbet	12.50
Decanter, 20 oz. with Stopper	57.50	Sugar, Footed or Flat	15.00
Demitasse Cup and Saucer	25.00	Tumbler, 3¾", 5 oz. or 9 oz.	12.50
Egg Cup	25.00	Tumbler, 4", 10 oz. Iced Tea	14.50
Goblet, 1 oz. Cordial	16.00	Tumbler, 5", 12 oz. Iced Tea	17.50
Goblet, 2 oz. Wine	13.50	Tumbler, 7 oz. Footed	13.50
Goblet, 3 oz. Cocktail	15.00	Tumbler, 9 oz. Footed	14.50
		Tumbler, 12½ oz. Footed	18.50
		Whiskey, 1½ oz. and 3 oz.	16.50

*Add about 50% more for Turquoise
**Cobalt double price listed

Please refer to Foreword for pricing information

FIRE-KING DINNERWARE "PHILBE" HOCKING GLASS COMPANY, 1937-1938

Colors: Blue, green, pink, crystal.

This is a beautiful pattern which is in limited supply. Collectors for this need a "long" pocket. However, whether you collect it or not, you need to be familiar with it lest you stumble onto a bargain and not know it!

The picture of the blue cookie jar is courtesy of Anchor Hocking. I had one years ago in green which I allowed a "friend" to talk me out of for the $10.00 I had in it because they were "collecting" it. I later found they "collected" it only long enough to sell it for the tidy sum I knew it to be worth. Oh, well; I'd as soon be called gullible as mercenary.

If you can say any pieces of this pattern are commonly found, then you'd have to lump the green grill plates, pink oval bowl and the blue 6½" footed iced tea in that group. The pitchers shown plus one other pink juice are all that are known so far. I'm certain there are others to be found.

The blue to the naked eye is a pretty, vivid blue and not the pale, "washed out" blue of the ovenware pieces. Much of the blue is silver trimmed.

Many of the dinnerware pieces have shapes similar to Cameo, another Hocking pattern. So, if you see a Cameo shaped blue pitcher which turns out not to be Cameo, chances are you've found a rare Fire-King Dinnerware pitcher!

	Crystal	Pink, Green	Blue
Bowl, 5½" Cereal	10.00	30.00	40.00
Bowl, 7¼" Salad	15.00	40.00	60.00
Bowl, 10" Oval Vegetable	15.00	37.50	55.00
Candy Jar, 4" Low, with Cover	75.00	127.50	157.50
Cookie Jar with Cover	100.00	200.00	350.00
Creamer, 3¼" Footed	25.00	37.50	57.50
Cup	20.00	52.50	100.00
Goblet, 7¼", 9 oz. Thin	37.50	117.50	150.00
Pitcher, 6", 36 oz. Juice	150.00	300.00	450.00
Pitcher, 8½", 56 oz.	250.00	350.00	500.00
Plate, 6" Sherbet	10.00	15.00	25.00
Plate, 8" Luncheon	12.00	17.50	30.00
Plate, 10" Heavy Sandwich	15.00	20.00	35.00
Plate, 10½" Salver	15.00	20.00	35.00
Plate, 10½" Grill	12.00	17.50	30.00
Plate, 11 5/8" Salver	12.00	17.50	32.50
Platter, 12" Closed Handles	15.00	27.50	50.00
Saucer, 6" (Same as Sherbet Plate)	10.00	15.00	25.00
Sugar, 3¼" Footed	25.00	45.00	65.00
Tumbler, 4", 9 oz. Flat Water	25.00	77.50	97.50
Tumbler, 3½" Footed Juice	30.00	90.00	125.00
Tumbler, 5¼", 10 oz. Footed	20.00	40.00	37.50
Tumbler, 6½", 15 oz. Footed Iced Tea	25.00	35.00	35.00

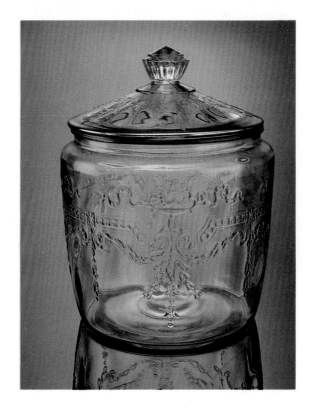

FIRE-KING OVEN GLASS ANCHOR HOCKING GLASS CORPORATION, 1941-1950's

Colors: Pale blue, crystal; some ivory and jade-ite.

Would you believe that this is the one pattern in Depression glass where prices have increased dramatically since the printing of the last book? Depression glass kitchen items are very desirable collectibles and the market is strong.

We again owe thanks to Anchor Hocking for the picture of the blue skillet and nipple cover. Now that we know these items were made, possibly our search will prove more fruitful! The jade-ite skillet is pictured in the new 2nd edition Kitchenware book. Only a few of those have turned up.

Price increases on the large covered roaster and the juice saver pie plate are the most dramatic in the book. Both are pictured. No. I don't "set" these prices. I merely observe and record what they sell for in the market place. (I just noticed that someone at the photography session put the lid on the roaster wrong. The handles sit side by side rather than atop each other so as to create a larger gripping surface. The "tabs" are to keep the handles from sliding on each other).

The one cup measure without a spout is called a "dry" measure and is rare.

The child's bake set ("Sunny Suzy Glass Baking Set") pictured in the 4th edition is bringing $35.00-40.00 in its original box.

I have re-listed the 4 3/8" individual pie plate and the 5 3/8" deep dish pie plate (as listed by Anchor Hocking) under "bowls" since I had so many calls and inquiries regarding these. The 5 3/8" one is pictured between the large roaster and the covered casserole on the table server. The smaller of these "bowls" is hard to find.

Novice collectors should know there are four different custard cups; and the mugs come in a thick and thicker version.

The uncovered casseroles were called "bakers" while those sold with lids were called "casseroles".

	Blue		Blue
Baker, 1 pt., Round or Square	3.50	Custard Cup, 5 oz.	3.00
Baker, 1 qt.	4.50	Custard Cup, 6 oz., 2 Styles	3.50
Baker, 1½ qt.	8.50	Loaf Pan, 9 1/8" Deep	15.00
Baker, 2 qt.	10.00	Measuring Bowl, 16 oz.	15.00
Bowl, 4 3/8", Individual Pie Plate	8.50	Nurser, 4 oz.	12.00
Bowl, 5 3/8", Cereal or Deep Dish Pie		Nurser, 8 oz.	15.00
Plate	8.50	Pie Plate, 8 3/8"	7.00
Cake Pan (Deep), 8¾" (Roaster)	12.00	Pie Plate, 9"	8.00
Casserole, 1 pt., Knob Handle Cover	10.00	Pie Plate, 9 5/8"	9.00
Casserole, 1 qt., Knob Handle Cover	10.00	Pie Plate, 10 3/8" Juice Saver	35.00
Casserole, 1½ qt., Knob Handle Cover	12.00	Perculator Top, 2 1/8"	3.50
Casserole, 2 qt., Knob Handle Cover	15.00	Refrigerator Jar & Cover, 4½" x 5"	7.50
Casserole, 1 qt., Pie Plate Cover	12.50	Refrigerator Jar & Cover, 5 1/8" x 9 1/8"	15.00
Casserole, 1½ qt., Pie Plate Cover	15.00	Roaster, 8¾"	25.00
Casserole, 2 qt., Pie Plate Cover	18.00	Roaster, 10 3/8"	40.00
Casserole, 10 oz., Tab Handle Cover	12.00	Table Server, Tab Handles (Hot Plate)	10.00
Coffee Mug, 7 oz., 2 Styles	17.50	Utility Bowl, 6 7/8"	7.50
Cup, 8 oz., Dry Measure, No Spout	25.00	Utility Bowl, 8 3/8"	8.50
Cup, 8 oz. Measuring, 1 Spout	10.00	Utility Bowl, 10 1/8"	12.00
Cup, 8 oz., Measuring, 3 Spout	16.00	Utility Pan, 8 1/8" x 12½"	12.00

FLORAGOLD, "LOUISA" JEANNETTE GLASS COMPANY, 1950's

Colors: Iridescent, some shell pink, ice blue and crystal.

There is a pattern in Carnival glass similar to this which is known as "Louisa"; hence the crossed nomenclature.

New pieces have been found in this pattern! One is a tall, ruffled edged comport and the other is a covered powder jar! Neither piece was for sale.

The smaller butter dish (5½″ x 3″ tall) is still unique at this time.

I have been asked time and again what the difference is between the 10 and 11 ounce tumblers. One ounce is obvious. The 10 ounce has a narrow band around the top which the 11 ounce does not have. The 15 ounce tumbler is very hard to find except in crystal where they sell in the $6.00-7.00 range.

There is a tid-bit in Floragold made from two ruffled bowls rather than the usual plate type. These are set around a white, wooden post.

Cups were sold with that large bowl and also the pitcher and were called "egg nog" sets. Therefore, cups are much more plentiful than saucers/sherbet plates.

That is a squared bowl in the picture next to the plate. Depth is lost at this camera angle.

Please don't write me about the oblong, footed, scalloped edge candy dish! There are TWO pictured in the last book. It's a commonly found item. I just couldn't turn one up in time for this picture! (It looks like the butter cover turned over with scalloped edges and four feet).

The salt and pepper can also be found with brown lids. Both white and brown are plastic and crack when over tightened. Perfect lids are harder to find than perfect shakers.

The vase looks like a large tumbler whose top was inwardly scalloped.

	Iridescent		Iridescent
Bowl, 4½″ Square	3.50	Coaster/Ash Tray, 4″	4.50
Bowl, 5½″ Round Cereal	17.50	Creamer	5.50
Bowl, 5½″ Ruffled Fruit	3.50	Cup	4.00
Bowl, 8½″ Ruffled Fruit	4.00	Pitcher, 64 oz.	22.50
Bowl, 8½″, Square	9.50	Plate, 5¾″ Sherbet	5.00
Bowl, 9½″ Deep Salad	25.00	Plate, 8½″ Dinner	16.50
Bowl, 9½″, Ruffled	6.50	Plate or Tray, 13½″	12.50
Bowl, 12″ Ruffled Large Fruit	6.50	Indent on 13½″ Plate	32.50
Butter Dish and Cover, ¼ lb.		Platter, 11¼″	13.50
Oblong	15.00	*Salt and Pepper, Plastic Tops	35.00
Butter Dish and Cover, Round	35.00	Saucer, 5¼″ (No Ring)	5.00
Butter Dish Bottom	12.00	Sherbet, Low Footed	8.00
Butter Dish Top	23.00	Sugar	5.00
Candlesticks, Double Branch Pr.	30.00	Sugar Lid	7.50
Candy or Cheese Dish and Cover,		Tumbler, 10 oz. Footed	11.50
6¾″	30.00	Tumbler, 11 oz. Footed	12.50
Candy, 5¼″ Long, 4 Feet	4.50	Tumbler, 15 oz. Footed	42.50
Candy Dish, 1 Handle	4.50	Vase or Celery	77.50

*Tops $7.50 each.

FLORAL, "POINSETTIA" JEANNETTE GLASS COMPANY, 1931-1935

Colors: Pink, green, delphite, jadite, crystal, amber, red, yellow.

Floral has ever been a popular and easily recognized pattern of Depression glass. It also has numerous pieces available to the collector which is another boon; plus it has the added enticement of the hunt for rarely seen or one-of-a-kind items as you can see from the long listing on the next page. To further aid the collector, this Floral pattern is readily available. You nearly always find some at the flea markets and shows.

Lest you think that bargains are never found today let me tell you of a pair of octagonal vases (one is pictured) in Floral which came from England and were sold at auction in June, 1983, for $150.00 each! Bargains do still abound. It pays to be educated. The Floral pattern is around the base of these vases.

The dresser set pictured is the only one of those to be found thus far. One powder dish measures 3" and the other 4¼". Several dresser trays have been found, however, so there must be other powder jars.

The sugar and the candy lids in Floral are interchangeable.

One 11" platter comes with scalloped indentations reminiscent of the Cherry Blossom platter. The normally found platter has smooth sides.

Jadite Floral cannisters are pictured in the new 2nd edition of my *Kitchen Glassware* book.

Novices should acquaint themselves with the flat bottomed tumbler pictured. Few of these are found. Notice also the two styles of flower vases, the flower frogs, the footed pink comport, the two lamps and their bulbs, the small green and crystal pitchers. These are all items you will not normally run into; but if you should, you need to know their worth!

Unusual items in Floral (so far) include the following:
    a) a set of DELPHITE Floral
    b) a YELLOW, two part relish
    c) an AMBER plate, cup and saucer
    d) green and crystal JUICE PITCHERS w/ground bottoms (shown)
    e) footed vases in green and crystal, flared at the rim (shown); some hold flower frogs with
        THE PATTERN ON THE FROGS
    f) a crystal lemonade pitcher
    g) lamps (shown in green and pink)
    h) a green GRILL plate
    i) an octagonal vase with a patterned, round foot (shown)
    j) a RUFFLED EDGED berry and master berry bowl (one shown)
    k) pink and green Floral ICE tubs (shown)
    l) oval vegetable with cover
    m) a rose bowl (shown)
    n) a 9" comport in pink and green (each shown)
    o) 9 oz. flat tumblers in green (shown)
    p) 3 oz. footed tumblers in green (shown)
    q) 8" round bowl in BEIGE (shown)
    r) CARAMEL colored dinner plate

See page 72 for prices.

FLORAL, "POINSETTIA" (Con't.)

	Pink	Green	Delphite	Jadite
Bowl, 4″ Berry (Ruffled 45.00)	8.50	9.00	25.00	
Bowl, 5½″ Cream Soup		250.00		
*Bowl, 7½″ Salad (Ruffled 50.00)	9.50	11.00	45.00	
Bowl, 8″ Covered Vegetable	22.50	25.00	37.50 (no cover)	
Bowl, 9″ Oval Vegetable	10.00	12.00		
Butter Dish and Cover	67.50	72.50		
Butter Dish Bottom	17.50	20.00		
Butter Dish Top	50.00	52.50		
Canister Set: Coffee, Tea, Cereal, Sugar, 5¼″ Tall, Each				25.00
Candlesticks, 4″ Pr.	45.00	62.50		
Candy Jar and Cover	27.50	30.00		
Creamer, Flat	8.00	9.50	57.50	
Coaster, 3¼″	7.50	8.00		
Comport, 9″	275.00	300.00		
†Cup	7.50	8.50		
Dresser Set (As Shown)		950.00		
Frog for Vase (Also Crystal $400.00)		575.00		
Ice Tub, 3½″ High Oval	375.00	400.00		
Lamp	117.50	117.50		
Pitcher, 5½″, 23 or 24 oz.		450.00		
Pitcher, 8″, 32 oz. Footed Cone	20.00	25.00		
Pitcher, 10¼″, 48 oz. Lemonade	160.00	177.50		
Plate, 6″ Sherbet	3.50	3.50		
Plate, 8″ Salad	6.50	7.00		
†Plate, 9″ Dinner	11.00	12.50	95.00	
Plate, 9″ Grill		47.50		
Platter (Like Cherry Blossom)	35.00	35.00		
Platter, 10¾″ Oval	11.00	12.50	95.00	
Refrigerator Dish and Cover, 5″ Square		45.00		12.50
††Relish Dish, Two Part Oval	9.50	9.50		
Salt and Pepper, 4″ Footed Pair	32.50	35.00		
Salt and Pepper, 6″ Flat	30.00			
†Saucer	6.00	6.50		
Sherbet	8.50	9.50	65.00	
Sugar	7.50	8.50	50.00 (open)	
Sugar/Candy Cover	9.50	12.50		
Tray, 6″ Square, Closed Handles	9.50	10.00		
Tumbler, 4½″, 9 oz. Flat		157.50		
Tumbler, 3½″, 3 oz. Footed		87.50		
Tumbler, 4″, 5 oz. Footed Juice	11.50	13.00		
Tumbler, 4¾″, 7 oz. Footed Water	11.00	13.50	125.00	
Tumbler, 5¼″, 9 oz. Footed Lemonade	25.00	27.50		
Vase, 3 Legged Rose Bowl		387.50		
Vase, 3 Legged Flared (Also in Crystal)		387.50		
Vase, 6 7/8″ Tall (8 Sided)		387.50		

†These have now been found in amber and red.
††This has been found in yellow.
*Cremax $85.00.

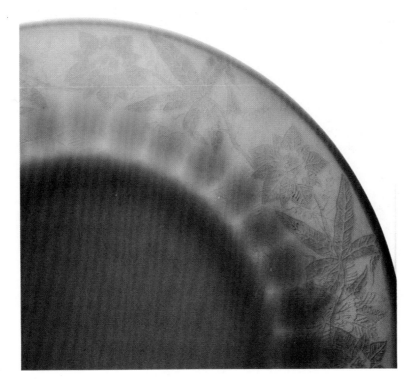

FLORAL AND DIAMOND BAND U.S. GLASS COMPANY, Late 1920's

Colors: Pink, green; some iridescent and black.

Interesting to note in the old advertisements below that one calls this "floral and diamond" whereas the other two reverse that to "diamond and floral". Iridized pieces are known to Carnival glass collectors as "Mayflower". Whatever the pattern is called, it is more like earlier Pattern glass than your usual Depression glass patterns. It's heavier and has bolder designs.

As is true of other patterns made by this company, there are no cups and saucers.

There appears to be more green available than pink; yet the shade of green often varies due to the less than precise methods of firing glass back then. Some of the green has a bluish cast making the pieces more aqua than green.

Small sugars and creamers have turned up in black.

Sugar lids, iced tea glasses and luncheon plates are the most difficult pieces to find. The iridized butter is the rarest piece in this pattern. Mould roughness is considered "normal" for this pattern.

	Green	Pink		Green	Pink
Bowl, 4½″ Berry	5.00	4.50	*Pitcher, 8″, 42 oz.	67.50	62.50
Bowl, 5¾″ Handled Nappy	7.00	6.50	Plate, 8″ Luncheon	12.50	10.00
Bowl, 8″ Large Berry	9.50	8.50	Sherbet	4.50	4.00
Butter Dish and Cover	87.50	85.00	Sugar, Small	6.50	6.00
Butter Dish Bottom	52.50	52.50	Sugar, 5¼″	8.50	8.00
Butter Dish Top	35.00	32.50	Sugar Lid	25.00	20.00
Compote, 5½″ Tall	9.50	7.50	Tumbler, 4″ Water	11.50	10.00
Creamer, Small	6.50	6.00	Tumbler, 5″ Iced Tea	15.00	14.00
Creamer, 4¾″	10.00	10.00			

*Iridescent — $125.00
Crystal — $100.00

Seven-Piece Berry Set
You'll really be most satisfied with the purchase of this set. It's very attractive, and affords a fitting and stylish addition to your present pieces. In green pressed glass, with diamond and floral design. Large bowl, 8 inches in diameter, and six sauce dishes to match, 4½ inches in diameter.
35N6838—Weight, packed, 7 pounds. Per set......68c

Five-Piece Table Set
Heavy pressed glass in light green, with pressed diamond and floral design. Creamer, covered sugar bowl and covered butter dish. Weight, packed, 9 pounds.
35N6836.........65c

Seven-Piece Water Set

Made from green pressed glass, with a floral and diamond design. You'll find that the sparkling scintillating pitcher and glasses are a set you'll be mighty proud to own when serving cold drinks. 3-pint pitcher. Six 8-ounce tumblers.
35N6837—Weight, packed, 12 pounds. Per set. $1.18

FLORENTINE NO. 1, "OLD FLORENTINE", "POPPY NO. 1"
HAZEL ATLAS GLASS COMPANY, 1932-1935

Colors: Pink, green, crystal, yellow, cobalt.

Since there are two Florentine patterns, both made by this company, beginners often have trouble distinguishing between the two. It helps to know that Florentine No. 1 was originally advertised as "Florentine Hexagonal" as opposed to "Florentine Round" or Florentine No. 2. If you look at the picture, there are eight pieces of Florentine No. 2 at the extreme left edge, the four blue pieces, the green and crystal tumbler and the two pink bowls. I originally included them in order to get Florentine No. 2 colors shown when we changed just this picture from black and white to color. It had the bonus effect of being very helpful for purposes of comparison. The shape differences are immediately apparent. Notice how gently the Florentine No. 2 compote and cream soup have been ruffled as compared with the scalloped ruffling of the edges of the sugars and creamers in Florentine No. 1. Florentine No. 1 tumblers are all footed, with the foot having the same gently serrated edges as the plate shown in detail in the pattern shot.

There are only eight sets of sugars and creamers to be found in Florentine No. 1. I said nine last time and one collector wrote me to say I should count again. He was right; (and me a math teacher, too)!

There are at least two extremely rare cobalt blue Florentine No. 1 pitchers. I saw one at a show in Denver; and a letter from California informed me of another. Several cobalt cups have surfaced, also. So, they're still there to be found!

That tall, footed iced tea pictured at the rear of the photograph is unusual. It's made in the Floral mold but has the Florentine pattern on it. How do I explain that? I don't. We do know that different companies sometimes exchanged molds. It's not likely that you'll find too many more; but in the event you stumble across another, don't pass it by! Collectors like these odd "conversation pieces".

	Crystal, Green	Yellow	Pink	Blue
Ash Tray, 5½"	16.50	25.00	24.00	
Bowl, 5" Berry	6.50	10.00	8.50	13.50
Bowl, 6" Cereal	9.50	12.50	12.50	
Bowl, 8½" Large Berry	15.00	20.00	22.50	
Bowl, 9½" Oval Vegetable & Cover	32.50	37.50	37.50	
Butter Dish and Cover	100.00	135.00	137.50	
Butter Dish Bottom	40.00	55.00	40.00	
Butter Dish Top	60.00	80.00	97.50	
Coaster/Ash Tray, 3¾"	12.50	15.00	20.00	
Creamer	7.50	10.00	10.00	
Creamer, Ruffled	17.50		22.50	45.00
Cup	6.00	7.00	6.50	57.50
Pitcher, 6½", 36 oz. Footed	32.50	40.00	37.50	425.00
Pitcher, 7½", 48 oz. Flat, Ice Lip or None	40.00	137.50	97.50	
Plate, 6" Sherbet	3.00	4.00	3.50	
Plate, 8½" Salad	5.50	9.50	9.00	
Plate, 10" Dinner	8.50	12.00	12.50	
Plate, 10" Grill	7.50	10.00	11.00	
Platter, 11½" Oval	9.50	13.50	15.00	
Salt and Pepper, Footed	30.00	42.50	45.00	
Saucer	2.00	3.00	3.00	
Sherbet, 3 oz. Footed	5.50	8.50	8.50	
Sugar	7.50	9.50	9.50	
Sugar Cover	11.00	13.50	12.00	
Sugar, Ruffled	17.50		20.00	42.50
Tumbler, 3¼", 5 oz. Footed	8.50			
Tumbler, 3¾", 5 oz. Footed Juice	8.00	15.00	15.00	
Tumbler, 4¾", 10 oz. Footed Water	11.50	15.00	17.50	
Tumbler, 5¼", 12 oz. Footed Iced Tea	16.00	20.00	22.50	
Tumbler, 5¼", 9 oz. Lemonade (Like Floral)			45.00	

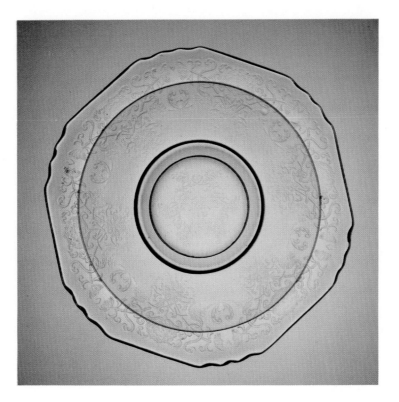

FLORENTINE NO. 2, "POPPY NO. 2"
HAZEL ATLAS GLASS COMPANY, 1934-1937

Colors: Pink, green, crystal; some cobalt, amber, ice blue.

On the day I was introducing this picture at a show in Michigan, a lady who had driven all the way from Indiana came to show me the rarely seen ruffled yellow bowl pictured. So, there are at least two! That probably means there are more to be found; pay attention! Actually, it looks as though they took a plate and ruffled the edges, a common bowl making procedure.

The pitchers on the left of the picture have Florentine No. 1 type handles; yet they have been found in original packing with Florentine No. 2 tumblers. Obviously, they can be used with both patterns. There are TWO sizes of the footed, more cone shaped pitchers in Florentine No. 2. The normally found one is 7 1/8″ tall and holds between 28 - 29½ ounces when filled to the brim. The rarely found one is chubbier and shorter, measuring only 6¼″ tall and holding between 24 - 25½ ounces. The ounce capacity varies, but the smaller pitcher is always that near inch shorter. If you turn to the 2nd edition cover in the back of this book, you can see the rare, ice blue colored pitcher that was bought in Mexico for $3.00.

Several pieces of the dark amber have surfaced, namely three tumblers (4½″, ftd., 9 oz.; 4″ flat, 9 oz.; 5″ flat, 12 oz.), a cup, saucer and sherbet.

The pattern shot was taken of a Federal "Madrid" shaped sherbet having a Hazel Atlas Florentine No. 2 design. This came from a Mexican flea market.

Lidless candies are NOT mayonnaise dishes although I have seen some labeled as such. How you use them is entirely your business. One ingenious dealer had even found a ladle to put in his candy bottom. Granted, lids are hard to find.

Some items are found with sprayed on color. See the blue shaker in the preceding picture. Paragraph one of the preceding pattern explains its being there in more detail. I've even seen one orange shaker with what is called "fired-on" color. Tops to butter dishes and oval vegetable bowls are interchangeable between respective pieces of the two Florentine patterns.

	Crystal, Green	Pink	Yellow	Blue		Crystal, Green	Pink	Yellow	Blue
Bowl, 4½″ Berry	8.00	9.00	13.50		Pitcher, 7½″, 48 oz.	40.00	97.50	130.00	
Bowl, 4¾″ Cream Soup	9.50	9.00	13.50		Pitcher, 8″, 76 oz.	72.50	197.50	177.50	
Bowl, 5″ Cream Soup, or Ruffled					Plate, 6″ Sherbet	2.50		4.00	
Nut		9.50		30.00	Plate, 6¼″ with Indent	13.50		22.50	
Bowl, 5½″	20.00		25.00		Plate, 8½″ Salad	5.00	6.00	7.00	
Bowl, 6″ Cereal	12.50	14.50	21.00		Plate, 10″ Dinner	9.50	12.00	11.00	
Bowl, 7½″ Shallow			50.00		Plate, 10¼″ Grill	6.50		8.00	
Bowl, 8″ Large Berry	14.50	16.50	16.50		Platter, 11″ Oval	10.00	11.00	13.50	
Bowl, 9″ Oval Vegetable and					Platter, 11½″ for Gravyboat			32.50	
Cover	32.50		42.50		Relish Dish, 10″, 3 Part or Plain	12.00	15.00	16.00	
Bowl, 9″ Flat	16.50				††Salt and Pepper, Pr.	35.00		40.00	
Butter Dish and Cover	82.50		117.50		Saucer (Amber: 15.00)	2.50		3.50	
Butter Dish Bottom	22.50		37.50		Sherbet, Footed (Amber: 39.50)	6.00		9.00	
Butter Dish Top	60.00		80.00		Sugar	6.00		8.50	
Candlesticks, 2¾″ Pair	32.50		42.50		Sugar Cover	10.00		14.50	
Candy Dish and Cover	77.50	99.50	127.50		Tray, Condiment for Shakers,				
Coaster, 3¼″	9.00	13.50	16.50		Creamer and Sugar (Round)			50.00	
Coaster/Ash Tray, 3¾″	12.50		20.00		Tumbler, 3½″, 5 oz. Juice	7.00	8.00	13.50	
Coaster/Ash Tray, 5½″	15.00		27.50		Tumbler, 3½″, 6 oz. Blown	8.50			
Comport, 3½″ Ruffled	12.50	6.50	17.50	45.00	†††Tumbler, 4″, 9 oz. Water	9.00	9.00	13.50	50.00
Creamer	6.50		8.50		††††Tumbler, 5″, 12 oz. Iced Tea	19.50		25.00	
Cup (Amber 35.00)	5.50		7.00		Tumbler, 3¼″, 5 oz. Footed	8.50		9.50	
Custard Cup or Jello	42.50		62.50		Tumbler, 4″, 5 oz. Footed	8.50		10.50	
Gravy Boat			35.00		Tumbler, 4½″, 9 oz. Footed	10.00		12.50	
Pitcher, 6¼″, 24 oz. Cone Footed			85.00		Vase or Parfait, 6″	20.00		52.50	
†Pitcher, 7½″, 28 oz. Cone Footed	18.50		21.50						

†Blue — $400.00
††Fired-on Orange or Blue, Pr. — 25.00
†††Amber: — 47.50
††††Amber: — 60.00

Please refer to Foreword for pricing information

FLOWER GARDEN WITH BUTTERFLIES, "BUTTERFLIES AND ROSES"

U.S. GLASS COMPANY, Late 1920's

Colors: Pink, green, blue-green, canary yellow, crystal, amber, black.

The prices on this pattern, which my wife likes, unfortunately, are going out of sight! It is hard to find, having just a piece or two turn up at major shows throughout the country. I know of several large collections and one man was gracious enough to say he'd allow me to photograph his for this book. Unfortunately, with my month long hospital stay, followed by six weeks of house confinement, I was unable to make the proper arrangements to do so. Maybe next time! Believe me, it's worth waiting to see!

We finally got a picture of that elusive, heart shaped candy! It came from the south and thoroughly delighted my sweetheart on our anniversary. Yes, it took a while to pull that off! You can see it as a pattern shot here.

I need to mention that the price for cologne bottles is for ones with a long, "dauber" stopper, not for ones with stoppers that have been ground off or broken. Reduce the price 30 percent on bottles without mint stoppers.

New pieces have turned up in black including a large vase, a cheese and cracker set and a domed comport.

My mother managed to find one plate that did not have the butterfly; and one couple managed to buy a six place setting in green for $25.00 at a garage sale!

	All Colors		All Colors
Ash Tray, Match-Pack Holders	157.50	Cup	77.50
Bowl, Rolled Edge Console,		Mayonnaise Set, 3 Piece	77.50
2 Styles	67.50	Plate, 7"	15.00
Candlesticks, 4" Pair	67.50	Plate, 8", Two Styles	17.50
Candlesticks, 8" Pair	87.50	Powder Jar, Footed	97.50
Candy Dish and Cover, 8"	77.50	Powder Jar, Flat	47.50
Candy Dish, Heart Shaped	267.50	Sandwich Server, Center Handle	75.00
Candy Dish, 6" Open	25.00	Saucer	37.50
Cheese and Cracker Set		Sugar, Open	77.50
(4" Compote, 10" Plate)	62.50	Tray, 5½" x 10" Oval	47.50
Cigarette Box, 2½" x 3½"		Tray, 11¾" x 7¾" Rectangular	57.50
(Black)	77.50	Vase, 6"	97.50
*Cologne Bottle, 7½" Tall Footed	157.50	Vase, 7" (Black)	97.50
Console Bowl, 10" Footed	72.50	Vase, 10"	117.50
Creamer	77.50		

*Stopper ½ price of bottle. Design on Black highlighted to emphasize pattern.

FOREST GREEN   ANCHOR HOCKING GLASS COMPANY CORPORATION, 1950-1957

Color: Forest green.

Many of the younger collectors are choosing to gather sets of this while it is relatively inexpensive. Dealers report that it's a steady selling glass year round, but it becomes an increasingly "hot" item at Christmas, particularly the punch bowl, stand and cups.

Soup bowls, dinner plates and said punch bowl with stand are getting more difficult to find and naturally, the price is climbing on these articles.

Pitchers and tumblers are plentiful, often sporting some "scene" in white.

The "Bubble" creamer and sugar where placed in the picture to remind you that another pattern is available in this color. There are kitchenware items as well. Notice the mixing bowls at the back.

This isn't Depression glass per se, being made much later. However, since so many are collecting it, I included it.

	Green		Green
Ash Tray	3.00	Plate, 10" Dinner	8.50
Batter Bowl	6.00	Platter, Rectangular	10.00
Bowl, 4¾" Dessert	3.50	Punch Bowl w/Stand	20.00
Bowl, 6" Soup	6.50	Punch Cup	2.00
Bowl, 7 3/8" Salad	6.50	Saucer	1.25
Creamer, Flat	4.50	Sugar, Flat	4.50
Cup	2.50	Tumbler, 5 oz.	2.00
Mixing Bowl Set, 3 Piece	17.50	Tumbler, 10 oz.	4.00
Pitcher, 22 oz.	12.50	Vase, 4" Ivy	3.00
Pitcher, 3 qt. Round	20.00	Vase, 6 3/8"	3.50
Plate, 6 5/8" Salad	2.00	Vase, 9"	5.00
Plate, 8 3/8" Luncheon	4.00		

FORTUNE   HOCKING GLASS COMPANY, 1937-1938

Colors: Pink, crystal.

There are fewer pieces in this picture than shown before, but the color shows truer here. Probably you can also tell from the picture that this pattern is a little hard to come by, particularly in plates and cups and saucers. It's an inexpensive pattern due to its being a short lived run at the factory and there being so few pieces to be found any more that collectors virtually ignore it.

Bowls appear more frequently than other items; so, if you'd like some pretty pink Depression bowls to serve from occasionally, you could probably soon find enough of those to allow you to enjoy the pattern.

Candy dish collectors latch onto the candy dishes; that's probably the best piece to own in the entire pattern.

	Pink, Crystal		Pink, Crystal
Bowl, 4" Berry	2.50	Cup	3.00
Bowl, 4½" Dessert	3.50	Plate, 6" Sherbet	2.00
Bowl, 4½" Handled	3.50	Plate, 8" Luncheon	4.00
Bowl, 5¼" Rolled Edge	4.00	Saucer	2.00
Bowl, 7¾" Salad or Large		Tumbler, 3½", 5 oz. Juice	3.50
Berry	5.00	Tumbler, 4", 9 oz. Water	4.50
Candy Dish and Cover, Flat	13.50		

"FRUITS" HAZEL ATLAS AND OTHER GLASS COMPANIES, 1931-1933

Colors: Pink, green; some crystal and iridized.

"Fruits" is a name given glass manufactured by several different companies of the time whose designs encompassed some variety of fruit. You'll find tumblers with pears, some iridized, or some with cherries; and there are pieces that have several fruits on the same dish, pears, grapes, cherries, etc. Its the "cherries only" tumblers that are more highly prized by collectors simply because they go with the "Fruits" pitcher which, so far, has only been found in green.

Berry bowls are hard to find in any color. "Item" collectors, (i.e. pitchers, candy dishes, butter dishes) drive up the prices on those items in all patterns.

A 5″, 12 oz. flat tumbler in green arrived too late to be included in this photograph. It's very unusual to find one that large.

	Green	Pink		Green	Pink
Bowl, 5″ Cereal	12.00	10.50	Sherbet	6.00	5.50
Bowl, 8″ Berry	32.50	30.00	Tumbler, 3½″ Juice	7.50	7.00
Cup	4.50	4.00	Tumbler, 4″ (One Fruit)	8.00	7.50
Pitcher, 7″ Flat Bottom	40.00		Tumbler, 4″ (Combination		
Plate, 8″ Luncheon	4.00	4.00	of Fruits)	8.50	8.50
Saucer	2.50	2.50	Tumbler, 5″, 12 oz.	35.00	22.50

HARP JEANNETTE GLASS COMPANY, 1954-1957

Colors: Crystal, crystal with gold trim, some shell pink and ice blue.

First of all, I don't know who named this pattern, but this design looks like a lyre to me rather than a "harp"; be that as it may, I'm thoroughly amazed at the number of people who are scrambling to gather pieces of this! They aren't all musicians, either, though I've had a number of them tell me at shows that the musical design is what draws them to the pattern.

Harp is a much later pattern than Depression glass, of course, and there are few pieces of it to collect. However, it does boast those cake stands which are reminiscent of Pattern glass, a glass that is even older than Depression! The design is on the foot of the pink and blue cake stands.

Collectors tell me they're having difficulty locating plates, cups, saucers and that two handled tray which is pictured. Demand is forcing prices up in this pattern.

	Crystal		Crystal
Ash Tray/Coaster	3.50	Plate, 7″	3.50
Coaster	2.00	Saucer	2.00
Cup	4.50	Tray, 2 Handled Rectangular	17.50
*Cake Stand, 9″	15.00	Vase, 6″	9.50

*Ice blue or shell pink $12.50

GEORGIAN, "LOVEBIRDS" FEDERAL GLASS COMPANY, 1931-1936

Colors: Green, crystal.

There are numerous collectors for Georgian. Much impetus toward collecting it was given in 1977 when the Peach State Depression Glass Club arranged for a setting of it to be given to the Smithsonian Institution in then President Jimmy Carter's name. Needless to say, much publicity was gained for the glass and a step toward preserving this American made glass was taken. (For a picture of "The President's Table" and a more detailed account of this club's coup, see the 4th edition of this book). There lies much of the reason that this pattern is now relatively scarce. What we see at markets is what was left over after all those "Georgians" completed their sets!

Beginning collectors tend to confuse this pattern with "Parrot". Georgian has round shaping and alternates birds with baskets of flowers in the design. "Parrot" is square shaped and has only birds in the design.

Dinner plates were made in two designs. One is like the pattern shot showing a full design; the other type has only the center motif and the garland. Both types are pictured.

Tumblers have only BASKETS in their design. Many people have missed owning tumblers because they were looking for the birds!

There are two styles of sugar bowls and unfortunately, the sugar lids are not interchangeable should you get so lucky as to find a lid.

The 6½" bowl, center front, with the straighter sides is the harder to find.

There's a giant, walnut lazy susan ("cold cuts server") which comes with this Georgian design. It's not a particularly pretty piece; but it's certainly worth finding; a similar one was pictured with "Madrid" pattern in the 5th edition.

The "conversation" piece most recently discovered in this pattern is a "mug". It was likely a creamer-to-be whose spout wasn't made. Nonetheless, it isn't "spouted"; so it's considered to be a mug.

	Green		Green
Bowl, 4½" Berry	5.00	Plate, 6" Sherbet	3.00
Bowl, 5¾" Cereal	13.50	Plate, 8" Luncheon	6.00
Bowl, 6½" Deep	45.00	Plate, 9¼" Dinner	16.50
Bowl, 7½" Large Berry	39.50	Plate, 9¼" Center Design Only	15.00
Bowl, 9" Oval Vegetable	45.00	Platter, 11½" Closed Handled	45.00
Butter Dish and Cover	67.50	Saucer	2.50
Butter Dish Bottom	40.00	Sherbet	8.50
Butter Dish Top	27.50	Sugar, 3", Footed	8.50
Cold Cuts Server, 18½" Wood with		Sugar, 4", Footed	9.00
Seven 5" Openings for 5" Coasters	477.50	Sugar Cover for 3"	22.50
Creamer, 3", Footed	8.50	Sugar Cover for 4"	32.50
Creamer, 4", Footed	9.50	Tumbler, 4", 9 oz. Flat	35.00
Cup	7.50	Tumbler, 5¼", 12 oz. Flat	60.00
†Hot Plate, 5" Center Design	30.00		

†Crystal - $18.50

HERITAGE FEDERAL GLASS COMPANY, Late 1930's - 1960's

Colors: Crystal, some pink, blue, green, cobalt.

People often ask me what I recommend their children start a set of when they'll be purchasing with their own limited funds. Heritage is a good pattern! It's extremely attractive, fairly easy to find, and it's relatively inexpensive. This crystal pattern "dresses" a table, too; it doesn't disappear; rather it commands attention, something I think a child would respond to quite naturally.

If you find any of those colored berry sets, latch onto them! Many Heritage collectors will be GLAD to take them off your hands! A lady in California wrote recently to tell me her mother had given her a pink Heritage bowl that she'd gotten at a bazaar for 50 cents---in 1955!

	Crystal	Pink	Blue Green
Bowl, 5″ Berry	4.50	15.00	30.00
Bowl, 8½″ Large Berry	12.50	40.00	57.50
Bowl, 10½″ Fruit	12.00		
Cup	3.50		
Creamer, Footed	11.50		
Plate, 8″ Luncheon	5.00		
Plate, 9¼″ Dinner	6.50		
Plate, 12″ Sandwich	8.50		
Saucer	2.00		
Sugar, Open Footed	9.50		

HEX OPTIC, "HONEYCOMB" JEANNETTE GLASS COMPANY, 1928-1932

Colors: Pink, green.

Kitchenware collectors are creating more demand for some of the Hex Optic items than are collectors for this pattern per se. Particularly attractive to them are the stacking refrigerator sets and the bucket reamer. Two of these reamers are pictured in the new 2nd edition of my Kitchenware book. Hex Optic was probably intended for kitchen use all along; hence it's fitting there so well.

A new tumbler has been discovered in Hex Optic! It's footed, holds 7 ounces and is 4¾″ tall. It was found in pink.

Iridized tumblers, oil lamps, and pitchers were made after 1950. The teal colored tumbler may possibly date with "Doric and Pansy" era. I can't confirm this, however.

A sunflower motif is a typical Jeannette marking for kitchenware items and can be seen in the 5″, 32 ounce pitcher in Hex Optic. The taller pitcher is footed and cone shaped. One has been pictured previously.

Scarce and higher priced items include the sugar shaker, rectangular butter, whiskey, stacking refrigerator sets, bucket reamer and larger pitcher.

	Pink, Green		Pink, Green
Bowl, 4¼″ Ruffled Berry	2.50	Plate, 6″ Sherbet	1.50
Bowl, 7½″ Large Berry	5.00	Plate, 8″ Luncheon	4.50
Bowl, 7¼″ Mixing	10.00	Platter, 11″ Round	5.00
Bowl, 8¼″ Mixing	14.00	Refrigerator Dish, 4″ x 4″	7.00
Bowl, 9″ Mixing	15.00	Refrigerator Stack Set, 3 Pc.	30.00
Bowl, 10″ Mixing	18.00	Salt and Pepper, Pr.	17.50
Bucket Reamer	37.50	Saucer	1.50
Butter Dish and Cover, Rectangular 1 lb. Size	35.00	Sugar, 2 Styles of Handles	4.00
		Sugar Shaker	50.00
Creamer, 2 Style Handles	4.00	Sherbet, 5 oz. Footed	3.50
Cup, 2 Style Handles	2.50	Tumbler, 3¾″, 9 oz.	3.50
Ice Bucket, Metal Handle	12.50	Tumbler, 4¾″, 7 oz., Footed	5.00
Pitcher, 5″, 32 oz. Sunflower Motif in Bottom	12.50	Tumbler, 5¾″ Footed	4.50
		Tumbler, 7″ Footed	5.50
Pitcher, 9″, 48 oz. Footed	27.50	Whiskey, 2″, 1 oz.	3.50

Please refer to Foreword for pricing information

HOBNAIL   HOCKING GLASS COMPANY, 1934-1936

These are items only made by Hocking. Many companies made patterns with a hobnail design, however. This is a very attractive glassware. However, you still don't see a lot of it at shows; so, if you are collecting it, you will probably have to specifically ask dealers for it. This is one of the patterns they tend to leave in the shop instead of carrying it to shows.

I've had numerous collectors ask me to help them find the red trimmed items. They are eye catching, aren't they! Sugars and creamers are particularly difficult to find with the trim.

You may notice that many of the pieces have shapes similar to those of "Moonstone". Since that pattern was introduced in 1941 and this one was out of the catalogues by 1937, it is likely that the molds for this were reworked and used again, thereby saving the company money.

Collectors of the pink should be aware that there was a hobnail pitcher and tumblers made by another company that will serve you well. It was pictured in the 5th edition. It's so alike that few would know the difference if you didn't point it out to them!

	Pink	Crystal		Pink	Crystal
Bowl, 5½" Cereal		2.50	Saucer (Sherbet Plate		
Bowl, 7" Salad		2.00	in Pink)	1.50	1.00
Cup	2.00	2.00	Sherbet	2.50	2.00
Creamer, Footed		2.50	Sugar, Footed		2.50
Decanter and Stopper, 32 oz.		12.50	Tumbler, 5 oz. Juice		3.00
Goblet, 10 oz. Water		4.50	Tumbler, 9 oz., 10 oz. Water		4.00
Goblet, 13 oz. Iced Tea		5.00	Tumbler, 15 oz. Iced Tea		5.00
Pitcher, 18 oz. Milk		12.50	Tumbler, 3 oz. Footed Wine		5.00
Pitcher, 67 oz.		17.50	Tumbler, 5 oz. Footed Cordial		4.00
Plate, 6" Sherbet	1.50	1.00	Whiskey, 1½ oz.		4.00
Plate, 8½" Luncheon	2.00	2.00			

HOLIDAY, "BUTTONS AND BOWS" JEANNETTE GLASS COMPANY, 1947-1949

Colors: Pink, iridescent; some shell pink opaque and crystal.

"Buttons and Bows" has long been a popular design in glass; so, it should come as no surprise that Holiday is an extremely popular design. Demand for it is great and the supply is fast dwindling even though it is a much later issued pattern than many in this book. My mother likes this. I still remember buying her six iced tea tumblers in the early '70's for $10.00 each and worrying that I'd paid too much for them! That was a lot on my school teacher's salary!

Oddly enough, you need to learn to recognize the candlesticks upside down as that's the way they're often set out by people who don't really know the glass. Just before this picture was snapped, I looked up to see the candles in their "sherbet" attitude and was reminded of this rather frequent occurrence. Candlesticks, by the way, are becoming scarce.

In the early '50's, iridizing glass to give it a more "Carnival" glass look was common procedure. Some Holiday pieces were iridized, namely the platter, footed juice and small milk pitcher (pictured), possibly to help get rid of remaining stock. Sometime later, an opaque, shell pink console bowl was made. These items are considered more novel than rare as not too many collectors desire them.

You should know that there are two styles of cups and the ones which fit the center rayed saucers will not fit the plain centered saucers.

Difficult items to find include the iced tea, cake plate, console bowl and the chop plate which is that huge plate standing between the two bowls. The cake plate has three feet and is shown in the center of the picture.

	Pink		Pink
Bowl, 5 1/8" Berry	7.00	Pitcher, 6¾", 52 oz.	25.00
Bowl, 7¾" Soup	27.50	Plate, 6" Sherbet	3.00
Bowl, 8½" Large Berry	14.50	Plate, 9" Dinner	9.50
Bowl, 9½" Oval Vegetable	12.00	Plate, 13¾" Chop	57.50
Bowl, 10¾" Console	65.00	Platter, 11 3/8" Oval	10.00
Butter Dish and Cover	35.00	Sandwich Tray, 10½"	9.00
Butter Dish Bottom	12.50	Saucer, Two Styles	3.00
Butter Dish Top	22.50	Sherbet	5.00
Cake Plate, 10½", 3 Legged	55.00	Sugar	6.00
Candlesticks, 3" Pair	50.00	Sugar Cover	8.50
Creamer, Footed	6.00	Tumbler, 4", 10 oz. Flat	14.50
Cup, Two Sizes	5.00	Tumbler, 4", Footed	25.00
Pitcher, 4¾", 16 oz. Milk	40.00	Tumbler, 6", Footed	52.50

93

HOMESPUN, "FINE RIB"   JEANNETTE GLASS COMPANY, 1939-1940

Colors: Pink, crystal.

We were setting up the glass for this Homespun shot at the photographers and I started to set in the "Homespun" crystal butter dish which I'd pictured before. It had the same knob and the same waffle design in the bottom and top; what it did NOT have was fine ribbing, rather, I was startled to see, minute little squares. The crystal may be a first cousin to Homespun; but it really isn't Homespun! Thus, I have to conclude that the only pieces made in crystal are the child's pieces and even that set doesn't seem to have a teapot and lid! They seem to have been rather stingy with their crystal for this pattern.

Further, close examination of the 96 oz. pitcher which doesn't contain the waffle design and Hazel Atlas's "Fine Rib" cobalt pitcher and tumblers shows them to be identical as far as I'm concerned. Is this then a case of subcontracting glass?

You'd probably be surprised at the numbers of people who like this pattern and who are content to search for it year after year, pleased at discovering just a piece now and then.

I have the teapot that fits under that child's teapot lid pictured. The lid got packed; the teapot stayed at home on the shelf! (There WAS a phone call interruption).

The footed, 4", 5 oz. tumblers with platters have turned up listing them as juices or cocktail sets. There are no sugar lids. There is a similar pink (also a green) powder jar with the wrong type knob whose lid will fit the sugar. It's another "cousin". Catalogue listings plainly show these sugars never had lids; further, they never made this in green.

	Pink, Crystal		Pink, Crystal
Bowl, 4½", Closed Handles	4.50	Platter, 13", Closed Handles	8.50
Bowl, 5" Cereal	7.50	Saucer	2.00
Bowl, 8¼" Large Berry	8.50	Sherbet, Low Flat	6.50
Butter Dish and Cover	40.00	Sugar, Footed	6.00
Coaster/Ash Tray	5.00	Tumbler, 4", 9 oz. Water	7.00
Creamer, Footed	6.50	Tumbler, 5¼", 13 oz. Iced Tea	12.50
Cup	4.00	Tumbler, 4", 5 oz. Footed	7.50
Pitcher, 96 oz.	27.50	Tumbler, 6¼", 9 oz. Footed	8.50
Plate, 6" Sherbet	2.00	Tumbler, 6½", 15 oz. Footed	13.50
Plate, 9¼" Dinner	9.50		

HOMESPUN CHILD'S TEA SET

	Pink	Crystal
Cup	22.50	15.00
Saucer	6.25	4.50
Plate	8.75	6.50
Tea Pot	21.50	
Tea Pot Cover	35.00	
Set: 14 Pieces	200.00	
Set: 12 Pieces		105.00

INDIANA CUSTARD, "FLOWER AND LEAF BAND"   INDIANA GLASS COMPANY, 1930's; 1950's

Colors: Ivory or custard, early 1930's; white, 1950's.

Now that cups and saucers are approaching $40.00 a set, you would expect more of them to show up; unfortunately, they don't seem to be available at any price!

The prices for this pattern, despite the sluggish economy, have continued to rise rather dramatically. I have had any number of antique dealers tell me in great detail how old and rare this "custard" glass is. I do know one thing, this pattern is scarce.

Many collectors don't have sherbets, including item collectors. (By the way, save for this pattern, sherbets are good "items" to collect in Depression Glass and most will even fit into the child's allowance limitations; many people prefer having one of every type rather than having to limit themselves to a single pattern).

	French Ivory		French Ivory
Bowl, 4 7/8" Berry	5.50	Plate, 5¾" Bread and Butter	4.50
Bowl, 5¾" Cereal	12.50	Plate, 7½" Salad	8.50
Bowl, 7½" Flat Soup	16.50	Plate, 8 7/8" Luncheon	8.50
Bowl, 8¾" Large Berry	20.00	Plate, 9¾" Dinner	13.50
Bowl, 9½" Oval Vegetable	20.00	Platter, 11½" Oval	22.50
Butter Dish and Cover	52.50	Saucer	6.00
Cup	29.00	Sherbet	67.50
Creamer	12.50	Sugar	8.50
		Sugar Cover	13.50

Please refer to Foreword for pricing information

IRIS, "IRIS AND HERRINGBONE"   JEANNETTE GLASS COMPANY, 1928-1932; 1950's; 1970's

Colors: Crystal, iridescent; some pink; recently bi-colored red/yellow and blue/green combinations.

First, let me point out an error in sizes that was mentioned to me by an avid collector. The straight sided cereal bowl, shown here between the sugar and creamer, which has always been listed as 6 inches, is, in reality, only 5 inches across. This bowl is not quite as hard to find as the soup, but nearly so. Some collectors, in fact, have never seen one.

All in all, Iris pattern has defied the economy and surged ahead in price. Even the nut bowl and fruit bowl sets and lamp shades are being swept from the market by avid Iris collectors.

You will find some pieces that have been acid treated, giving them a satin-like appearance. Collectors pay very little attention to these including the rarely seen 8" plate! Also, some newly made, bi-colored vases and candy bottoms have been made with the color being sprayed on over crystal. These don't have the rayed bottoms of the old; so there is no difficulty encountered there.

I thought you might like to see a rare demitasse saucer. This one is unusual in the fact that it has painted flowers! The lack of the demitasse saucers was explained when I ran into a '47 ad showing the cups on plain copper saucers for "al fresco dining". Ruby, blue, amethyst colored cups can be found and are pictured on the 2nd edition cover at the back of this book.

The 4¼", 3 oz. cocktail omitted from the listing last time is shown between the butter dish and vase.

Notice the unusual pink vase. A 9½" scalloped fruit bowl in pink was pictured on the rare page at the back of the 5th edition. The white milk glass vases being found are products of the early 1970's.

Both beaded top berry bowls are hard to find. Eight ounce iridized water goblets are appearing in the market a few at a time.

Don't pass by crystal coasters without checking them for Iris pattern either!

	Crystal	Iridescent		Crystal	Iridescent	Pink, Green
Bowl, 4½" Berry, Beaded Edge	30.00	6.50	Fruit or Nut Set	27.50		
Bowl, 5" Ruffled Sauce	5.50	5.00	Goblet, 4" Wine	12.50	13.50	
Bowl, 5" Cereal	27.50		Goblet, 4¼", 3 oz., Cocktail	15.00		
Bowl, 7½" Soup	67.50	20.00	Goblet, 4½" Wine	12.50		
Bowl, 8" Berry, Ruffled	9.50	8.50	Goblet, 5¾", 4 oz.	14.50		
Bowl, 8" Berry, Beaded Edge	47.50	9.50	Goblet, 5¾", 8 oz.	15.00	22.50	
*Bowl, 9½" Salad	8.50	8.00	Lampshade	27.50		
Bowl, 11" Ruffled Fruit	8.50	6.00	Pitcher, 9½" Footed	20.00	25.00	
Bowl, 11" Fruit, Straight Edge	30.00		Plate, 5½" Sherbet	6.00	5.00	
Butter Dish and Cover	30.00	32.50	Plate, 8" Luncheon	32.50		
Butter Dish Bottom	7.50	10.00	Plate, 9" Dinner	30.00	17.50	
Butter Dish Top	22.50	22.50	Plate, 11¾" Sandwich	12.00	11.00	
Candlesticks, Pr.	17.50	22.50	Saucer	4.00	3.50	
Candy Jar and Cover	67.50		Sherbet, 2½" Footed	13.50	9.00	
Coaster	32.00		Sherbet, 4" Footed	11.00		
Creamer, Footed	7.00	8.00	Sugar	7.00	6.00	
Cup	8.50	7.50	Sugar Cover	6.50	6.00	
**Demitasse Cup	15.00	50.00	Tumbler, 4" Flat	47.50		
**Demitasse Saucer	35.00	60.00	Tumbler, 6" Footed	11.50	11.50	
			Tumbler, 7" Footed	14.00	13.50	
			Vase, 9"	15.00	14.00	40.00

*Pink — $37.50
**Ruby, Blue, Amethyst priced as Iridescent

Please refer to Foreword for pricing information

JUBILEE LANCASTER GLASS COMPANY, Early 1930's

Color: Yellow, pink.

We can't seem to keep this pattern on the shelf in the shop! As soon as I get it, someone admires it and away it goes.

I'd heard reports of pink; so I was delighted to find the pink sugar to confirm what I'd heard. Lancaster made several "similar" patterns and its hard to be certain when someone points to a piece of Jubilee and says, "My grandmother gave me a set of that; only mine is pink!" Jubilee has an open area in the center of the flower. There are pieces turning up which seem to be Jubilee but which have a total flower design which has no open center. I trust you could blend these without too much problem; but strictly speaking, they aren't Jubilee but something else. Most collectors aren't quibbling over differences at this point. Read on.

There are two pieces in the picture which probably aren't Jubilee either. Can you spot them? I put them here deliberately to show you the minute differences and to show the skeptic how well they do "go together". One is the creamer dead center of the picture. True, there is ribbing and the handle and foot differ. It's the flower I want you to see. Notice there's a big petal and then a shorter, tiny petal. Jubilee flower petals tend to be all the same size. Have you spotted the other piece? It's the cocktail goblet which has this same big/little type flower. Yes, purists like to know these details.

Two new pieces of Jubilee are the candle holder (shown) and a footed sherbet/champagne! Notice that the mayonnaise does have the serving spoon!

New collectors should know that there are two different goblets. One is 6" and holds 10 ounces. The other is a more bulbous 6 1/8 inches, but it holds 12½ ounces. So far, I've only encountered three of the larger ones; so they must be scarce. Both are pictured.

	Yellow		Yellow
Bowl, 9" Handled Fruit	32.50	Plate, 7" Salad	6.50
Candlestick, Pr.	37.50	Plate, 8¾" Luncheon	8.50
Cheese & Cracker Set	30.00	Plate, 13" Sandwich	20.00
Creamer	16.50	Saucer	3.00
Cup	11.50	Sherbet/Champagne, 4¾"	7.50
Goblet, 6", 10 oz.	22.50	Sugar	16.00
Goblet, 6 1/8", 12½ oz.	25.00	Tray, 11", 2 Handled Cake	20.00
Mayonnaise & Plate	62.50	Tray, Center Handled Sandwich	25.00
w/Original Ladle	75.00		

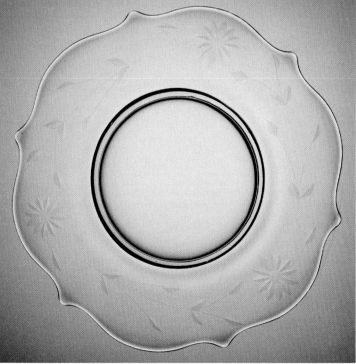

LACE EDGE, "OPEN LACE"   HOCKING GLASS COMPANY, 1935-1938

Colors: Pink, some crystal.

For those who have asked over the years, I have included a Lace Edge vase. This one has been "satin-ized", a process that turns more people off than on; but at least you'll know what the 7″ vase looks like. A console bowl and candlesticks can also be found frosted. You see high prices on these pieces; but they hold little appeal for collectors and should bring considerably less than those same pieces without the frosting process. (That's why you see this vase. I found someone who felt the same as I).

The 9″ comport shown in the pattern shot is an extremely rare find. Please don't pass any of these by as the last report I had on this one had an asking price of an ounce of gold!

A new size bowl has turned up in crystal! It measures 8¼″ across and stands 2¼″ tall.

There are several items in Lace Edge that even dealers confuse with other Depression patterns. First is the tumbler previously discussed under Coronation. You will notice that the rays on the tumbler climb only a third of the way up the glass. We left the saucer from under the cup so that you could see clearly what a short distance the rays travel up Lace Edge cups. On Queen Mary cups, the pattern with which these cups are confused, the rays climb nearly to the top of the cup.

Novices should be aware that the 7¾″ salad bowl and the butter bottom are one in the same. Both are pictured in the foreground. Also, because of the open area lacing in the design, this pattern damages easily. That is not so much to say the laces break off as they chip and crack through from edge to edge. Therefore, it is imperative that you exam each lace of a piece before paying mint prices for it.

In the back of the picture at either side you can see the 7½″, three part relish and the ribbed salad bowl. Demand for both of these has spiraled and the price has reacted upward. The larger ribbed bowl is plentiful; that is not so of the 7¾″ version!

Many companies manufactured a laced type pattern (see "Laced Edge" by Imperial); however, Hocking made this Lace Edge pattern sometimes only in pink, occasionally in pink and crystal. Therefore, if you find similar pieces in green, blue, yellow or black, you have found a piece made by some other glass firm.

	Pink*		Pink*
**Bowl, 6 3/8″ Cereal	12.50	Fish Bowl, 1 gal. 8 oz.	
Bowl, 7¾″, Ribbed	30.00	(Crystal Only)	15.00
Bowl, 7¾″ Salad	13.50	Flower Bowl, Crystal Frog	16.50
Bowl, 8¼″, (Crystal)	5.00	Plate, 7¼″ Salad	12.50
Bowl, 9½″ Plain or Ribbed	12.00	Plate, 8¾″ Luncheon	12.00
***Bowl, 10½″, 3 Legs, (Frosted, $25.00)	125.50	Plate, 10½″ Dinner	17.50
Butter Dish or Bon Bon		Plate, 10½″ Grill	11.50
with Cover	45.00	Plate, 10½″ 3 Part Relish	17.50
Butter Dish Bottom	13.50	Plate, 13″, 4 Part Solid Lace	17.50
Butter Dish Top	31.50	Platter, 12¾″	17.50
***Candlesticks, Pr. (Frosted $40.00)	117.50	Platter, 12¾″, 5 Part	16.50
Candy Jar and Cover, Ribbed	32.50	Relish Dish, 7½″, 3 Part Deep	37.50
Comport, 7″	15.00	Saucer	7.50
Comport, 7″ and Cover, Footed	27.50	***Sherbet, Footed	47.50
Comport, 9″	500.00	Sugar	14.50
Cookie Jar and Cover	39.50	Tumbler, 3½″, 5 oz. Flat	7.50
Creamer	14.50	Tumbler, 4½″, 9 oz. Flat	8.50
Cup	16.00	Tumbler, 5″, 10½ oz. Footed	40.00
		Vase, 7″, (Frosted $35.00)	217.50

*Satin or frosted items 50% lower in price
**Officially listed as cereal or cream soup
***Price is for absolute mint condition

LACED EDGE, "KATY BLUE" IMPERIAL GLASS COMPANY, Early 1930's

Colors: Blue w/opalescent edge; green w/opalescent edge.

When scuttlebutt circulated that Imperial was going out of business, I headed for the factory to obtain what information I could on Imperial's lines of glassware. A former employee was kind enough to help me locate and copy much of what I needed on this Laced Edge pattern which I was beginning to see turning up at shows and flea markets.

This is an attractive pattern. There doesn't seem to be a lot of it around; but maybe people just aren't aware its collectible. Cruel as it seems, the pattern's collectibility has been enhanced by the company's difficulties. Too, it was made in a blue color that many people like and its fancy, intricate, opened work design make it a collector's dream. All these factors have contributed to the prices presently being asked for this glassware!

Imperial called the new white edging technique "Sea Foam" and did this opalescent type edging to many of its blue, green and pink lines of glass.

Serving pieces in this are not easily found; and very little of the green Laced Edge has turned up to date.

Bowl, 4½", Fruit	9.00	Plate, 10", Dinner	20.00
Bowl, 7", Soup	15.00	Plate, 12", Luncheon (per	
Bowl, 9", Vegetable	30.00	catalogue description)	22.50
Bowl, 11", Divided Oval	27.50	Platter, 13"	35.00
Bowl, 11", Oval	30.00	Saucer	4.00
Cup	15.00	Sugar	15.00
Creamer	15.00	Tidbit, w/8" & 10" plates	42.50
Mayonnaise, 3 Pc.	35.00	Tumbler, 9 oz.	20.00
Plate, 6½", Bread & Butter	8.00	Vase, 5½"	22.50
Plate, 8", Salad	12.00		

LAKE COMO HOCKING GLASS COMPANY, 1934-1937

Color: White with blue scene.

Any number of people would collect this pattern if they could just find more of it. It sells very well in the shop when I can find it!

I still have been unable to locate the regular cup! If you have one, please let me know. The cup shown is called a St. Denis style.

	White
Bowl, 6" Cereal	5.00
Bowl, 9¾" Vegetable	12.50
Creamer, Footed	8.50
Cup, Regular	6.50
Cup, St. Denis	7.50
Plate, 7¼" Salad	5.00
Plate, 9¼" Dinner	9.50
Platter, 11"	15.00
Salt & Pepper, Pr.	22.50
Saucer	3.00
Saucer, St. Denis	3.50
Sugar, Footed	8.50

Please refer to Foreword for pricing information

LAUREL McKEE GLASS COMPANY, 1930's

Colors: French ivory, jade green, white opal and poudre blue.

Any one of the kitchenware collecting enthusiasts will immediately recognize these colors as being typical of McKee's cannisters and such. As you can see, they also made dinnerware items decorated with this Laurel wreath whose design alone proclaimed their dishes worthy of honor.

A couple of jadite 4½", 9 oz. tumblers have turned up as well as the jadite children's set shown. I realize there's some duplication in the two pictures, but with the emphasis being noted on children's ware items, I felt it incumbent to show these a little more precisely. Of course, the Scotty Dog decal items are the most highly prized. However, you very seldom run into these any more.

Poudre blue Laurel is seldom seen; yet sets can be obtained in ivory and green with a little patience.

Hardest to find pieces include tumblers, shakers, candlesticks and the three legged console bowl. The cheese dish bottom is simply the 7½" salad plate.

The blue plate shown below is a commemorative piece with Jeannette McKee's picture embossed on it and stating a week of celebration (Aug. 28 - Sept. 5) on acheiveing fifty years (1888 - 1938). It is an unusual find and sells for $20.00.

	White Opal, Jade Green	French Ivory	Poudre Blue
Bowl, 5" Berry	3.50	4.50	6.50
Bowl, 6" Cereal	4.50	5.00	8.00
Bowl, 6", Three Legs	6.50	8.00	
Bowl, 8" Soup		13.50	
Bowl, 9" Large Berry	9.50	12.50	17.50
Bowl, 9¾" Oval Vegetable	12.00	15.00	22.50
Bowl, 10½", Three Legs	20.00	25.00	32.50
Bowl, 11"	16.50	27.50	27.50
Candlestick, 4" Pair	16.50	22.50	27.50
Cheese Dish and Cover	37.50	47.50	
Creamer, Short	6.50	7.50	
Creamer, Tall	7.50	8.50	12.50
Cup	4.00	5.00	11.00

	White Opal, Jade Green	French Ivory	Poudre Blue
Plate, 6" Sherbet	2.50	3.50	4.50
Plate, 7½" Salad	3.00	5.00	7.50
Plate, 9 1/8" Dinner	4.50	5.00	9.50
Plate, 9 1/8" Grill	3.50	4.50	7.50
Platter, 10¾" Oval	13.50	16.50	20.00
Salt and Pepper	45.00	35.00	
Saucer	2.00	2.50	4.00
Sherbet	6.50	9.50	
Sugar, Short	6.50	7.50	12.50
Sugar, Tall	7.50	8.50	13.50
Tumbler, 4½", 9 oz. Flat	30.00	22.50	
Tumbler, 5", 12 oz. Flat		27.50	

CHILDREN'S LAUREL TEA SET

	Plain	Decorated Rims	Scotty Dog Decal	Green
Creamer	20.00	30.00	37.50	30.00
Cup	15.00	20.00	27.50	20.00
Plate	7.50	12.50	17.50	12.50
Saucer	5.50	7.50	12.50	7.50
Sugar	20.00	30.00	37.50	30.00
14 Piece Set	150.00	220.00	300.00	220.00

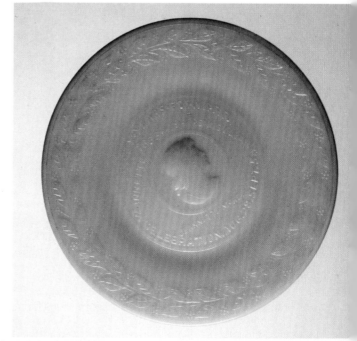

Please refer to Foreword for pricing information

LINCOLN INN FENTON GLASS COMPANY, Late 1920's

Colors: Red, cobalt, light blue, amethyst, black, green, pink, crystal, amber, jade (opaque)

I recently visited with a lady whose grandfather had worked at Fenton. In a house filled with Fenton, her good dishes were crystal Lincoln Inn!

We were excited about discovering the amber Lincoln Inn pitcher before. Now there are two blue ones to report and several crystal ones. It seems that a little more of this is turning up recently as more people learn to recognize the pattern.

Happily, red and cobalt items seem the easiest to find although red shakers are something of a nemesis. Another oddity, as compared with other Depression patterns, is that stemmed pieces are more easily obtained than regular luncheon items. This could be a boon for people who enjoy collecting "something" but who have little interest in owning an entire set. No doubt the goblets could be blended with many types of tableware plus one could then experience the collector's thrill of finding something!

New listings for the pattern include a 9″ shallow bowl and a 4½″ cone shaped sherbet!

As you can see from the tall sherbet, the red tends to have an amberina (red/yellow) cast in some pieces, particularly stemware. With some glass collectors, this tends to be more of a "bonus" than a detriment.

For those who have never seen green Lincoln Inn, please notice the shakers! Both styles of tops are found on the shakers.

	Blue, Red	All Other Colors		Blue, Red	All Other Colors
Ash Tray	10.00	5.00	Nut Dish, Footed	12.50	6.50
Bon Bon, Handled Square	11.00	6.50	Pitcher, 7¼″, 46 oz.		350.00
Bon Bon, Handled Oval	11.00	6.50	Plate, 6″	4.50	2.50
Bowl, 5″ Fruit	6.00	4.00	Plate, 8″	6.50	4.00
Bowl, 6″ Cereal	7.50	5.00	Plate, 9¼″	8.50	6.00
Bowl, 6″ Crimped	8.50	5.50	Plate, 12″	14.50	8.50
Bowl, Handled Olive	8.50	5.50	Salt/Pepper, Pair	130.00	77.50
Bowl, Finger	7.50	6.50	Saucer	3.00	2.00
Bowl, 9″, Shallow		10.00	Sherbet, 4½″, Cone Shape		7.50
Bowl, 9¼″ Footed	13.50	11.50	Sherbet, 4¾″	13.50	8.00
Bowl, 10½″ Footed	20.00	13.50	Sugar	16.50	11.50
Candy Dish, Footed Oval	11.00	6.50	Tumbler, 4 oz. Flat Juice	11.50	6.50
Comport	8.50	5.50	Tumbler, 5 oz. Footed	12.50	8.00
Creamer	16.50	11.50	Tumbler, 7 oz. Footed	13.50	8.00
Cup	10.00	6.50	Tumbler, 9 oz. Footed	14.50	9.50
Goblet, Water	17.50	11.00	Tumbler, 12 oz. Footed	17.50	12.00
Goblet, Wine	13.50	8.50	Vase, 12″ Footed	60.00	40.00

Please refer to Foreword for pricing information

LORAIN, "BASKET", No. 615 INDIANA GLASS COMPANY, 1929-1932

Colors: Green, yellow; some crystal.

I have my doubts as to just how old the crystal divided relish is. It doesn't "look" like older crystal to me; and another bothersome thing is that I have encountered too many of them on a recent trip through Indiana. I put it here to elicit your input and hopefully gain more valid information on the subject. Crystal Lorain heretofore was rarely seen although some snack sets (rectangular shape with an off center indent for a cup) had been found with flashed borders in primary colors of red, yellow, blue and green.

The luminescent yellow color of Lorain draws most collectors. Bowls, the 8″ deep berry in particular (pictured upturned at back), are very hard to find. Everyone wishes they'd bought them at the first book price of $5.50! (Some people even wish they'd bought two first edition books, one to use and one to keep in mint condition to sell for the unbelievable price they're bringing)!

Prices for Lorain, as for most other patterns, have held a gentle, steady rise during the past economic woes of the country. People with funds to spare have continued to buy. Even in my limited travels this spring (from North Carolina to California) I can feel an undercurrent of activity that bodes well for our field of collecting. I see definite signs of a healthier economy just in my limited area of the business world. Many wondered, but most of the glass held its value or even showed a slight increase during these hard times past. In fact, one man I met at a recent show told me he figured he'd lost money by putting it in the bank instead of glass. His glass investments had earned him a great deal more money over the past ten years than had his savings accounts! No! I'm not advocating sinking the life savings. Personally, I'm a great believer in eggs in many baskets; but it was interesting to hear another say what I already knew!

The sherbet with "Lorain" design and a "Lace Edge" border in avocado green or white are of recent origin and Indiana must have made bushels of them!

	Crystal, Green	Yellow		Crystal, Green	Yellow
Bowl, 6″ Cereal	22.50	40.00	Plate, 10¼″ Dinner	27.50	40.00
Bowl, 7¼″ Salad	29.00	40.00	Platter, 11½″	17.50	27.50
Bowl, 8″ Deep Berry	62.50	97.50	Relish, 8″, 4 Part	13.50	22.50
Bowl, 9¾″ Oval Vegetable	27.50	37.50	Saucer	3.50	4.50
Creamer, Footed	11.00	17.00	Sherbet, Footed	13.50	24.50
Cup	8.50	11.50	Snack Tray, Crystal/Trim	11.00	
Plate, 5½″ Sherbet	4.00	6.00	Sugar, Footed	11.00	16.50
Plate, 7¾″ Salad	7.00	11.00	Tumbler, 4¾″, 9 oz. Footed	13.50	21.50
Plate, 8 3/8″ Luncheon	12.50	20.00			

MADRID FEDERAL GLASS COMPANY, 1932-1939; Indiana Glass Company, 1980's

Colors: Green, pink, amber, crystal, "Madonna" blue.

Ostensibly as their contribution to the Bi-Centennial celebration in 1976, Federal Glass Company redesigned molds to make the "Recollection" glassware. Their "Recollection" was a new, sharper molded MADRID pattern in AMBER glass with a tiny little '76 date marking in the design of each piece. We now think this was a last ditch effort to save their company by trying to cash in on the collectibles market. The amber color was a hair darker than the older Madrid and since the glass WAS marked, there was little reason for collectors to panic. They merely had to be more careful that they didn't buy new butter tops on old butter bottoms. (The new butter top mold marks run through the North and South poles of the knob while the old mold marks formed an "equator" around the middle of the knob). You could get a twenty piece starter set, 4 dinners, salads, cups, saucers and soups for $19.00. The butter and cover cost you $6.00.

Shortly thereafter, Federal Glass Company went out of business and "Recollection" butter dishes were selling at the local dish barns for $1.99 in early 1979. Even at that, the pieces were no bargain as an investment, of course.

Unfortunately, Indiana Glass Company bought Federal's "Recollection" molds, removed the date from them and is now selling crystal again. They've added some items, a footed cake stand and shakers; but you need to be aware that these are newly manufactured. The new crystal is sharper designed and has a "bluer" tint than the old; but for the time being, I'm taking crystal out of the listing prices so some newcomers to collecting don't get "taken" by the unscrupulous. This doesn't mean that old crystal Madrid is worthless by any stretch of the imagination. It's still old and reputable dealers know its worth.

Most of the "Madonna" blue items have long since disappeared into collections.

The gravy boat and platter shown here came to Kentucky by way of Iowa which, for some reason, seems to be the state in which they're often found! The walnut lazy susan (pictured in the 5th edition) is often found in Kentucky, Virginia and West Virginia indicating that these items were regionally distributed. I know Madrid was given for premiums in my area in the '30's by the Kroger Company.

Notice the hot dish coasters with the indents. Probably cups were supposed to sit here making it a snack type server. I see someone placed a sherbet there equally well.

Check for chips around the pointed ridges and on the knobs of the lidded items.

	Crystal, Amber	Pink	Green	Blue		Crystal, Amber	Pink	Green	Blue
Ash Tray, 6" Square	122.50		77.50		Pitcher, 8½", 80 oz. Ice Lip	50.00		177.50	
Bowl, 4¾" Cream Soup	10.00				Plate, 6" Sherbet	2.50	3.00	3.00	6.50
Bowl, 5" Sauce	5.00	5.50	5.00	7.50	Plate, 7½" Salad	8.00	8.00	7.50	12.50
Bowl, 7" Soup	9.50		10.00	12.50	Plate, 8 7/8" Luncheon	5.50	6.00	7.50	12.50
Bowl, 8" Salad	11.50		15.00	22.50	Plate, 10½" Dinner	24.00		26.00	37.50
Bowl, 9 3/8" Large Berry	14.50	17.50			Plate, 10½" Grill	8.00		13.50	
Bowl, 9½" Deep Salad	18.50				Plate, 10¼" Relish	8.50	8.50	9.50	
Bowl, 10" Oval Vegetable	12.50	12.00	13.50	20.00	††Plate, 11¼" Round Cake	8.50	8.50	16.50	
†Bowl, 11" Low Console	11.50	8.00			Platter, 11½" Oval	10.00	9.00	12.50	17.50
Butter Dish and Cover	60.00		67.50		Salt/Pepper, 3½" Footed	57.50		77.50	110.00
Butter Dish Bottom	30.00		32.50		Salt/Pepper, 3½" Flat	37.50		55.00	
Butter Dish Top	30.00		35.00		Saucer	2.50	3.00	3.50	5.00
†Candlesticks, 2¼" Pair	15.00	13.50			Sherbet, Two Styles	6.50		7.50	9.50
Cookie Jar and Cover	32.50	25.00			Sugar	6.50		7.50	10.00
Creamer, Footed	6.00		8.00	11.50	Sugar Cover	24.50		25.00	72.50
Cup	5.00	6.00	6.50	10.00	Tumbler, 3 7/8", 5 oz.	11.50		27.50	17.50
Gravy Boat and Platter	825.00				Tumbler, 4¼", 9 oz.	11.00	11.00	17.50	17.50
Hot Dish Coaster	25.00		27.50		Tumbler, 5½", 12 oz., 2				
Hot Dish Coaster w/Indent	27.50		27.50		Styles	16.50		23.50	20.00
Jam Dish, 7"	16.00		13.50	22.00	Tumbler, 4", 5 oz. Footed	17.50		31.50	
Jello Mold, 2 1/8" High	8.50				Tumbler, 5½", 10 oz. Footed	19.50		30.00	
††Pitcher, 5½", 36 oz. Juice	30.00				Wooden Lazy Susan, 7 Hot				
Pitcher, 8", 60 oz. Square	37.50	32.50	114.50	137.50	Dish Coasters	500.00			
Pitcher, 8½", 80 oz.	50.00		177.50						

†(Iridescent priced slightly higher)
††Crystal — $150.00

Please refer to Foreword for pricing information

MANHATTAN, "HORIZONTAL RIBBED"   ANCHOR HOCKING GLASS COMPANY, 1938-1941

Colors: Crystal, pink; some green, ruby and iridized.

Yes! Manhattan is getting to be a heavily collected pattern and it has stepped from the ranks of relative anonymity! However, I hadn't envisioned it attaining the ranks of rare glass that I usually have for a cover shot! Unfortunately, our cover shot didn't turn out and while I wasn't home to be consulted, a publishing decision was made to go with this shot which looked "fantastic" on the cover. So, welcome to the ranks of the cover elite, Manhattan! (It'll delight my brother. It's his pattern)! It does make a nice cover though, doesn't it?

Pictured here is the first iridized piece of Manhattan I'd ever encountered along with the green tumbler previously shown. Are there pitchers in these colors? A ruby juice pitcher has turned up as well as several other pieces like the red plate shown.

That large relish tray, shown here with pink inserts and on the cover with ruby ones, is a big seller in our shop. Collectors tend to prefer the ruby inserts when they can be found.

In the previous book we pictured a covered candy and a small wine glass that were made by another company but which blend nicely with this pattern. This time, notice the double branched candlestick. This was made by L.E. Smith Company but has such a look of Manhattan that people are buying them to go with their sets; so, I included it here. Anchor Hocking made the small, squared candle pictured for this pattern.

Probably the hardest item to find in Manhattan is the small 42 ounce pitcher in pink. I took plates, cups and saucers in pink out of the listing last time because collectors had convinced me that even though pink was in the factory listings, these particular pieces just no longer existed if, indeed, they ever had. Please notice the pink cup! So, we'll list these items again!

Notice the little sauce dish with the metal frame which originally held a spoon of some kind. You will often find bowls with various metal embellishments.

Notice the ash tray with the Anchor Hocking embossing. These bring slightly higher prices due to their "advertising" nature.

	Crystal	Pink		Crystal	Pink
Ashtray, 4″	4.50		Relish Tray, 14″, 5 Part	9.00	15.00
Bowl, 4½″ Sauce	5.00	6.00	*Relish Tray Insert	3.50	4.50
Bowl, 5 3/8″ Berry			Pitcher, 42 oz.	14.50	25.00
with Handles	5.50	6.50	Pitcher, 80 oz. Tilted	20.00	32.50
Bowl, 7½″ Large Berry	6.00	6.50	Plate, 6″ Sherbet	2.50	
Bowl, 8″, Closed Handles	11.00	12.50	Plate, 8½″ Salad	6.00	6.50
Bowl, 9″ Salad	9.50	10.00	Plate, 10¼″ Dinner	6.50	
Bowl, 9½″ Fruit	15.00	16.50	Plate, 14″ Sandwich	9.50	10.00
Candlesticks, 4½″			Salt/Pepper, 2″ Pr.		
(Double) Pr.	9.50		(Square)	13.50	27.50
Candy Dish, 3 Legs	5.00	6.00	Saucer	2.50	12.50
Candy Dish and Cover	20.00		Sherbet	5.00	5.50
Coaster, 3½″	2.00	3.00	Sugar, Oval	4.00	6.00
Comport, 5¾″	8.50	10.00	**Tumbler, 10 oz. Footed	7.00	9.00
Creamer, Oval	4.00	6.00	Vase, 8″	8.50	
Cup	7.50	25.00	Wine, 3½″	7.50	
Relish Tray, 14″, 4 Part	7.00	8.50			

**Green or iridized — $5.50
*Ruby — $3.50

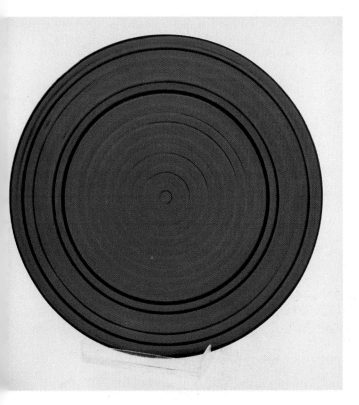

MAYFAIR FEDERAL GLASS COMPANY, 1934

Colors: Crystal, amber, green.

You're looking at a really rare Depression glass pattern which still can be reasonably obtained as far as your purse is concerned! That isn't to say it is plentiful and therein lies the reason the price has stayed down. People are discouraged from attempting to collect it. However, my wife recently met a lady in Texas who'd nearly completed her set in a two year time period. So, it still can be done! I've always thought it an extremely attractive pattern with those roses and arches. It looks like the perfect wedding gift!

The reason the pattern is so limited resides in the fact Hocking had patented the name "Mayfair" which caused Federal to redesign these glass molds into what became the Rosemary pattern. The green items pictured here (as well as one cup, cream soup and sugar in amber) represent what is called the "transitional period" or the glass made BETWEEN Mayfair and Rosemary. You'll notice that these pieces have arching in the bottom of each piece rather than the waffle design and there is no waffling between the top arches. If you turn to the picture of Rosemary, you'll see that the glass under the arches has been left perfectly plain. We traditionally include the TRANSITIONAL pieces with the Mayfair pattern because they more closely resemble them than they do Rosemary. Would you have noticed the difference had I not pointed it out to you? For the puristic collector, strictly speaking, it must have waffling to be Mayfair. However, so far, cream soup dishes have only been found in the transitional mode.

The footed sugar has no handles. Yes, it does resemble a sherbet. One lady told me she collected six sugar bowls before she found out they weren't sherbets! She kept wondering where all the sugar bowls were.

	Amber	Crystal	Green
Bowl, 5″ Sauce	4.00	3.00	5.00
Bowl, 5″ Cream Soup	12.50	9.00	12.50
Bowl, 6″ Cereal	12.00	6.00	13.50
Bowl, 10″ Oval Vegetable	12.50	9.00	13.50
Creamer, Footed	9.00	7.00	8.50
Cup	5.00	3.50	6.50
Plate, 6¾″ Salad	3.50	2.25	4.50
Plate, 9½″ Dinner	9.50	6.50	8.50
Plate, 9½″ Grill	9.00	7.00	7.50
Platter, 12″ Oval	12.50	9.00	13.50
Saucer	2.00	1.25	2.00
Sugar, Footed	9.00	7.00	8.50
Tumbler, 4½″, 9 oz.	10.00	6.50	13.50

MAYFAIR, "OPEN ROSE" HOCKING GLASS COMPANY, 1931-1937

Colors: Ice blue, pink; some green, yellow, crystal. *(See Reproduction Section)*

In the yellow and green Mayfair, you are looking at some of the most expensive and rare items in Depression glass! It was believed that you couldn't collect an entire set in these colors. Obviously, it was an erroneous assumption! (A yellow bottom has been found for the butter dish just since this was photographed).

In the blue Mayfair, you have perhaps the most beloved color of any in Depression glass; (it's always held first place in my mind); and in the pink Mayfair, you had the most universally owned pattern of any in Depression glass! Many people are now collecting it due to having inherited a piece or two in pink from a grandmother or aunt! It seems likely that half the population of the thirties had a piece of Mayfair in their possession. If you bought cookies at the store, you got a cookie jar; if you sent in a coupon from soap, you got a hat shaped bowl. The local hardware stores sold it as well as the five and dime; movie houses gave away a piece each week if you bought a ticket for their show; gasoline stations gave pieces with the purchase of so many gallons of gas; ad infinitum! Mayfair enjoyed an extremely long run at the factory and the pattern was made into numerous items (which required expenditure for various molds). All of this points to the fact it was an extremely popular pattern back then; and I can tell you that it's an extremely popular pattern now!

Rare pieces include any piece in green or yellow (EXCEPT those four green items priced in the listing for under $25.00); ROUND cups; THREE FOOTED bowls, sugar LIDS, decanter (came with bath salts) STOPPERS; 1 and 4½ ounce goblets; and the only FOOTED shaker ever to be found! Because there are so many collectors for this pattern and demand is great, these rare pieces command high prices.

WARNING: the cookie jar (green and pink) and the whiskey (green, pink, blue, cobalt) have been reproduced. See the Reproduction section at the back of this book for further discussion.

Some pieces of Mayfair were acid dipped or "satinized". They originally came with painted flowers which dishwashers have subsequently removed. Collectors pay little attention to these and therefore these items bring about 30 percent less than prices listed.

Crystal shakers and juice pitchers sell for about half the prices listed for pink.

New collectors, notice the price difference on the various sizes of goblets. Some are very rarely found! Noting prices in all patterns will generally clue you to what is hard to find. You might notice that the previously listed 6″ plate and saucer only measures 5¾″.

More Mayfair price listings are found on page 118.

	Pink*	Blue	Green	Yellow
Bowl, 5″ Cream Soup	30.00			
Bowl, 5½″ Cereal	14.50	30.00	50.00	50.00
Bowl, 7″ Vegetable	15.00	32.50	87.50	87.50
Bowl, 9″, 3 1/8″ High, 3 Leg Console	1,950.00			
Bowl, 9½″ Oval Vegetable	16.00	37.50	77.50	77.50
Bowl, 10″ Vegetable	14.00	40.00		87.50
Bowl, 10″ Same Covered	60.00	75.00		225.00
Bowl, 11¾″ Low Flat	35.00	45.00	20.00	80.00
Bowl, 12″ Deep Scalloped Fruit	37.50	50.00	22.50	90.00
Butter Dish and Cover or 7″ Covered Vegetable	45.00	200.00	900.00	900.00
Butter Bottom With Indent			250.00	250.00
Butter Dish Top	30.00	167.50	650.00	650.00
Cake Plate, 10″ Footed	17.40	40.00	50.00	
Candy Dish and Cover	35.00	130.00	425.00	300.00
Celery Dish, 9″ Divided			100.00	100.00

*Frosted or satin finish items slightly lower

Please refer to Foreword for pricing information

MAYFAIR, "OPEN ROSE" (Con't.)

	Pink*	Blue	Green	Yellow
**Celery Dish 10″ or 10″ Divided	18.50	27.50	87.50	87.50
Cookie Jar and Lid	30.00	147.50	457.50	500.00
Creamer, Footed	14.50	47.50	150.00	150.00
Cup	12.50	35.00	125.00	125.00
Decanter and Stopper, 32 oz.	92.50			
Goblet, 3¾″, 1 oz. Liqueur	347.50		347.50	
Goblet, 4″, 2½ oz.	72.50			
Goblet, 4″, 3½ oz. Cocktail	52.50		257.50	
Goblet, 4½″, 3 oz. Wine	52.50		257.50	
Goblet, 5¼″, 4½ oz. Claret	377.50		377.50	
Goblet, 5¾″, 9 oz. Water	40.00		257.50	
Goblet, 7¼″, 9 oz. Thin	127.50	97.50		
Pitcher, 6″, 37 oz.	32.50	87.50	357.50	357.50
Pitcher, 8″, 60 oz.	35.00	975.50	317.50	317.50
Pitcher 8½″, 80 oz.	65.00	127.50	357.50	357.50
Plate, 5¾″ (Often Substituted as Saucer)	8.00	13.50	67.50	67.50
Plate, 6½″ Round Sherbet	9.00			
Plate, 6½″ Round, Off Center Indent	19.50	20.00	62.50	
Plate, 8½″ Luncheon	15.50	25.00	57.50	57.50
Plate, 9½″ Dinner	40.00	42.50	97.50	97.50
Plate, 9½″ Grill	24.00	24.00	52.50	52.50
Plate, 11½″ Handled Grill				80.00
Plate, 12″ Cake w/Handles	25.00	40.00	25.00	
***Platter, 12″ Oval, Open Handles	15.00	35.00	117.50	117.50
Platter, 12½″ Oval, 8″ Wide, Closed Handles			157.50	157.50
Relish, 8 3/8″, 4 part or Non-Partitioned	17.50	32.50	97.50	95.00
Salt and Pepper, Flat Pair	40.00	175.00	600.00	600.00
Salt and Pepper, Footed Pair	2,000.00			
Sandwich Server, Center Handle	27.50	45.00	20.00	87.50
Saucer (Cup Ring)	18.50		100.00	100.00
Saucer (See 5¾″ Plate)				
Sherbet, 2¼″ Flat	87.50	52.50		
Sherbet, 3″ Footed	12.50			
Sherbet, 4¾″ Footed	55.00	47.50	127.50	127.50
Sugar, Footed	15.00	45.00	150.00	150.00
Sugar Lid	850.00		900.00	900.00
Tumbler, 3½″, 5 oz. Juice	28.00	72.50		
Tumbler, 4¼″, 9 oz. Water	21.00	62.50		
Tumbler, 4¾″, 11 oz. Water	87.50	85.00	157.50	157.50
Tumbler, 5¼″, 13½ oz. Iced Tea	29.50	85.00		
Tumbler, 3¼″, 3 oz. Footed Juice	52.50			
Tumbler, 5¼″, 10 oz. Footed	24.50	67.50		157.50
Tumbler, 6½″, 15 oz. Ftd. Iced Tea	28.50	80.00	177.50	
Vase (Sweet Pea)	125.00	65.00	150.00	
Whiskey, 2¼″, 1½ oz.	57.50			

*Frosted or satin finish items slightly lower
**Divided Pink Celery — $67.50
***Divided Crystal — $12.50

Please refer to Foreword for pricing information

MISS AMERICA (DIAMOND PATTERN) HOCKING GLASS COMPANY, 1935-1937

Colors: Crystal, pink; some green, ice blue and red.   *(See Reproduction Section)*

Miss America is a very popular Depression glass pattern. We often sell pieces of this in our shop to people who are just looking for a pretty piece of glass and who really could care less about its origins or "history"! As you can see from the old advertisement pictured below, this was Hocking's answer to a "hobnail" design. Indeed, beginning collector's often confuse this pattern with Westmoreland's "English Hobnail". (Even sunburst center rays characterize Miss America pieces; and the goblets have three rings at the top as you can see from those pictured).

Notice from the picture that the coasters have 6 raised inside rings. Coasters aren't that easily found and the unwitting often stack them with the much cheaper sherbet plates.

Please take note of the large red console bowl found with the original label! There isn't a lot of red Miss America known to exist; so, when new pieces are found, they're immediately grabbed by knowledgeable collectors. Sugars, creamers, 3½″ wines, 4½″ juice glasses, 10 oz. goblets, luncheon plates, the curved-in fruit bowl and now the console bowl are items seen thus far in red. I've heard a former factory worker had an eight piece setting in red Miss America!

There's an unusual sprayed-on amethyst goblet in the picture with the pink. A jadite plate was shown in the 5th edition. So far, these weird colors elicit more conversation than anything else. There are few collectors for light green Miss America.

Prices for Miss America butter dishes suffered some when the reproductions first came out. Some collectors were afraid of being duped and didn't buy and some collectors were content to own the cheaper reproduction. However, most collectors can now tell old from new; and there are numerous collectors once again searching for the older butter dishes. More detailed information on reproductions in Miss America is contained in the back of the book. Other items which have been reproduced include the shakers, the pitcher without the ice lip and the water tumbler.

There is still much demand for candy dishes in pink. Learn to check the knob handles. They've occasionally been glued back on!

At least six of those rarely seen 11¾″ divided relish dishes in pink have shown up in Ohio in the past three years!

	Crystal	Pink	Green	Red		Crystal	Pink	Green	Red
Bowl, 4½″ Berry			7.00		****Plate, 10¼″ Dinner	9.50	17.50		
*Bowl, 6¼″ Berry	6.00	13.50	9.00		Plate, 10¼″ Grill	7.50	12.50		
Bowl, 8″ Curved in at Top	30.00	45.00		300.00	Platter, 12¼″ Oval	10.00	15.00		
Bowl, 8¾″ Straight Deep					Relish, 8¾″, 4 Part	7.50	13.50		
Fruit	22.50	37.50			Relish, 11¾″ Round Divided	12.50	125.00		
Bowl, 10″ Oval Vegetable	10.00	16.50			Salt and Pepper, Pr.	22.50	42.50	257.50	
**Butter Dish and Cover	187.50	375.00			Saucer	2.50	4.50		
Butter Dish Bottom	6.00	13.50			Sherbet	6.50	12.50		
Butter Dish Top	181.50	361.50			Sugar	6.00	12.50		125.00
Cake Plate, 12″ Footed	16.50	27.50			****Tumbler, 4″, 5 oz. Juice	12.50	35.00		
Candy Jar and Cover,					Tumbler, 4½″, 10 oz.				
11½″	47.50	97.50			Water	12.00	24.00	13.50	
Celery Dish, 10½″					Tumbler, 6¾″, 14 oz.				
Oblong	7.50	15.00			Iced Tea	20.00	45.00		
Coaster, 5¾″	12.50	18.50							
Comport, 5″	10.00	15.00							
Creamer, Footed	6.50	12.50		125.00					
Cup	7.50	15.00	8.00						
Goblet, 3¾″, 3 oz. Wine	14.00	47.50		150.00					
Goblet, 4¾″, 5 oz. Juice	16.00	47.50		150.00					
Goblet, 5½″, 10 oz.									
Water	17.50	37.50		150.00					
Pitcher, 8″, 65 oz.	50.00	87.50							
Pitcher, 8½″, 65 oz. w/Ice									
Lip	57.50	92.50							
***Plate, 5¾″ Sherbet	3.00	5.00	5.00						
Plate, 6¾″			6.00						
Plate, 8½″ Salad	5.00	14.00	8.00	57.50					

*Also has appeared in Cobalt Blue — $100.00
**Absolute mint price
***Also in Ice Blue — $30.00
****Also in Ice Blue — $75.00

**Glass Luncheon Set
Crystal or Rose Tint**

A practical Luncheon Set with hobnail design — sunburst center. Choice of crystal or rose glass. Set serves 4. Consists of four each of 8½-in. salad plates, footed tumblers 5⅜-in. tall, 3⅜-in. tea cups, 5¼-in. saucers. Shipping weight 15 pounds.

550 A 4906—Crystal.
16-Piece Set **$1.29**
550 A 4907—Rose.
16-Piece Set **1.29**

Please refer to Foreword for pricing information

MODERNTONE, "SAILBOAT" MODERTONE, & "LITTLE HOSTESS PARTY DISHES", HAZEL ATLAS GLASS COMPANY, 1934-1942; Late 1940's - Early 1950's

Colors: Amethyst, cobalt blue; some crystal, pink and platonite fired-on colors.

Moderntone is dwindling which is beginning to trigger rises in price. Watch out for pieces too badly scratched to command mint prices!

Notice the cobalt saucer and plate pictured with the SAILBOAT design. These pieces are beginning to attract the attention of some collectors. Only the saucer is decorated; the cup remains plain. The saucer sells for $8.00-$10.00; and the luncheon plates sell for $13.00-$16.00. (There are various sized Hazel Atlas tumblers and a pitcher bearing sailboats that can be blended with these dishes, also).

The tumbler and small whiskey glass pictured were made in cobalt, pink, green and crystal. These were not officially listed as Moderntone. Collectors have adopted these for this pattern, however.

The child's water set pictured in the metal holder was often found packaged with a Colonial Block creamer to be used as a child's pitcher for this set!

The butter dish has a rim of glass around which the metal lid fits; so, don't buy a cereal bowl with a lid resting atop it as a butter. The cheese dish needs to have that wooden insert to be labeled a cheese dish, also. Notice that the cheese and butter lids differ.

A man asked me at a Michigan show about the "Little Hostess Party Set" child's dishes in Moderntone, what colors went together, which sets were marked, which had two or three rings, etc! With all this interest in the Moderntone children's dishes, I figured I'd better get out my wife's set and get it pictured! Her set of 16 pieces consisted of four each cups, saucers and plates plus sugar, creamer, teapot and lid. She received it as a gift in 1952 and she believes the people had gotten it as a premium gift via "Big Top" peanut butter. The colors in her set are gray, turquoise, gold and orange; the sugar and creamer are orange and teapot and lid are turquoise. Each piece of her set is marked with the "H over A" Hazel Atlas mark. Her cups all have two rings. I recently purchased a different set of 16. The colors in it are chartreuse, gray, dark green and maroon. The teapot and lid are maroon; the sugar and creamer are chartreuse. The pieces are all marked; the cups all have two rings. However, my mother bought a pastel set of 14 pieces, having no teapot. The colors of her set are pale pink, pale green, pale yellow and blue; the sugar and creamer are pale pink. None of her pieces are marked; and all of her cups have THREE rings! These sets were all made of platonite with fired-on colors. It's my understanding that the pastel sets did not have teapots originally. Lids for the teapots seem to be the hardest pieces to find; and the maroon teapot seems to hold a little more charm for collectors than the turquoise.

Crystal Moderntone is seldom noticed save for the ash tray; don't pass that!

	Cobalt	Amethyst	Platonite Fired On Colors		Cobalt	Amethyst	Platonite Fired On Colors
Ash Tray, 7¾", Match Holder in Center	87.50			Plate, 5¾" Sherbet	3.50	3.00	.75
Bowl, 4¾" Cream Soup	11.00	9.50		Plate, 6¾" Salad	6.50	4.50	1.00
Bowl, 5" Berry	13.50	6.50	.75	Plate, 7¾" Luncheon	5.00	5.00	1.25
Bowl, 5" Cream Soup, Ruffled	15.00	11.50	1.75	Plate, 8 7/8" Dinner	9.00	6.50	2.50
				Plate, 10½" Sandwich	15.00	10.00	3.50
Bowl, 6½" Cereal	32.00	25.00	2.00	Platter, 11" Oval	17.50	11.50	2.00
Bowl, 7½" Soup	32.00	25.00	2.50	Platter, 12" Oval	25.00	18.00	2.00
Bowl, 8¾" Large Berry	22.50	17.50	4.00	Salt and Pepper, Pr.	25.00	25.00	9.00
Butter Dish with Metal Cover	57.50			Saucer	2.00	2.00	.75
Cheese Dish, 7" with Metal Lid	67.50			Sherbet	7.50	6.50	2.00
				Sugar	7.50	6.50	2.00
Creamer	7.50	6.00	2.00	Sugar Lid in Metal	20.00		
Cup	7.50	6.00	1.00	Tumbler, 5 oz.			2.50
Cup (Handle-less) or Custard	9.50	9.00		Tumbler, 9 oz.	15.00		3.00
				Tumbler, 12 oz.	22.00	20.00	3.00
				Whiskey, 1½ oz.	11.50		3.00

LITTLE HOSTESS PARTY SET

	Pastel	Dark		Pastel	Dark
Cup, 1¾"	2.50	3.00	Sugar, 1¾"	3.00	3.50
Saucer, 3 7/8"	1.00	2.00	Teapot and Lid, 3½"		30.00
Plate, 5¼"	2.00	3.00	Set, 14 Pc.	30.00	60.00
Creamer, 1¾"	3.00	3.50	Set, 16 Pc.		60.00

Please refer to Foreword for pricing information

MOONDROPS NEW MARTINSVILLE, 1932-1940

Colors: Amber, pink, green, cobalt, ice blue, red, amethyst, crystal, dark green, light green, jadite, smoke, black.

From glancing at the picture and the listing, the first impression one gets is that this is a plentiful pattern---easily collected. Unfortunately, this is far from the truth! New Martinsville made a variety of pieces, but evidently they didn't make a lot of any piece for you only occasionally run into a piece of Moondrops and usually its a goblet or tumbler. Plates and other flat pieces are virtually impossible to find!

A new piece to turn up is a three footed powder jar in amber!

So far, only smoke tumblers have been found; no matching pitcher has surfaced.

Collectors for Moondrops concentrate mostly on the red and blue colors; item collectors adore these plumed top butter dishes. "Bee hive" stoppers are the least desirable type to find. "Rocket" and "Winged" type pieces are better liked.

Crystal Moondrops brings 30 - 35 percent less than the prices listed for "all other colors".

	Blue/Red	All Other Colors		Blue/Red	All Other Colors
Ash Tray	27.50	10.00	Goblet, 5 1/8", Metal Stem Wine	12.00	8.50
Bowl, 5¼" Berry	6.00	4.00	Goblet, 5½", Metal Stem Wine	13.50	8.50
Bowl, 6¾" Soup	10.00	8.00	Goblet, 6¼", 9 oz. Water	17.50	13.50
Bowl, 7½" Pickle	12.00	9.50	Mug, 5 1/8", 12 oz.	25.00	15.00
Bowl, 8 3/8" Footed, Concave Top	13.00	12.00	Perfume Bottle, "Rocket"	45.00	25.00
Bowl, 8½" Three Footed Divided			Pitcher, 6 7/8", 22 oz. Small	125.00	70.00
Relish	12.50	9.50	Pitcher, 8 1/8", 32 oz. Medium	137.50	97.50
Bowl, 9½" Three Legged Ruffled	17.50	12.50	Pitcher, 8", 50 oz. Large with Lip	147.50	105.00
Bowl, 9¾" Oval Vegetable	22.50	17.50	Pitcher, 8 1/8", 53 oz. Large, No Lip	145.00	110.00
Bowl, 9¾" Covered Casserole	67.50	45.00	Plate, 5 7/8" Bread and Butter	3.50	3.00
Bowl, 9¾" Two Handled Oval	32.50	25.00	Plate, 6 1/8" Sherbet	4.00	2.50
Bowl, 11½" Boat Shaped Celery	20.00	17.50	Plate, 6" Round, Off-Center Indent for		
Bowl, 12" Round Three Footed			Sherbet	5.00	4.00
Console	32.50	22.50	Plate, 7 1/8" Salad	6.00	4.00
Bowl, 13" Console with "Wings"	57.00	30.00	Plate, 8½" Luncheon	9.00	5.00
Butter Dish and Cover	357.50	225.00	Plate, 9½" Dinner	12.50	8.50
Butter Dish Bottom	57.50	35.00	Plate, 15" Round Sandwich	25.00	13.50
Butter Dish Top	300.00	190.00	Plate, 15" Two Handled Sandwich	27.50	20.00
Candles, 2" Ruffled Pair	22.50	17.50	Platter, 12" Oval	17.50	12.50
Candles, 4½" Sherbet Style Pr.	19.50	15.00	Powder Jar, 3 Footed	35.00	25.00
Candlesticks, 5" "Wings" Pr.	52.50	32.50	Saucer	3.50	3.00
Candlesticks, 5¼" Triple Light Pr.	65.00	35.00	Sherbet, 2 5/8"	10.00	6.50
Candlesticks, 8½" Metal Stem Pr.	25.00	20.00	Sherbet, 4½"	15.00	8.50
Candy Dish, 8" Ruffled	15.00	12.50	Sugar, 2¾"	13.50	8.50
Cocktail Shaker, with or without			Sugar, 4"	11.50	6.50
Handle, Metal Top	25.00	17.00	Tumbler, 2¾", 2 oz. Shot	10.00	6.50
Comport, 4"	12.50	7.50	Tumbler, 2¾", 2 oz. Handled Shot	12.50	7.50
Comport, 11½"	27.50	17.50	Tumbler, 3¼", 3 oz. Footed Juice	11.50	7.50
Creamer, 2¾" Miniature	14.00	9.00	Tumbler, 3 5/8", 5 oz.	10.00	6.00
Creamer, 3¾" Regular	12.00	7.50	Tumbler, 4 3/8", 7 oz.	11.00	7.50
Cup	9.00	7.50	Tumbler, 4 3/8", 8 oz.	12.00	8.50
Decanter, 7¾" Small	50.00	32.50	Tumbler, 4 7/8", 9 oz. Handled	13.50	9.50
Decanter, 8½" Medium	57.50	32.50	Tumbler, 4 7/8", 9 oz.	13.50	10.00
Decanter, 11¼" Large	67.50	37.50	Tumbler, 5 1/8", 12 oz.	17.50	11.00
Decanter, 10¼" "Rocket"	77.50	47.50	Tray, 7½", For Miniature		
Goblet, 2 7/8", ¾ oz. Liqueur	17.50	12.50	Sugar/Creamer	22.50	15.00
Goblet, 4", 4 oz. Wine	15.00	9.50	Vase, 7¾" Flat, Ruffled Top	42.50	32.50
Goblet, 4¾", "Rocket" Wine	25.00	17.50	Vase, 9¼" "Rocket" Style	77.50	55.00
Goblet, 4¾", 5 oz.	12.50	8.00			

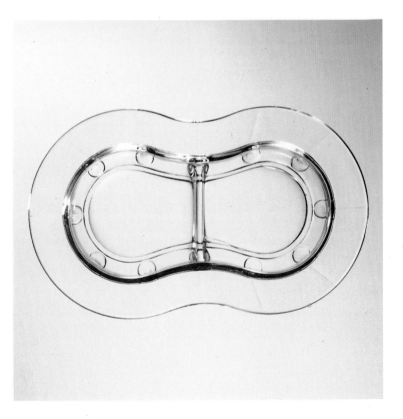

MOONSTONE ANCHOR HOCKING GLASS CORPORATION, 1941-1946

Color: Crystal with opalescent hobnails, some green.

The four pieces pictured with the "Moonstone" labels are courtesy of a collector in Ohio. Since we seem to have a "Bubble" bowl and a "Lace Edge" sherbet labeled as "Moonstone", it would seem they meant the process of opalizing to be called "Moonstone" as well as the pattern. There definitely could be more of these type pieces around, so watch for them. Finding them won't necessarily make you rich; but the pieces are of interest to collectors.

We do know that goblets, cups, saucers, plates, creamers and sugars were made in this in green and sold under the name "Ocean Green". Again, these pieces at present are scarce but considered to be more novel than rare.

The uncrimped 5½" berry bowl is the only item that appears to be in short supply in Moonstone at the moment. This pattern is attractive and sells well in our shop.

The cologne bottle pictured, as well as pitchers, shakers and some stemmed water goblets, were made by Fenton Glass Company rather than Anchor Hocking. However, collectors of Moonstone are including these items in their collections and I see no harm in it. The listing here is strictly for Anchor Hocking pieces. (The cologne bottle is presently selling for $10.00-12.00).

The picture below is courtesy of Anchor Hocking Glass Corporation.

	Opalescent Hobnail		Opalescent Hobnail
Bowl, 5½" Berry	7.00	Cup	6.00
Bowl, 5½" Crimped Dessert	6.00	Goblet, 10 oz.	14.50
Bowl, 6½" Crimped Handled	7.00	Heart Bonbon, One Handle	7.00
Bowl, 7¾" Flat	8.00	Plate, 6¼" Sherbet	3.00
Bowl, 7¾" Divided Relish	7.50	Plate, 8" Luncheon	8.50
Bowl, 9½" Crimped	12.50	Plate, 10" Sandwich	15.00
Bowl, Cloverleaf	8.50	Puff Box and Cover, 4¾" Round	15.00
Candleholder, Pr.	15.00	Saucer (Same as Sherbet Plate)	3.00
Candy Jar and Cover, 6"	17.50	Sherbet, Footed	6.00
Cigarette Jar and Cover	14.50	Sugar, Footed	6.00
Creamer	6.00	Vase, 5½" Bud	8.50

Please refer to Foreword for pricing information

126

MT. PLEASANT, "DOUBLE SHIELD"   L.E. SMITH COMPANY, 1920's-1934

Colors: Black amethyst, amethyst, cobalt blue, green, pink.

The pattern insert is of a handled server with Dogwood or Apple Blossom decoration very similar to that MacBeth Evans used on their glass. A bowl has also turned up having the same etching.

I once said Mt. Pleasant was "never" give away glassware. It has always been better glassware, the type bought in the finer department stores. Never say "never"! I've learned it was a premium item for a store in western New York!

Even though the "double shield" image is sometimes hard to spot on the underside of pieces, the scalloped edges with alternating one and two points make this pattern easy to locate. Notice the gold trimmed luncheon items (with the crystal cup, no less) are an exception, however. Only the sugar and creamer have the fancy edge in this 18 piece set.

A collector in New York tells me there are numerous other items to be found, particularly bowls; but I have been unable to get specifics. Let me hear if you find something unlisted.

	Pink, Green	Black Amethyst, Amethyst, Cobalt		Pink, Green	Black Amethyst, Amethyst, Cobalt
Bon Bon, Rolled Up Handles	9.50	15.00	Cup	4.50	7.50
Bowl, 3 Footed, Rolled-In			Plate, 8″ Scalloped or Square	7.50	9.50
Edges, As Rose Bowl	12.50	16.00	Plate, 8″, Solid Handles	7.50	15.00
Bowl, 8″ Scalloped, Two Handles	12.50	16.50	Plate, 10½″ Cake with		
Bowl, 8″ Two Handled Square	12.50	16.50	Solid Handles	13.50	20.00
Candlesticks, Single Stem Pr.	13.50	16.50	Salt and Pepper Shakers		
Candlesticks, Double Stem Pr.	20.00	30.00	(Two Styles)	17.50	25.00
Creamer (Scalloped Edges)	8.50	12.50	Saucer, Square or Scalloped	2.50	3.50
Cup (Waffle-Like Crystal)	3.50		Sherbet, Scalloped Edges	6.00	11.00
			Sugar (Scalloped Edges)	9.50	12.50

NEW CENTURY, and incorrectly, "LYDIA RAY"   HAZEL ATLAS GLASS COMPANY, 1930-1935

Colors: Green; some crystal, pink, amethyst and cobalt.

Pitchers and tumblers are items which usually appear in cobalt and amethyst although some cups have surfaced!

The covered casserole, decanter and wine goblets are the hardest pieces to find. Ash trays are rarely seen!

The crystal "powder jar" is a sherbet with a sugar lid but they are found often enough to have been sold in this fashion.

Ovide pattern has been incorrectly called New Century elsewhere. You might wish to refer to that pattern now to see how different it is from this. It will matter if you order one and get the other!

	Green, Crystal	Pink, Cobalt, Amethyst		Green, Crystal	Pink, Cobalt, Amethyst
Ash Tray/Coaster, 5 3/8″	25.00		Plate, 7 1/8″ Breakfast	5.50	
Bowl, 4½″ Berry	4.50		Plate, 8½″ Salad	5.50	
Bowl, 4¾″ Cream Soup	8.50		Plate, 10″ Dinner	9.50	
Bowl, 8″ Large Berry	9.50		Plate, 10″ Grill	7.50	
Bowl, 9″ Covered Casserole	45.00		Platter, 11″ Oval	10.00	
Butter Dish and Cover	47.50		Salt and Pepper, Pr.	25.00	
Cup	4.50	8.50	Saucer	2.00	4.00
Creamer	5.50		Sherbet, 3″	5.00	
Decanter and Stopper	37.50		Sugar	5.00	
Goblet, 2½ oz. Wine	11.50		Sugar Cover	8.50	
Goblet, 3¼ oz. Cocktail	12.50		Tumbler, 3½″, 5 oz.	7.50	6.50
Pitcher, 7¾″, 60 oz. with			Tumbler, 4 1/8″, 9 oz.	7.50	6.50
or without Ice Lip	25.00	22.50	Tumbler, 5″, 10 oz.	9.50	9.00
Pitcher, 8″, 80 oz. with			Tumbler, 5¼″, 12 oz.	13.50	10.00
or without Ice Lip	27.50	27.50	Tumbler, 4″, 5 oz. Footed	8.50	
Plate, 6″ Sherbet	2.00		Tumbler, 4 7/8, 9 oz. Footed	10.50	
			Whiskey, 2½″, 1½ oz.	6.00	

Please refer to Foreword for pricing information

NEWPORT, "HAIRPIN" HAZEL ATLAS GLASS COMPANY, 1936-1940

Colors: Cobalt blue, amethyst; some pink, "Platonite" white and fired-on colors.

I met a collector who had been working on a set of cobalt Newport for two years. He'd acquired everything except eight cereal bowls that he needed. He'd only found two. Does that tell you anything regarding the scarcity of cereal bowls? One is pictured on the rack behind the creamer.

The 4¼" berry bowl shown is the only piece I've seen in pink. White shakers from this pattern are often purchased to "fill in" for the absence of any in Petalware. Otherwise, white Newport attracts little attention.

Amethyst Newport is attractive but in shorter supply than cobalt; it's also attracting the attention of some Morrocan amethyst collectors, too; so competition is increasing for these items!

	*Cobalt	Amethyst		*Cobalt	Amethyst
Bowl, 4¼" Berry	8.00	7.50	Plate, 11½" Sandwich	19.50	14.50
Bowl, 4¾" Cream Soup	9.50	8.50	Platter, 11¾" Oval	22.50	18.00
Bowl, 5¼" Cereal	17.50	12.50	Salt and Pepper	32.50	30.00
Bowl, 8¼" Large Berry	22.50	20.00	Saucer	2.50	2.50
Cup	6.50	5.00	Sherbet	8.50	7.50
Creamer	9.50	8.00	Sugar	9.50	8.00
Plate, 6" Sherbet	3.50	3.00	Tumbler, 4½", 9 oz.	20.00	17.50
Plate, 8½" Luncheon	6.00	6.50			

*White 60% of Cobalt price.

NORMANDIE, "BOUQUET AND LATTICE" FEDERAL GLASS COMPANY, 1933-1940

Colors: Iridescent, amber, pink, crystal.

I recently saw a stack of eight dinner plates in pink Normandie sell to one lucky collector who had been seeking them for over two years! He was very glad he'd made the effort to be at that particular Depression glass show! Pink sugar lids are equally hard!

The iridized Normandie has begun to pick up sales at shows. Collectors used to ignore it, but no longer. I have always been told that Carnival glass collectors consider this to be "late" Carnival, also; so, competition is increased for this glass. Salad plates in the iridized Normandie are hard to locate.

	Amber	Pink	Iridescent		Amber	Pink	Irdescent
Bowl, 5" Berry	4.00	5.00	5.00	Platter, 11¾"	10.00	14.00	10.00
*Bowl, 6½" Cereal	7.50	9.50	7.50	Salt and Pepper, Pr.	35.00	45.00	
Bowl, 8½" Large Berry	10.00	13.00	9.50	Saucer	2.00	2.50	2.00
Bowl, 10" Oval Veg.	11.00	20.00	13.50	Sherbet	5.50	7.50	7.00
Creamer, Footed	6.00	8.50	7.50	Sugar	5.00	6.00	6.50
Cup	5.50	6.50	6.00	Sugar Lid	57.50	89.50	
Pitcher, 8", 80 oz.	47.50	67.50		Tumbler, 4", 5 oz.			
Plate, 6" Sherbet	2.00	2.00	2.00	Juice	12.00	25.00	
Plate, 8" Salad	6.00	7.50	22.50	Tumbler, 4¼", 9 oz.			
Plate, 9¼" Luncheon	5.00	8.50	7.50	Water	11.00	20.00	
Plate, 11" Dinner	13.00	42.50	13.00	Tumbler, 5", 12 oz.			
Plate, 11" Grill	8.50	10.50	10.50	Iced Tea	15.00	30.00	

*Mistaken by many as butter bottom.

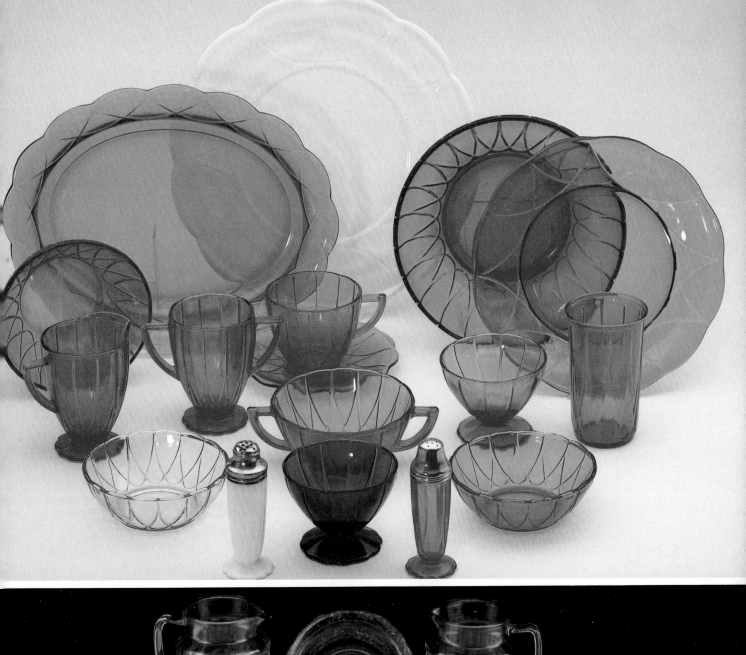

NO. 610, "PYRAMID" INDIANA GLASS COMPANY, 1926-1932

Colors: Green, pink, yellow; some crystal; black, 1974-75 by Tiara.

All pieces in yellow Pyramid are hard to find, particularly the lid for that ice bucket pictured!

Eleven ounce tumblers are rarely seen in any color. Don't pass them should you be so lucky as to see them for sale.

I've only seen two crystal pitchers in all my travels. Many pitcher collectors would love to add one to their collections! Other crystal pieces are much easier to find.

Remember that the prices listed are for mint items and this is another pattern whose edges and seams and points collect nicks and chips. Examine pieces you find carefully.

Indiana made pieces in black for Tiara Home Products in 1974 and 1975. If you purchase these, just remember they are relatively new pieces of glass!

	Crystal, Pink	Green	Yellow
Bowl, 4¾" Berry	12.50	13.50	22.00
Bowl, 8½" Master Berry	17.50	20.00	40.00
Bowl, 9½" Oval	22.50	22.50	42.50
Bowl, 9½" Pickle	22.50	22.50	42.50
Creamer	16.50	16.50	24.00
Ice Tub	57.50	67.50	167.50
Ice Tub and Lid			500.00
Pitcher	142.50	167.50	350.00
Relish Tray, 4 Part Handled	27.50	37.50	50.00
Sugar	16.50	17.50	24.50
Tray for Creamer and Sugar	16.00	20.00	40.00
Tumbler, 8 oz. Footed	16.50	24.50	40.00
Tumbler, 11 oz. Footed	32.50	42.50	

NO. 612, "HORSESHOE" INDIANA GLASS COMPANY, 1930-1933

Colors: Green, yellow; some pink, crystal.

There was a time when you often saw this pattern out at markets and it generated great activity! Collectors scurried to complete their sets! They were right to scurry as most of this has disappeared into collections. Bowls, candy dishes, tumblers (particularly the 9 oz. flat) are very hard to obtain at any price.

There are three sizes of vegetable bowls even though the company only listed two. They are the 7½", the 8½", and a 9½". I've held and measured all three! They nest in similar fashion to the mixing bowls of that time period.

As is true of many Indiana patterns, it was merely given a number as it's name. Collectors have dubbed the pattern "Horseshoe".

Grill plates are scarce and do not contain the center motif. They're like the platter pictured.

Many collectors still need the butter dish to complete their sets. If you spot one at a market, buy it. Collectors will beat a path to your door!

	Green	Yellow		Green	Yellow
Bowl, 4½" Berry	16.50	13.50	Plate, 8 3/8" Salad	6.00	7.00
Bowl, 6½" Cereal	14.50	15.00	Plate, 9 3/8" Luncheon	7.50	7.50
Bowl, 7½" Salad	12.50	15.00	Plate, 10 3/8" Dinner	14.50	15.00
Bowl, 8½" Vegetable	16.00	22.50	Plate, 10 3/8" Grill	17.50	20.00
Bowl, 9½" Large Berry	22.50	25.00	Plate, 11" Sandwich	9.00	11.50
Bowl, 10½" Oval Vegetable	12.50	16.00	Platter, 10¾" Oval	14.50	15.00
Butter Dish and Cover	500.00		Relish, 3 Part Footed	15.00	25.00
Butter Dish Bottom	150.00		Saucer	3.00	3.50
Butter Dish Top	350.00		Sherbet	10.00	11.50
Candy in Metal Holder			Sugar, Open	10.00	10.50
Motif on Lid —			Tumbler, 4¼", 9 oz.	67.50	
Also, Pink— ($97.50)	117.50		Tumbler, 4¾", 12 oz.	77.50	
Creamer, Footed	11.50	12.50	Tumbler, 9 oz. Footed	12.50	14.50
Cup	7.00	7.50	Tumbler, 12 oz. Footed	69.50	72.50
Pitcher, 8½, 64 oz.	185.00	200.00			
Plate, 6" Sherbet	3.00	4.50			

NO. 616, "VERNON" INDIANA GLASS COMPANY, 1930-1932

Colors: Green, crystal, yellow.

What you see pictured here is what is possible to own! You occasionally find pieces of crystal trimmed in silver. None of this glass is plentiful; but it is possible to still gather a set together with a little patience. It's very attractive.

The yellow is like Lorain; it has an almost fluorescent glow about it.

Sugar and creamer collectors give extra competition for those items!

	Green	Crystal	Yellow
Creamer, Footed	20.00	10.50	17.50
Cup	13.50	5.50	12.00
Plate, 8″ Luncheon	6.50	5.50	7.25
Plate, 11″ Sandwich	20.00	12.50	18.50
Saucer	4.50	2.75	4.50
Sugar, Footed	19.50	10.00	17.50
Tumbler, 5″ Footed	24.00	11.50	22.50

NO. 618, "PINEAPPLE & FLORAL" INDIANA GLASS COMPANY, 1932-1937

Colors: Crystal, amber; some fired-on red, green; Late 60's: avocado.

To date, I have only seen cup, saucer, dinner plate, creamer, sugar, and small tumbler in fired-on red. If you know of other pieces, let me hear from you!

In green, only the plates have appeared. Avocado colored comports were selling in local dish barns as late as 1970, however. They also turn up in various flashed and iridized colors.

Bowls and tumblers are getting difficult to find. Tumblers often have extreme mold roughness along the seams of the glass.

You will find a large, cone shaped vase which fits into a metal stand in Pineapple and Floral. It was a popular item with florists and funeral parlors.

This is an attractive pattern which "dresses up" a table!

	Crystal	Amber, Red		Crystal	Amber, Red
Ash Tray, 4½″	13.00	16.00	Plate, 11½″ Indentation	20.00	
Bowl, 4¾″ Berry	20.00	14.00	Plate, 11½″ Sandwich	12.50	13.50
Bowl, 6″ Cereal	18.50	15.00	Platter, 11″ Closed Handles	10.00	11.50
Bowl, 7″ Salad	3.00	8.50	Platter, Relish, 11½″,		
Bowl, 10″ Oval Vegetable	18.00	15.00	Divided	14.00	9.50
Comport, Diamond Shaped	1.50	6.50	Saucer	3.00	3.00
Creamer, Diamond Shaped	6.50	8.50	Sherbet, Footed	15.00	15.00
Cream Soup	17.50	17.50	Sugar, Diamond Shaped	6.50	8.50
Cup	7.50	7.00	Tumbler, 4¼″, 8 oz.	22.50	25.00
Plate, 6″ Sherbet	3.00	4.00	Tumbler, 5″, 12 oz.	27.50	
Plate, 8 3/8″ Salad	5.00	6.00	Vase, Cone Shaped	22.50	
*Plate, 9 3/8″ Dinner	10.00	12.50	Vase Holder (17.50)		

*Green — $20.00

Please refer to Foreword for pricing information

OLD CAFE HOCKING GLASS COMPANY, 1936-1938; 1940

Colors: Pink, crystal, ruby red.

Notice that the Royal Ruby cups were promoted on crystal saucers!

The Old Cafe juice and 80 oz. pitchers were pictured in the 5th edition (rare page at the back of the book). Choice items!

The lamp was made from a vase inverted and drilled to accept cord and socket.

There is a cookie jar with "Old Cafe" type panels but with a cross hatched lid design which some people are collecting to "go with" this pattern.

	Crystal, Pink	Royal Ruby		Crystal, Pink	Royal Ruby
Bowl, 3¾" Berry	2.00	4.00	Pitcher, 6", 36 oz.	47.50	
Bowl, 5", One or Two Handles	3.00		Pitcher, 80 oz.	67.50	
Bowl, 5½" Cereal	4.00	8.50	Plate, 6" Sherbet	1.50	
Bowl, 9", Closed Handles	7.50	11.50	Plate, 10" Dinner	12.50	
Candy Dish, 8" Low	5.00	10.00	Saucer	2.00	
Cup	3.00	6.00	Sherbet, Low Footed	4.00	
Lamp	9.50	17.50	Tumbler, 3" Juice	4.00	
Olive Dish, 6" Oblong	4.00		Tumbler, 4" Water	5.00	
			Vase, 7¼"	8.50	13.50

OLD ENGLISH, "THREADING" INDIANA GLASS COMPANY

Colors: Green, amber; some pink, crystal, forest green.

A new piece shown here is the ruffled comport in amber!

Also, some crystal decorated pitcher and tumbler sets have surfaced.

The dip and chip (cheese and cracker) set is shown in the right of the picture. Unfortunately, the two pieces aren't the same color! We can now assume there is a pink comport to accompany the indented pink plate, however!

The lid for the pitcher has the same cloverleaf knob as the sugar pictured. The pitcher lid will be notched for pouring purposes. It will not interchange with the candy lid as it is also slightly larger.

Possibly the center handled server is the hardest piece of Old English to find.

	Pink, Green, Amber		Pink, Green, Amber
Bowl, 4" Flat	10.00	Pitcher and Cover	80.00
Bowl, 9" Footed Fruit	19.50	Plate, Indent for Compote	17.50
Bowl, 9½" Flat	22.50	Sandwich Server, Center Handle	27.50
Candlesticks, 4" Pr.	22.50	Sherbet	14.50
Candy Dish & Cover, Flat	37.50	Sugar	11.00
Candy Jar with Lid	35.00	Sugar Cover	19.50
Candy Jar, 9¾", 2 Handles	25.00	Tumbler, 4½" Footed	12.50
Compote, 3½" Tall, 7" Across	12.50	Tumbler, 5½" Footed	19.50
Creamer	11.50	Vase, 5 3/8", Fan Type, 7"	
Fruit Stand, 11" Footed	30.00	Across	32.50
Goblet, 5¾", 8 oz.	17.50	Vase, 12" Footed	30.00
Pitcher	50.00		

"ORCHID" PADEN CITY GLASS COMPANY, Early 1930's

Colors: Yellow, cobalt blue, green, pink, red and black.

New pieces to be excited about are red Orchid candlesticks and black and red Orchid vases, items readers have shown me since the last book! Thanks! I didn't know "Orchid" could be found in red or black.

I have also located blue orchid plates on "crows foot" blanks. They're squared like the bowl pictured.

Although this pattern is limited in supply, I suspect there are other pieces than those listed here. Let me know what you find!

	Pink, Green, Yellow	Red, Black Cobalt Blue
Bowl, 4 7/8" Square	9.00	17.50
Bowl, 8¾" Square	12.50	30.00
Candlesticks, 5¾" Pair	22.50	37.50
Creamer	12.50	27.50
Comport, 6¼"	13.50	22.50
Ice Bucket, 6"	27.50	49.50
Mayonnaise, 3 Pc.	17.50	32.50
Plate, 8", Square		20.00
Sugar	12.50	27.50
Vase, 10"	37.50	67.50

OVIDE, incorrectly dubbed "New Century" HAZEL ATLAS GLASS COMPANY, 1930-1935

Colors: Green, black, white, platonite trimmed with fired-on colors.

Everyone loves the Art Deco decorated pieces of Ovide. However, besides what is pictured here, I have only run into a sugar and creamer; I've talked with two different collectors who have stumbled onto entire sets. It is most definitely scarce; but you might be the third to find an entire set!

Many restaurants were attracted to the Platonite's heat resistant properties. Therefore, you can find plates like the plainer white one pictured in the back.

I've seen the black decorated with sterling floral designs. The design will be marked "sterling" around the top edge. You'll notice that even the fired-on Platonite cup and saucer have been edged in gold. Platonite pieces have been fired with various colors. Turn to Moderntone for examples.

	Green	Black, Decorated White		Green	Black, Decorated White
Bowl, 4¾" Berry		6.50	Plate, 6" Sherbet	1.00	2.50
Bowl, 5½" Cereal		6.50	Plate, 8" Luncheon	1.50	5.00
Bowl, 8" Large Berry		13.50	Plate, 9" Dinner		7.50
Candy Dish and Cover	14.50	22.50	Platter, 11"		9.50
Cocktail, Footed Fruit	1.50	6.50	Salt and Pepper, Pr.	7.50	20.00
Creamer	2.50	7.50	Saucer	1.25	3.00
Cup	1.50	5.50	Sherbet	1.50	6.50
			Sugar, Open	2.50	7.50

Please refer to Foreword for pricing information

OYSTER AND PEARL ANCHOR HOCKING GLASS CORPORATION, 1938-1940

Colors: Pink, crystal, ruby red, white with fired-on pink or green.

Oddly enough, the really avid collectors of Oyster and Pearl that I've run into have all been men! One lady enlisted my help in finding her husband a piece he'd been wanting for ages. What you see pictured was collected by a man whose wife couldn't stand "the stuff"!

Most Depression glass collectors like the pink and red salad sets, i.e., the big bowl and underplate. I've also heard of them being used as a small punch bowl and liner; (I trust they used paper cups). However, the bowls with fired-on colors are either loved or despised!

Those oblong relish dishes are useful, attractive and great as gifts! On top of that, the price is also right.

	Crystal, Pink	Royal Ruby	White With Fired On Green Or Pink
Bowl, 5¼" Heart Shaped, One Handled	5.00		5.00
Bowl, 6½" Deep Handled	8.00	12.50	
Bowl, 10½" Deep Fruit	15.00	29.50	10.00
Candleholder, 3½" Pr.	15.00	29.50	12.50
Plate, 13½" Sandwich	10.00	25.00	
Relish Dish, 10¼" Oblong	5.50		

"PARROT", SYLVAN   FEDERAL GLASS COMPANY, 1931-1932

Colors: Green, amber; some crystal and blue.

I mentioned the blue Parrot sherbet in the last book; well, the lady owner was kind enough to lend it to me to be photographed! Enjoy!

Federal named this pattern Sylvan (a woods dweller); and, of course, that's apt. However, it's universally called "Parrot" by collectors; and thus it's listed here by its "nickname" since few could locate it by its real name.

Prices for "Parrot", like other Depression glass patterns, have increased only slightly, but steadily during the past economic crisis. This is probably due less to economics than to the limited supply available at the present time. Many people are reluctant to start collecting a pattern which is no longer easily found. On the other hand, this relative scarcity enhances this pattern's attractiveness to other collectors who consider glassware for investment purposes. Demand for a pattern has much to do with price; and because this pattern has ever been admired by collectors, prices hold! Don't skip collecting a pattern just because it's getting scarce. It may take time, but sets aren't impossible to collect yet; and the day may well come when people will be proud to own a single setting of a rare pattern, much like they value a cut glass bowl, today!

There are very few "Parrot" pitchers to be found. Collectors who have them in their collections probably number fewer than fifty. A few years ago, a "stash" of 37 green pitchers turned up in an old hardware store and even with careful handling, two of them soon broke. That indicated to me why so few pitchers have been found; there's some fragility factor at work either in the design or the heating/cooling processing of these. These "Parrot" pitchers are like an endangered species and should be treated accordingly! To date, no amber pitcher has turned up.

After the pitcher, the hot plate and tall sherbet/champagne are the hardest items to locate. (They're conspicuously absent from this picture).

The pointed ridges on the cups, sherbets, sugar lids, et cetera, should be carefully checked for damage. They tend to flake and chip; and again, don't pay MINT prices for DAMAGED or noticeably REPAIRED glassware! Sugar lids, in particular, fit the latter category. I have no quarrel with repairing glass; it salvages much that would otherwise be lost to us. However, repaired glass should always be so marked; and you should exercise caution as to who repairs your glass. Some so called repairmen are grinders and butchers. Ask to see examples of their work and then decide. Are edges rounded and smoothed to near mint condition; or are they left flattened and sharp? Are chips and flakes ground away leaving dips in the surface; or is the entire edge reworked to insure uniformity? Does their equipment leave minute "scars" and "hairline" cracks; or is the resultant work indeed as "smooth as glass"?

Green "Parrot" grill plates, oddly enough, are round. Amber grill plates are squared like the plates. There are fewer pieces of amber to be found; but there are fewer collectors for the amber color though I think it equally attractive! Notice the thinner footed tumbler in amber which is extremely hard to find!

	Green	Amber		Green	Amber
Bowl, 5″ Berry	12.50	10.00	Plate, 10¼″ Square	32.50	32.50
Bowl, 7″ Soup	25.00	25.00	Platter, 11¼″ Oblong	27.50	40.00
Bowl, 8″ Large Berry	47.50	49.50	Salt and Pepper, Pr.	177.50	
Bowl, 10″ Oval Vegetable	35.00	40.00	Saucer	8.50	8.50
Butter Dish and Cover	227.50	557.50	*Sherbet, Footed Cone	16.50	15.00
Butter Dish Bottom	27.50	200.00	Sherbet, 4¼″ High	127.50	
Butter Dish Top	200.00	257.50	Sugar	20.00	19.50
Creamer, Footed	20.00	22.50	Sugar Cover	85.00	117.50
Cup	22.50	22.50	Tumbler, 4¼″, 10 oz.	77.50	77.50
Hot Plate, 5″	357.50		Tumbler, 5½″, 12 oz.	97.50	97.50
Pitcher, 8½″, 80 oz.	750.00		Tumbler, 5¾″ Footed		
Plate, 5¾″ Sherbet	10.00	10.00	Heavy	87.50	89.50
Plate, 7½″ Salad	14.00		Tumbler, 5½″, 10 oz.		
Plate, 9″ Dinner	27.50	25.00	Thin (Madrid Mold)		75.00
Plate, 10½″ Round Grill	17.50				
Plate, 10½″ Square Grill		16.00			

*Blue $75.00.

PATRICIAN, "SPOKE" FEDERAL GLASS COMPANY, 1933-1937

Colors: Pink, green, amber ("Golden Glo"), yellow.

Federal's "Golden Glo" Patrician is still the most popular color with today's collector and save for a few pieces, it is relatively easy to find! The plates remain among the least expensive in Depression glass! In many patterns, now, dinner plates are becoming scarce!

Pieces less easily found in amber include the large berry bowl, footed tumblers, pitchers, cookie jars and cereal bowls. The cereal bowl, by the way, is 6 inches in diameter and deep; the jam dish is 6½" across and the same height as the butter bottom but without the indent.

Pitchers with applied handles (shown in crystal) are seen less frequently than those with molded handles. Neither type are frequently found. They both have a 75 ounce capacity; but the molded handle type stands only 8" high, whereas the applied handle pitcher stands 8¼"tall.

No pink cookie jar has yet been found. Notice the price listings for the shakers and butter dishes in that color.

Check all sugar lids for damage and repair.

Take the time to notice the intricate borders and the Roman Chariot wheel the designer was careful to incorporate in this pattern named after a Roman nobleman. There's quite a bit of history as well as artistic accomplishment reflected here.

	Amber, Crystal	Pink	Green		Amber, Crystal	Pink	Green
Bowl, 4¾" Cream Soup	10.00	15.00	15.00	Plate, 9" Luncheon	7.00	6.50	6.50
Bowl, 5" Berry	7.50	9.50	7.50	Plate, 10½" Dinner	5.00	16.00	20.00
Bowl, 6" Cereal	15.00	17.50	17.50	Plate, 10½" Grill	7.50	9.50	9.50
Bowl, 8½" Large Berry	25.00	17.50	17.50	Platter, 11½" Oval	10.00	10.00	12.50
Bowl, 10" Oval				Salt and Pepper, Pr.	40.00	75.00	42.50
Vegetable	17.50	15.00	15.00	Saucer	5.00	5.00	5.00
Butter Dish and Cover	67.50	200.00	89.50	Sherbet	9.00	10.00	10.00
Butter Dish Bottom	45.00	150.00	50.00	Sugar	6.50	7.00	7.00
Butter Dish Top	22.50	50.00	39.50	Sugar Cover	27.50	40.00	40.00
Cookie Jar and Cover	52.50		275.00	Tumbler, 4", 5 oz.	20.00	20.00	20.00
Creamer, Footed	6.50	8.50	9.50	Tumbler, 4½", 9 oz.	19.50	18.50	18.50
Cup	8.00	7.50	8.00	Tumbler, 5½", 14 oz.	27.50	30.00	29.50
Jam Dish	15.00	20.00	25.00	Tumbler, 5¼", 8 oz.			
Pitcher, 8", 75 oz.	77.50	97.50	80.00	Footed	30.00		37.50
Pitcher, 8¼", 75 oz.	77.50	97.50	87.50				
Plate, 6" Sherbet	6.50	4.50	4.50				
Plate, 7½" Salad	9.50	12.50	9.50				

"PATRICK", LANCASTER GLASS COMPANY, Early 1930's

So called "Patrick" is a brother pattern to "Jubilee". How the pattern ever got such a masculine appellation for such an effeminate etching is beyond me! This pattern is characterized by a three flowered bouquet in the center of the design which is accompanied by flowers at either side attached to sprangled fronds. Although there are seemingly more pieces to be found in "Patrick" than in "Jubilee', it hasn't enjoyed the collecting fervor of "Jubilee" yet!

Since serving pieces in both patterns are so hard to find, many collectors are turning to the plainer yellow pieces of Depression glass to use with their sets. These pieces used to be ignored; but no longer. You seldom see any piece of Depression glass that isn't collectible!

	Yellow/ Pink		Yellow/ Pink
Bowl, 9", Handled Fruit	20.00	Mayonnaise, 3 Pc.	25.00
Bowl, 11", Console	22.50	Plate, 7", Sherbet	5.00
Candlesticks, Pr.	30.00	Plate, 7½", Salad	6.00
Candy Dish, 3 Ftd.	32.50	Plate, 8", Luncheon	6.50
Cheese & Cracker Set	25.00	Saucer	2.00
Creamer	10.50	Sherbet, 4¾"	10.50
Cup	8.00	Sugar	10.00
Goblet, 4", Cocktail	15.00	Tray, 11", 2 Handled	15.00
Goblet, 4¾", 6 oz., Juice	15.00	Tray, 11", Ctr. Handled	20.00
Goblet, 6", 10 oz., Water	17.50		

"PEACOCK REVERSE", LINE 412 PADEN CITY, 1930's

Colors: Cobalt blue, red, yellow.

Line #412 had what is commonly called this "crow's foot" design. The etching would also have had a number at the company. I have seen a number of "crow's foot" pieces since the last publication of this book; however, I've seen only a very few pieces of "Peacock Reverse" and except for a divided candy dish in yellow discovered at a Louisville flea market, every piece has been in red. I feel certain there are other pieces and colors to be discovered in the pattern. Please let me know what you find! (That yellow candy, by the way, is pictured in the new Pocket Guide and in the Elegant Glassware book which is where this pattern truly belongs)!

	Red, Blue		Red, Blue
Bowl, 4 7/8" Square	20.00	Plate, 5¾" Sherbet	16.50
Bowl, 8¾" Square	47.50	Saucer	10.00
Bowl, 8¾" Square with Handles	52.50	Sherbet, 4 5/8" Tall, 3 3/8" Diameter	32.50
Candlesticks, 5¾" Sq. Base, Pr.	72.50	Sherbet, 4 7/8" Tall, 3 5/8" Diameter	32.50
Candy Dish, 6½" Squared	49.50	Sugar, 2¾" Flat	47.50
Creamer, 2¾" Flat	47.50	Tumbler, 4", 10 oz. Flat	42.50
Cup	25.00		

149

PETALWARE MACBETH-EVANS GLASS COMPANY, 1930-1940

Colors: Monax, cremax, pink, crystal, cobalt and fired-on red, blue, green and yellow.

The red edged pieces of Petalware in the top photograph were marketed as "Florette" and are perhaps the most desirable of all Petalware dishes to own! You generally find a piece here and there rather than bunches of items at one time. Notice how attractive the fired-on red sherbet is when grouped with these red trimmed pieces. Seeing it alone at a market isn't nearly so stimulating.

In the bottom photograph you see the cobalt mustard dish (sans its metal lid) which my wife uses to individually serve fruit, custard, or sherbet at home. Also notice the gold trimmed cremax pieces which more collectors admire than they do the perfectly plain cremax color. There, too, are representatives of pink Petalware which is in so limited a supply as to make collecting it very time consuming.

The red "ribbon" decorator plates were sold with eight different fruits---among them a "Florence Cherry" which appealed to me for obvious reasons!

Several collectors are specifically looking for the "blue bird" items of Petalware (see plate in picture); so don't pass those by when you're shopping.

No shakers are found for Petalware; however, many collectors blend Newport shakers in Monax with their sets.

Many lamp shades are to be found with Petalware design from small individual types to large Chinese coolie hat shapes. These are more interesting than collectible, today, due to a dearth of the type lamps these fit. The small shades are generally priced $8.00-10.00; and the larger ones around $15.00. I'm certain some Petalware collector out there has a unique use for these. Let me hear about it so I can pass the information to other collectors.

I'm often asked for an idea of pattern to collect that is attractive, inexpensive and easily found. Here it is! Monax Petalware fits the criteria to a tee. Not only that, but it can be "dressed up" simply with a bright table cloth, center piece flowers and food! It's like nothing you find in the stores today and friends and guests will love it!

	Pink, Crystal	Plain	CREMAX, MONAX Fired-On Decorations		Pink, Crystal	Plain	CREMAX, MONAX Fired-On Decorations
Bowl, 4½" Cream Soup	4.50	5.50	7.50	Plate, 8" Salad	1.75	3.00	6.00
Bowl, 5¾" Cereal	3.50	4.50	6.50	Plate, 9" Dinner	3.00	3.50	7.50
Bowl, 7" Soup		6.50	10.00	Plate, 11" Salver	4.00	5.00	10.00
*Bowl, 8¾" Large Berry	7.50	12.50	15.00	Plate, 12" Salver		6.50	12.50
Cup	2.50	4.50	6.00	Platter, 13" Oval	5.50	7.50	12.50
**Creamer, Footed	2.50	4.50	7.50	Saucer	1.50	1.50	2.50
Lamp Shade (Many Sizes) $8.00 to $15.00				Sherbet, 4" Low Footed		10.00	
Mustard with Metal Cover				**Sherbet, 4½" Low Footed	3.00	4.50	7.50
in Cobalt Blue Only $5.00				**Sugar, Footed	2.50	4.50	7.50
Pitcher, 80 oz. (Crystal				Tidbit Servers or Lazy Susans,			
Decorated Bands)	20.00			Several Styles 12.00 to 17.50			
Plate, 6" Sherbet	1.50	2.00	4.00	***Tumblers (Crystal			
				Decorated Bands) 2.50 to 7.50			

*Also in cobalt at 32.50
**Also in cobalt at 19.50
***Several Sizes

"PRETZEL", NO. 622 INDIANA GLASS COMPANY, 1930's-1970's

Color: Crystal.

This is another of Indiana's numbered patterns that has been nicknamed so long that it is now "Pretzel" and nothing else. A pitcher and three sizes of tumblers are listed in Indiana's catalogues, but none have surfaced. They'd be quite a find!

The plentiful leaf shaped olive dish, the 8½", 2 handled pickle and the 10¼" celery tray have all been made in recent years. Some of the later pieces have clusters of fruits in the bottom, also.

Sherbet cups and the 9 3/8" berry bowl are the hardest pieces to locate.

	Crystal		Crystal
Bowl, 7½", Soup	3.50	Plate, 6"	1.00
Bowl, 9 3/8", Berry	7.50	Plate, 8 3/8", Salad	2.50
Celery, 10¼", Tray	2.50	Plate, 9 3/8", Dinner	3.50
Creamer	4.50	Plate, 11½", Sandwich	5.00
Cup	3.50	Saucer	1.00
Olive, 7", Leaf Shape	1.50	Sherbet, Flat	3.00
Pickle, 8½", 2 Hdld.	2.00	Sugar	3.50
Plate, Tab Hdld., Liner	2.00		

PRIMO, "PANELLED ASTER", U.S. GLASS COMPANY, Early 1930's

Colors: Green, yellow.

This small line of glassware has some unique shapes! There is a coaster/ash tray combination found packed with the tumblers that is plain, having no design, that is not usually recognized as belonging to the pattern.

My wife is positive she's seen a center handled server in it, also; I'm awaiting a picture as proof!

A lot of mold roughness is found on most pieces.

	Yellow/ Green		Yellow/ Green
Bowl, 4½"	6.50	Plate, 10", Dinner	10.00
Bowl, 7¾"	12.50	Plate, 10", Grill	7.50
Cake Plate, 10", 3 Ftd.	13.50	Saucer	2.00
Coaster/Ash Tray	6.00	Sherbet	6.50
Creamer	7.50	Sugar	7.50
Cup	6.50	Tumbler, 5¾", 9 oz.	9.00
Plate, 7½"	5.00		

PRINCESS HOCKING GLASS COMPANY, 1931-1935

Colors: Green, topaz and apricot yellow, pink; some blue.

I never do a show that someone doesn't walk up and ask what the name of this pattern is because their grandmother or someone "had" a piece of it. The next question is, "Is this what's called Depression Glass?" It still astounds me that there are MULTITUDES of people still in this world who haven't the faintest idea what Depression glass is or that it has any value!

Pay attention to those footed pitchers. They are extremely unusual and so far are only found in pink and green. Some have been found bearing frosted panels down each side. Tumblers have been seen with matching panels, too.

Also shown is the rarely seen blue cookie jar and cup and saucer. I talked with a dealer who turned down a set of the blue at a Texas show because he knew it came from Mexico and was leary of it. That brings us to the fact that there is quite a bit of "odd" glass coming from below the border, namely the Florentine sherbet from a Madrid shaped mold, the blue Florentine pitcher, a crystal bowl similar to No. 612. As I see it, there are two thoughts on this, either it's reproduction or it was made by the various companies for a specific market there. Quite a bit of Depression glass is found in Canada; I'm getting letter after letter from England from people who are discovering it there and are wanting books for more information. People find it in Scotland, the Virgin Islands, Hawaii and Alaska. So, it seems likely that there were markets for the glass in these other areas. Perhaps there was a specific market for blue Princess below our borders.

There are two distinctly different colors of yellow Princess. That usually found is the topaz yellow pictured. There is a more apricot, amber color, too.

The 4½" berry bowl is becoming hard to find in all colors. Some dealers call the undivided relish a "soup" bowl.

The 5½" spice shakers which closely match Princess were sold with "Dove" black pepper rather than by Hocking with Princess pattern as far as I can tell.

Satinized pieces, represented in the picture by the pink sugar and creamer, are virtually ignored by collectors. These items bring 10 to 20 percent less.

	Green	Pink	Yellow Amber		Green	Pink	Amber
Ash Tray, 4½"	50.00	57.50	67.50	Plate, 11½" Grill, Closed Handles	7.50	5.00	6.00
Bowl, 4½" Berry	16.50	10.00	27.50	Plate, 11½" Handled Sandwich	9.50	7.50	8.50
Bowl, 5" Cereal or Oatmeal	18.50	13.50	22.50	Platter, 12" Closed Handles	12.50	11.00	30.00
Bowl, 9" Octagonal Salad	22.50	16.50	67.50	Relish, 7½" Divided	17.50	12.50	47.50
Bowl, 9½" Hat Shaped	25.00	14.50	75.00	Relish, 7½" Plain	52.50		92.50
Bowl, 10" Oval Vegetable	17.50	15.00	37.50	Salt and Pepper, 4½" Pair	37.50	30.00	50.00
Butter Dish and Cover	67.50	65.00	425.00	Spice Shakers, 5½" Pair	27.50		
Butter Dish Bottom	22.50	20.00	200.00	†††Saucer (Same as Sherbet Plate)	5.00	4.00	4.00
Butter Dish Top	45.00	45.00	225.00	Sherbet, Footed	13.50	11.00	27.50
Cake Stand, 10"	14.50	12.00		Sugar	8.50	6.50	9.50
Candy Dish and Cover	35.00	37.50		Sugar Cover	12.50	11.50	12.50
Coaster	22.50	52.50	67.50	Tumbler, 3", 5 oz. Juice	20.00	14.50	22.50
†Cookie Jar and Cover	35.00	40.00		Tumbler, 4", 9 oz. Water	18.50	12.50	20.00
Creamer, Oval	8.50	9.50	9.50	Tumbler, 5¼", 13 oz. Iced Tea	23.50	16.50	25.00
††Cup	9.00	6.50	7.50	Tumbler, 4¾", 9 oz. Sq. Ftd.	50.00	42.50	
Pitcher, 6", 37 oz.	35.00	25.00	500.00	Tumbler, 5¼", 10 oz. Footed	21.50	16.00	17.50
Pitcher, 7 3/8", 24 oz. Footed	400.00	400.00		Tumbler, 6½", 12½ oz. Footed	47.50	30.00	57.50
Pitcher, 8", 60 oz.	37.50	35.00	60.00	Vase, 8"	22.00	17.50	
Plate, 5½" Sherbet	5.00	3.50	4.50				
Plate, 8" Salad	8.50	6.50	7.50				
Plate, 9½" Dinner	17.50	11.00	11.00				
††Plate, 9½" Grill	9.50	6.50	6.50				

†Blue — $400.00
††Blue — $60.00
††† Blue — $45.00

Please refer to Foreword for pricing information

QUEEN MARY (PRISMATIC LINE), "VERTICAL RIBBED"
HOCKING GLASS COMPANY, 1936-1940

Colors: Pink, crystal; some ruby red.

I don't believe pink shakers exist in Queen Mary. I think those "pictured" in earlier editions must have been crystal with their red tops fooling the camera into making them look pink. None of us can truly remember their having been pink; and since no others have turned up. . .!

At a Texas show one lady was delighted to find Queen Mary dinner plates that she claimed to have been looking for over two years! Perhaps that should tell us something! Pink dinner plates are the only item to show a significant rise in price since the last edition, too; so, definitely we're being told they're scarce!

Footed tumblers are also scarce.

Beginning collectors should know that there are two sizes of cups to be found in this "Prismatic Line" as Hocking called it. The smaller cup is the easiest to locate and it fits on a saucer with a cup ring. The larger cup fits on Hocking's typical saucer/sherbet plate, one plate serving a dual purpose.

During the Royal Ruby promotion of the early '40's, some pieces were made in ruby. I've seen the candlestick. In the early '50's, a 3½" round ash tray was made in Forest Green and Royal Ruby.

	Pink	Crystal		Pink	Crystal
Ash Tray, 2" x 3¾" Oval	3.50	2.00	Cup (2 sizes)	5.00	4.50
*Ash Tray, 3½" Round		2.00	Plate, 6" and 6 5/8"	2.50	2.50
Bowl, 4" One Handle or None	3.00	2.00	Plate, 8½" Salad	4.00	3.50
Bowls, 5" Berry, 6" Cereal	3.50	2.50	Plate, 9¾" Dinner	17.50	6.50
Bowl, 5½", Two Handles	4.00	3.00	Plate, 12" Relish, 3 Sections	8.50	6.00
Bowl, 7" Small	5.00	4.00	Plate, 12" Sandwich	6.50	5.50
Bowl, 8¾" Large Berry	7.50	6.00	Plate, 14" Serving Tray	8.00	7.50
Butter Dish or Preserve and			Relish Tray, 12", 3 Part	8.50	8.50
Cover	75.00	20.00	Relish Tray, 14", 4 Part	8.50	8.50
Butter Dish Bottom	6.00	4.00	Salt and Pepper, Pr.	82.50	12.50
Butter Dish Top	69.00	16.00	Saucer	1.50	1.50
Candy Dish and Cover	20.00	12.00	Sherbet, Footed	4.00	3.50
**Candlesticks, 4½" Double			Sugar, Oval	4.50	4.00
Branch, Pr.		10.00	Tumbler, 3½", 5 oz. Juice	4.00	2.50
Celery or Pickle Dish, 5" x 10"	4.50	3.50	Tumbler, 4", 9 oz. Water	5.50	4.00
Cigarette Jar, 2" x 3" Oval	5.50	3.50	Tumbler, 5", 10 oz. Footed	13.50	10.00
Coaster, 3½"	2.50	2.00			
Coaster/Ash Tray, 4¼"					
Square	4.50	4.50			
Comport, 5¾"	5.00	4.50			
Creamer, Oval	4.50	4.00			

*Ruby Red - $5.00; Forest Green - $3.00
**Ruby Red - $27.50

157

RAINDROPS, "OPTIC DESIGN" FEDERAL GLASS COMPANY 1929-1933

Colors: Green, crystal.

I've now looked eight years for a mate to this shaker. Yes, "Raindrops" shakers are that rare. However, since there are relatively few collectors for this pattern, the price for such a rare Depression glass item remains low! (One collector did tell me he had one in his collection; but it was not for sale).

"Raindrops" humps are ROUNDED little hills occuring on the inside of pieces or undersides of plates. This pattern is often confused with "Thumbprint"/Pear Optic pattern which had ELONGATED impressions which are slightly "scooped out" in the center like "thumbprints".

I've known of three "Raindrops" sugar lids in all the years I've dealt with Depression glass. It's one of the rarest lids to be found in this glass. However, due to few collectors for this pattern, these rare lids won't command anywhere near the prices accorded a Monax American Sweetheart or Mayfair sugar lid. DEMAND, not necessarily RARITY, determine price in Depression glass.

	Green		Green
Bowl, 4½" Fruit	2.00	Salt and Pepper, Pr.	37.50
Bowl, 6" Cereal	3.00	Saucer	1.50
Cup	3.00	Sherbet	3.50
Creamer	4.50	Sugar	3.50
Plate, 6" Sherbet	1.50	Sugar Cover	20.00
Plate, 8" Luncheon	2.50	Tumbler, 3", 4 oz.	3.00
		Whiskey, 1 7/8"	3.50

"RIBBON" HAZEL ATLAS GLASS COMPANY Early 1930's

Colors: Green; some black, crystal, pink.

I'm encountering pieces of "Ribbon" more and more in my travels which encourages my belief that a set of this is not such an impossibility as was once believed. Too, I see more people buying it than ever before. You used to find only a piece or two at a time; now, there are usually three or four pieces grouped together.

You will notice the similarity of shapes to Hazel Atlas's Cloverleaf and Ovide patterns. The company seems to have gotten a lot of mileage out of their molds which was sensible since molds were costly but could be reworked for a different design.

Pink and black shakers are in demand by item collectors only. Shakers are the only items noted so far in pink.

As I visit collector's homes, more and more I'm being served something from one of these inexpensive patterns which they are using and enjoying daily!

	Green	Black		Green	Black
Bowl, 4" Berry	2.00		Salt and Pepper, Pr.	15.00	27.50
Bowl, 8" Large Berry	6.00	13.00	Saucer	1.50	
Candy Dish and Cover	20.00		Sherbet, Footed	3.00	
Creamer, Footed	3.50	9.00	Sugar, Footed	3.00	9.00
Cup	2.50		Tumbler, 5½", 10 oz.	5.50	
Plate, 6¼" Sherbet	1.25		Tumbler, 6½", 13 oz.	6.50	
Plate, 8" Luncheon	2.00	8.00			

RING, "BANDED RINGS" HOCKING GLASS COMPANY 1927-1933

Colors: Crystal, crystal w/pink, red, blue, orange, yellow, black, silver, etc. rings; green, some pink, "Mayfair" blue, red.

Interest in this pattern is increasing and the prices are beginning to reflect this. Many pitcher collectors virtually ignored this pattern when it was cheaply priced. Now, they're having a terrible time finding these pitchers for their collections. If the pitchers shown were reversed, i.e., the pink one like the green and the green like the pink, you'd have the very rarely seen Ring pitchers. These shown are of the variety commonly found. So far, only pitchers and tumblers have been located in pink.

Unusual colors of red and "Mayfair" blue Ring have only been noted in luncheon plates and tumblers. Let me hear from you if you find other items, please.

Ring shakers are difficult to locate. At one time it was a common practice to rob Ring shakers of their tops to put them on the more prestigious Mayfair shakers. No more! Ring collectors want their shakers intact; and suddenly, dealers found they weren't so plentiful!

Banded Ring was advertised as "New Fiesta", suitably festooned with colorful sombreros and gaily skirted dancing girls outfitted in like colors of orange, yellow and green! There are various colors of bands. Don't even TRY to get them all to match. Go for an over-all appearance of color.

Ring with the silver trim is very chic, particularly the stemmed pieces.

Notice that Ring has ice buckets, cocktail shakers and decanters---everything the Prohibition era precluded! Well, if you'd been officially "dry" from 1919 to 1933, maybe it was time for a "New Fiesta" and drink accoutrements!

	Crystal	Crystal Decor., Green		Crystal	Crystal Decor., Green
Bowl, 5" Berry	2.00	3.00	Sandwich Server, Center		
Bowl, 7" Soup	6.00	7.50	Handle	9.50	17.50
Bowl, 8" Large Berry	4.00	6.00	Saucer	1.50	2.00
Butter Tub or Ice			Sherbet, Low (for 6½"		
Bucket	8.50	13.50	Plate)	4.00	4.50
Cocktail Shaker	7.50	13.50	Sherbet, 4¾" Footed	4.00	6.00
Cup	2.50	3.50	Sugar, Footed	3.00	4.00
Creamer, Footed	3.50	4.50	Tumbler, 3½", 5 oz.	2.50	3.50
Decanter and Stopper	14.50	25.00	Tumbler, 4¼", 9 oz.	3.50	4.50
Goblet, 7" to 8" (Varies)			Tumbler, 5 1/8", 12 oz.	4.00	4.50
9 oz.	4.50	9.50	Tumbler, 3½" Footed		
Ice Tub	8.50	12.00	Cocktail	4.00	4.50
Pitcher, 8", 60 oz.	8.50	15.00	Tumbler, 5½" Footed		
*Pitcher, 8½", 80 oz.	10.50	17.50	Water	3.50	4.50
Plate, 6¼" Sherbet	1.25	2.50	Tumbler, 6½", Footed		
Plate, 6", Off Center			Iced Tea	5.00	8.50
Ring	1.50	3.50	Whiskey, 2", 1½ oz.	3.50	5.00
**Plate, 8" Luncheon	1.50	2.50			
***Salt and Pepper, Pr., 3"	12.50	22.50			

*Also found in Pink. Priced as Green.
**Red — 17.50. Blue — 22.50.
***Green — 57.50.

ROCK CRYSTAL, "EARLY AMERICAN ROCK CRYSTAL"

McKEE GLASS COMPANY, 1920's and 1930's in colors

Colors: Four shades of green, aquamarine, vaseline, yellow, amber, pink and satin frosted pink, red slag, dark red, red, amberina red, crystal, frosted crystal, crystal with goofus decoration, crystal with gold decoration, amethyst, milk glass, blue frosted or "Jap" blue and cobalt blue.

Just so you'd know it could be done, we put a set together in red! Actually, it was found mostly intact as you see it here having belonged to a former employee. Notice the varying shades of red, from the amberina plate at the back (small center) to the very dark covered pitcher and candy dish bottom. Notice, also, that the pieces come with scalloped or plain edges. Many collectors refer to the small centered plates as "serving" plates and to the larger centered plates as dinner plates.

I realize that my listings here are not entirely complete as to actual pieces made. There are numerous bowls, for instance, with varying edges, heights and diameters. I chose to give a representative sample that could be easily read rather than the reams of information that would be more than you'd want to know (or wade through or pay for in extra book cost)!

Do notice the lovely punch bowl pictured in crystal and the tankard type pitchers in forest green and amber which are so rare. The canary yellow pitcher is also elusive.

You will find the blue berry set residing in silver metal holders. Cobalt blue items include the candlestick and a large, footed, scalloped edged fruit bowl which was shown in the last book. That same bowl has been found in a tomato slag red!

We were recently able to replace the small footed fruit bowl in crystal that belonged to my wife and which was smashed at the last photography session. It is seldom a piece is damaged in one of those horrendous three days of setting up thousands of pieces of glass to be photographed. I hope you fully appreciate the money, time, effort and skill each of these color photographs represent, not just on my part, but on the part of friends who lend glass or help during sessions to employees who spend hours on their knees trying to arrange the pieces so that the camera can "see" them most advantageously.

	Crystal	All Other Colors	Red
*Bon Bon, 7½″ S.E.	12.50	20.00	37.50
Bowl, 4″ S.E.	7.50	10.00	20.00
Bowl, 4½″ S.E.	8.00	10.00	22.50
Bowl, 5″ S.E.	9.50	12.50	25.00
**Bowl, 5″ Finger Bowl with 7″ Plate, P.E.	15.00	20.00	35.00
Bowl, 7″ Pickle or Spoon Tray	15.00	22.00	37.50
Bowl, 7″ Salad S.E.	15.00	22.50	30.00
Bowl, 8″ Salad S.E.	15.00	22.00	35.00
Bowl, 9″ Salad S.E.	17.50	23.00	40.00
Bowl, 10½″ Salad S.E.	18.50	25.00	45.00
Bowl, 11½″ Two Part Relish	20.00	27.00	35.00
Bowl, 12″ Oblong Celery	20.00	27.00	42.50
***Bowl, 12½″ Footed Center Bowl	35.00	65.00	150.00
Bowl, 13″ Roll Tray	22.50	35.00	
Bowl, 14″ Six Part Relish	22.50	37.50	
Butter Dish and Cover	197.50		
Butter Dish Bottom	100.00		
Butter Dish Top	97.50		
****Candelabra, Two Lite Pr.	32.50	50.00	100.00
Candelabra, Three Lite Pr.	35.00	55.00	110.00
Candlestick, 5½″ Low Pr.	27.50	45.00	67.50
Candlestick, 8½″ Tall Pr.	57.50	75.00	137.50
Candy and Cover, Round	25.00	45.00	100.00
Cake Stand, 11″, 2¾″ High, Footed	19.50	32.50	57.50

Please refer to Foreword for pricing information

ROCK CRYSTAL, "EARLY AMERICAN ROCK CRYSTAL" (Con't.)

	Crystal	All Other Colors	Red
Comport, 7″	27.50	37.50	52.50
Creamer, Flat S.E.	20.00		
Creamer, 9 oz. Footed	15.00	25.00	42.50
Cruet and Stopper, 6 oz. Oil	39.50		
Cup, 7 oz.	12.00	15.00	32.50
Goblet, 7½ oz., 8 oz. Low Footed	13.50	22.50	45.00
Goblet, 11 oz. Low Footed Iced Tea	15.00	22.00	55.00
Jelly, 5″ Footed S.E.	13.50	20.00	35.00
Lamp, Electric	57.50	127.50	250.00
Parfait, 3½ oz. Low Footed	8.50		
Pitcher, Quart S.E.	77.50	135.00	
Pitcher, ½ Gal., 7½″ High	95.00	145.00	
Pitcher, 9″ Large Covered	125.00	175.00	300.00
Pitcher, Fancy Tankard	137.50	325.00	450.00
Plate, 6″ Bread and Butter S.E.	4.50	6.50	11.00
Plate, 7½″ P.E. & S.E.	6.50	9.00	13.50
Plate, 8½″ P.E. & S.E.	7.50	9.50	20.00
Plate, 9″ S.E.	12.50	17.50	35.00
Plate, 10½″ S.E.	13.50	18.50	37.50
Plate, 11½″ S.E.	14.50	20.00	40.00
Plate, 10½″ Dinner S.E. (Large Center Design)	37.50	45.00	62.50
Punch Bowl and Stand, 14″	265.00		
Salt and Pepper (2 styles)	40.00	75.00	
Salt Dip	20.00		
Sandwich Server, Center Handled	20.00	30.00	75.00
Saucer	4.50	6.50	10.00
Sherbet or Egg, 3½ oz. Footed	9.50	17.50	30.00
Spooner	27.50		
Stemware, 1 oz. Footed Cordial	15.00	25.00	40.00
Stemware, 2 oz. Wine	14.00	23.00	35.00
Stemware, 3 oz. Wine	15.00	25.00	37.50
Stemware, 3½ oz. Footed Cocktail	12.00	17.50	35.00
Stemware, 6 oz. Footed Champagne	12.50	17.50	27.50
Stemware, 8 oz. Large Footed Goblet	13.50	22.50	45.00
Sundae, 6 oz. Low Footed	9.50	15.00	27.50
Sugar, 10 oz. Open	13.00	20.00	35.00
Sugar, Lid	25.00	35.00	50.00
Syrup with Lid	52.50		
Tumbler, 2½″ oz. Whiskey	9.50	15.00	35.00
Tumbler, 5 oz. Juice	12.00	18.00	32.50
Tumbler, 5 oz. Old Fashioned	12.00	18.00	35.00
Tumbler, 9 oz. Concave or Straight	15.00	22.00	37.50
Tumbler, 12 oz. Concave or Straight	20.00	25.00	45.00
Vase, Cornucopia	35.00	50.00	
Vase, 11″ Footed	32.50	40.00	117.50

*S.E. McKee designation for scalloped edge
**P.E. McKee designation for plain edge
***Red Slag — $300.00. Cobalt — $137.50
****Cobalt — $75.00

ROSE CAMEO BELMONT TUMBLER COMPANY, 1931

Color: Green.

Since shards of Rose Cameo have turned up in "digs" at the old factory site of the Hazel Atlas plant, it seems likely that company may have made this even though the patent was registered to the Belmont Tumbler Company.

Tumblers are the most frequently seen item. There are two styles, one having a slightly flared edge. It is pictured.

The hard to find straight sided bowl is turned on edge behind the tumbler. Notice the bottom surface is much wider than on the other bowls shown.

This pattern is still confused with Cameo. Rose Cameo has a rose inside the cameo rather than the little dancing girl; hence the name "Rose" Cameo.

	Green		Green
Bowl, 4½" Berry	3.50	Sherbet	4.50
Bowl, 5" Cereal	5.50	Tumbler, 5" Footed (2 Styles)	9.50
Bowl, 6", Straight Sides	7.50		
Plate, 7" Salad	4.50		

ROSEMARY, "DUTCH ROSE" FEDERAL GLASS COMPANY 1935-1937

Colors: Amber, green, pink; some iridized.

Due to the increasing popularity of green and the scarcity of pink, I have separated these colors in the price listing. Amber is the most plentiful color in this pattern; but pink and green are most in demand.

Rosemary pattern resulted from Federal's having to change their Mayfair pattern after learning that Hocking had beaten them to the patent office with the name "Mayfair". You will notice that Rosemary has perfectly plain glass at the base of its pieces save for the center Rose motif. It has neither the "arches" of the "transitional" Mayfair pieces nor the "arches and waffling" of the traditional Mayfair pieces.

The pink footed item with the creamer is the sugar bowl. In this pattern the sugar has no handles. It's not a tumbler nor a sherbet. It's the sugar bowl!

Cream soup bowls, oval vegetables and cereal dishes and tumblers are all hard to find! Pink tumblers have made the biggest jump in price.

Few iridized salad plates are to be found today.

	Amber	Green	Pink		Amber	Green	Pink
Bowl, 5" Berry	4.00	4.50	4.00	Plate, Dinner	5.50	10.00	8.50
Bowl, 5" Cream Soup	7.50	13.50	12.50	Plate, Grill	6.00	10.00	8.00
Bowl, 6" Cereal	10.00	12.50	10.00	Platter, 12" Oval	9.50	14.50	11.50
Bowl, 10" Oval Vegetable	8.50	15.00	12.00	Saucer	2.00	3.50	2.00
Creamer, Footed	6.50	9.50	7.50	Sugar, Footed	6.50	9.50	7.50
Cup	4.00	7.00	4.50	Tumbler, 4¼", 9 oz.	10.00	13.50	18.00
Plate, 6¾" Salad	4.00	6.00	3.50				

ROULETTE, "MANY WINDOWS" HOCKING GLASS COMPANY, 1935-1939

Colors: Green; some pink and crystal.

It's amazing how much you learn about a pattern when you purchase a set and sell it! For instance, I learned that sherbets and luncheon plates abound and therefore, most collectors already have them. I learned that I could've sold all the other items ten times over! There are numerous collectors out there searching for Roulette! Actually, it's a very attractive pattern when you get a bunch of it together!

New collectors please notice that the rouletting occurs toward the upper third of the pitcher. There is a pitcher with a cubed design at the bottom that is sometimes mistaken for Roulette. There is also a cobalt pitcher with an embossed design (rather than impressed) which is much like Roulette. Neither are Roulette, however!

Shot glasses, footed tumblers and saucers are singularly hard to find.

Pink Roulette has appeared only in pitcher and tumbler sets so far. Do notice the one small crystal glass pictured. That wee glass may indicate a pitcher! Watch for it.

	Pink, Green, Crystal
Bowl, 9″ Fruit	8.50
Cup	4.00
Pitcher, 8″, 64 oz.	22.50
Plate, 6″ Sherbet	2.00
Plate, 8½″ Luncheon	4.00
Plate, 12″ Sandwich	7.50
Saucer	2.00
Sherbet	4.00
Tumbler, 3¼″, 5 oz. Juice	4.50
Tumbler, 3¼″, 7½ oz. Old Fashioned	6.00
Tumbler, 4 1/8″, 9 oz. Water	12.50
Tumbler, 5 1/8″, 12 oz. Iced Tea	10.00
Tumbler, 5½″, 10 oz. Footed	9.50
Whiskey, 2½″, 1½ oz.	6.50

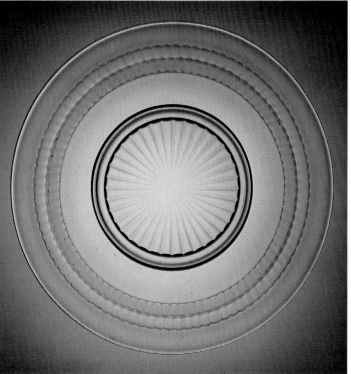

169

"ROUND ROBIN" MANUFACTURER UNKNOWN, Probably early 1930's

Colors: Green, some iridescent.

Yes! There's a sherbet pictured and a plate and a green sugar bowl, finally! Actually, I ran into a four place setting in Ohio and SIX never before seen sherbets in southern Kentucky, no less!

This pattern is interesting in that it has footed cups and the domino drip tray, rather "fancy" pieces for such a small pattern.

	Green	Iridescent		Green	Iridescent
Bowl, 4″ Berry	3.50	4.00	Plate, 8″ Luncheon	2.50	3.00
Cup, Footed	3.00	4.00	Plate, 12″ Sandwich	3.50	4.50
Creamer, Footed	4.50	5.50	Saucer	1.50	1.50
Domino Tray	17.50		Sherbet	3.50	4.00
Plate, 6″ Sherbet	1.50	1.50	Sugar	4.50	5.00

ROXANA HAZEL ATLAS GLASS COMPANY, 1932

Colors: Yellow, crystal; some white.

This is one of the patterns you'll have to ask for by name at shows. Most dealers won't have it with them, but may have pieces at home or in their shops.

The 6″ cereal bowl is pictured here on the stand at the left. Unfortunately, the camera doesn't allow for depth and it looks more like a plate than a bowl.

Notice the sherbet pictured. If you find other pieces in this pattern, I'd appreciate hearing from you. To date, these are all that are known.

This would be a fun little pattern to search out and use at breakfast with cereal or for brunch with fruit and salad!

	Yellow	White		Yellow
Bowl, 4½″ x 2 3/8″	5.00	10.00	Plate, 6″ Sherbet	2.50
Bowl, 5″ Berry	3.50		Saucer	2.50
Bowl, 6″ Cereal	5.50		Sherbet, Footed	3.50
			Tumbler, 4″, 9 oz.	7.50

ROYAL LACE   HAZEL ATLAS GLASS COMPANY, 1934-1941

Colors: Cobalt blue, crystal, green, pink; some amethyst.

Royal Lace is one of those Depression glass patterns that sells itself. Everyone seems to like it! Even crystal is in demand in this pattern, something that can be said for few other patterns save, perhaps, for Miss America and Manhattan. You or your progenitor could have bought a 44 piece set in 1934 for $2.99! (Lest you treat that price too lightly, my grandfather-in-law sold his tobacco crop in 1932 at a penny a pound, for literally months of labor! These dishes would have been totally out of the question for his family---and millions like his)!

In spite of what the picture would indicate, pitchers are not that easily found, particularly the bulbous type. Yet, even the 48 ounce straight side, (yes, 48 ounce, not 54 ounce as stated in old catalogue listings), is rapidly disappearing from the market.

Blue Royal Lace is a favorite color with collectors and it seems plentiful enough. Many people favor the green, but most of that has disappeared into collections of people who started gathering glass a dozen years ago when Depression glass collecting first came into vogue with the general populace. (Of course, you do meet "old timers" who started collecting in the early '60's when you bought it at auctions for $2.00 for the basket loads)!

The odd looking piece in the center of the photo is the toddy set. It should have a ladle with a cherry red knob like the one on the metal top. The cookie jar is the insert. It's found in amethyst and cobalt with eight roly-poly cups which are usually plain, but which can be found bearing the tiny "Ships" motif.

You can see from the price listing that butter dishes are prime items to own.

Remember to check the inside rims of plates, bowls and butter dishes for chips and flakes which may have been caused by stacking and use or they may have come from the mold with tiny damage. At any rate, these imperfections affect the price.

One couple found an unusual ruffled cream soup in pink Royal Lace; you might like to watch for others.

	Crystal	Pink	Green	Blue	Amethyst
Bowl, 4¾" Cream Soup	7.50	11.50	22.50	22.50	
Bowl, 5" Berry	6.00	12.00	16.50	22.50	
Bowl, 10" Round Berry	10.00	12.50	20.00	35.00	
Bowl, 10", 3 Leg Straight Edge	12.50	18.50	30.00	42.50	
Bowl, 10", 3 Leg Rolled Edge	75.00	25.00	60.00	157.50	
Bowl, 10", 3 Leg Ruffled Edge .	17.50	19.50	37.50	142.50	
Bowl, 11" Oval Vegetable	12.50	15.00	19.50	35.00	
Butter Dish and Cover	52.50	95.00	225.00	357.50	
Butter Dish Bottom	37.50	60.00	150.00	225.00	
Butter Dish Top	25.00	35.00	75.00	132.50	
Candlestick, Straight Edge Pair	18.50	25.00	42.50	75.00	
Candlestick, Rolled Edge Pair	37.50	35.00	50.00	95.00	
Candlestick, Ruffled Edge Pair	22.50	35.00	50.00	87.50	
Cookie Jar and Cover	25.00	37.50	52.50	215.00	
Cream, Footed	8.00	11.00	17.50	25.00	
Cup	5.00	9.50	14.00	22.50	
Pitcher, 48 oz., Straight Sides	30.00	40.00	67.50	82.50	
Pitcher, 8", 68 oz.	40.00	39.50	75.00	117.50	
Pitcher, 8", 86 oz.	42.50	55.00	95.00	127.50	
Pitcher, 8½", 96 oz.	45.00	62.50	120.00	157.50	
Plate, 6" Sherbet	2.50	3.50	6.00	8.50	
Plate, 8½" Luncheon	4.00	6.50	9.50	22.50	
Plate, 10" Dinner	7.50	11.50	17.50	30.00	
Plate, 9 7/8" Grill	5.50	8.50	15.00	22.50	
Platter, 13" Oval	12.00	15.00	25.00	35.00	
Salt and Pepper, Pr.	32.50	37.50	112.50	197.50	
Saucer	2.50	3.50	5.00	7.50	
Sherbet, Footed	7.00	9.00	17.50	25.00	
Sherbet in Metal Holder	3.50			20.00	25.00
Sugar	7.00	7.50	15.00	22.50	
Sugar Lid	13.00	22.50	27.50	77.50	
Tumbler, 3½", 5 oz.	7.50	12.50	20.00	27.50	
Tumbler, 4 1/8", 9 oz.	8.50	10.00	17.50	25.00	
Tumbler, 4 7/8", 10 oz.	12.50	17.00	27.50	45.00	
Tumbler, 5 3/8", 12 oz.	12.50	20.00	25.00	40.00	
Toddy or Cider Set: Includes Cookie Jar, Metal Lid, Metal Tray, 8 Roly-Poly Cups and Ladle				100.00	120.00

ROYAL RUBY ANCHOR HOCKING GLASS COMPANY, 1938-1960's; 1977

Color: Ruby red.

The term "Royal Ruby" refers to the red glassware made by the Anchor Hocking Company only. Many people erroneously group any red glass under that term. Anchor Hocking initially started promoting Royal Ruby in 1938 and continued the promotion through the early 1940's.

The piece you see at the bottom of the page is a ball vase containing a citronella candle which was lit to scare away mosquitoes as you sat on the patio. This probably explains why there are so many of these vases to be found today. Whether the product had any affect on mosquitoes, I don't know.

The squared red items were a 1950's issue, made at the same time as the Forest Green items of like shape. Presently, there is not as much demand for the red as for the green; but in talking with dealers, the squared items appear to be in shorter supply than the older round ones. Many dealers tell me people buy this specifically for their Christmas tables.

The 5¼" bowl located behind the round dinner plate was sold in a set of seven bowls, one larger 10" bowl included, as a popcorn set.

The 13¾" salad plate with the 11½" salad bowl has become one of Royal Ruby's most sought after items; and the oval vegetable bowl is encountered very infrequently. They're absent from most collections at the moment!

The price for the ball stemmed goblet has remained about the same; but I know my once abundant supply has dwindled; so, be forewarned.

In 1977 Anchor Hocking re-introduced 4½" and 8" bowls in red Bubble; 7, 9, 12 and 16 ounce plain tumblers; an ivy ball vase; a punch cup and a square ash tray. All these items supposedly carry the anchor trademark of the company and, in general, were lighter in weight and color than the older glassware.

Not all footed sugars take the slotted lid and some lids simply will not fit the sugar; so buying pieces separately presents a problem.

	Red
Ash Tray, 4½" Square	2.50
Bowl, 4¼" Berry	4.00
Bowl, 5¼"	6.50
Bowl, 7½" Soup	9.50
Bowl, 8" Oval Vegetable	12.50
Bowl, 8½" Large Berry	12.50
Bowl, 10" Deep	15.00
Bowl, 11½" Salad	18.00
Creamer, Flat	6.00
Creamer, Footed	7.50
Cup (Round or Square)	3.50
Goblet, Ball Stem	6.50
Lamp	20.00
Pitcher, 22 oz. Tilted or Upright	20.00
Pitcher, 3 qt. Tilted	25.00
Pitcher, 3 qt. Upright	30.00
Plate, 6½" Sherbet	2.00
Plate, 7" Salad	3.50
Plate, 7¾" Luncheon	4.00
Plate, 9" or 9¼" Dinner	7.50
Plate, 13¾"	12.50
Punch Bowl and Stand	35.00
Punch Cup	2.00
Saucer (Round or Square)	1.50
Sherbet, Footed	6.50
Sugar, Flat	6.00
Sugar, Footed	7.50
Sugar Lid	7.50
Tumbler, 2½ oz. Footed Wine	8.50
Tumbler, 3½ oz. Cocktail	6.50
Tumbler, 5 oz. Juice, 2 Styles	5.00
Tumbler, 9 oz. Water	5.00
Tumbler, 10 oz. Water	5.00
Tumbler, 13 oz. Iced Tea	8.50
Vase, 4" Ball Shaped	4.50
Vase, 6½" Bulbous, Tall	7.50
Vases, Several Styles (Small)	5.00
Vases, Several Styles (Large)	10.00

Please refer to Foreword for pricing information

"S" PATTERN, "STIPPLED ROSE BAND" MACBETH-EVANS GLASS COMPANY, 1930-1933

Colors: Crystal; crystal w/trims of silver, blue, green, amber; pink; some amber, green, fired-on red, Monax, and light yellow.

"S" Pattern is a delicate, lovely little pattern that has been virtually ignored by collectors except for the pitchers, tumblers and cake plates. It's really a shame because it has a simple charm, a delicacy that I find appealing and think collectors would, too, if they'd stop to consider this pattern! The silver rimmed pieces are elegant looking in a complete table setting! This is another pattern I can heartily recommend to people with limited funds to spend but who want a pretty pattern to collect. It would probably be especially suitable for young people.

The pink and green pitchers in the back are the rarely seen variety. Tumblers have been found to match both, now. (You can see the green pictured). A boxed set of six pink tumblers turned up; oddly enough, three were silk screened with the "S" Pattern, and three were perfectly plain! The normally found "S" Pattern pitcher has the fat shape of the American Sweetheart pitcher. One was pictured in the 4th edition along with a tid-bit server and an unusual Monax plate.

There are two sizes of cake plates to be found in "S" Pattern. Unlike it's sister Dogwood pattern, the harder to find one is the 13″ rather than the 11″. That amber cake plate pictured is the only one of those I've ever seen.

Two distinct shades of yellow occur in "S" pattern, a very light, pretty yellow and a more honey amber color, like the cake plate. There seems to be more amber available than the other, lighter color; therefore, there are more collectors for the amber.

	Crystal	Yellow, Amber, Crystal With Trims
*Bowl, 5½″ Cereal	2.50	3.50
Bowl, 8½″ Large Berry	6.50	12.50
*Creamer, Thick or Thin	4.00	5.50
*Cup, Thick or Thin	2.50	3.50
Pitcher, 80 oz. (Like "Dogwood") (Green or Pink 495.00)	37.50	67.50
Pitcher, 80 oz. (Like "American Sweetheart")	47.50	52.50
Plate, 6″ Sherbet (Monax: 14.00)	1.50	2.00
**Plate, 8″ Luncheon	2.00	2.50
Plate, 9¼″ Dinner	3.50	4.50
Plate, Grill	2.50	4.50
Plate, 11″ Heavy Cake	30.00	32.50
***Plate, 13″ Heavy Cake	47.50	57.50
*Saucer	1.50	2.00
Sherbet, Low Footed	3.50	4.50
*Sugar, Thick and Thin	4.00	5.50
Tumbler, 3½″, 5 oz.	2.50	4.50
Tumbler, 4″, 9 oz. (Green or Pink: 57.50)	3.50	5.50
Tumbler, 4¼″, 10 oz.	3.50	6.00
Tumbler, 5″, 12 oz.	4.50	6.50

*Fired-on red items will run approximately two times price of amber.
 **Deep Red — $50.00.
***Amber — $77.50

SANDWICH HOCKING GLASS COMPANY, 1939-1964; 1977

Colors:

| Crystal | 1950's-1960's | Pink | 1939-1940 | Forest Green | 1950's-1960's |
| Amber | 1960's | Royal Ruby | 1939-1940 | White (opaque) | 1950's |

Notice the pattern shot of a never before seen 9 ounce footed AMBER tumbler!

Thankfully, the Sandwich most collected is that of Anchor Hocking. (When you turn the page, you'll understand that statement a little better). Crystal is the color most sought with Forest Green presently running a close second. Some investment minded collectors noted the shortage of all items in green (save for the five pieces which were packaged in Mother's Oats and sold all over the nation) and set out to latch onto those items which caused quite a flurry of activity in green Sandwich for a time. The five commonly found items in green Sandwich include: the 5 oz. juice, 9 oz. water, 4-7/8″ berry bowl and the custard cup and liner. That same liner in CRYSTAL, however, is an elusive piece of glass.

I explained the scarcity of the pitchers in forest green in the 3rd and 4th editions. The larger pitcher has turned out to be even more scarce than the juice; but a small hoard of them which turned up from a warehouse recently took care of the present demand. (Some of the stories you hear of how people find these supplies down in sub level, rat infested, tenement buildings in neighborhoods even the daring would approach cautiouly should make us better appreciate these diligent dealers who are today's part sleuth, part adventurer).

No lid has been found for the green cookie jar. It was promoted as a vase.

There is an opaque white punch bowl set (stand, bowl, 12 cups) which is presently selling for $25.00-30.00. It sold in my area in the mid '60's for $1.79 with an oil change and lubrication at the Ashland Oil station.

Notice the iridized blue cup and saucer of unknown origin. No one has contacted me with knowledge of other pieces. Was it a luncheon set?

Anchor Hocking got briefly into the re-issue business by making a Sandwich cookie jar again. The newer version is larger than the old, however; there's no reason to mistake the two. The newer one has a height of 10¼″, a 5½″ opening and a 20″ circumference at it largest part. The older Sandwich cookie jar is only 9¼″ tall, has a mouth of 4-7/8″ and is only 19″ in circumference.

On the subject of re-issues, I would like to state the following:

It's only my opinion, of course, but I feel companies only hurt themselves with re-issues. They sacrifice their integrity or the "trust" factor they have with the collecting public which numbers in the millions; and they sabotage all that free prideful publicity the collectors give them when bragging to friends about their collections made by thus and so glass company during such and such years. That's got to be PRICELESS material (feed-back) to that company since it's BOUND to make persons hearing that "testimony" sit up and take notice of any other glassware that company advertises or is historical-ly associated with. Really, it's beyond me to understand the reasoning behind re-issues. If they ab-solutely HAVE to use old molds, they should always make pieces in **untried** colors. That way, the pieces MIGHT become collectible and thus would be marketable to larger numbers of people. Trying for old colors, besides showing no imagination, just destroys everybody's taste for any of it! What's being accomplished? A large scale destruction of an invaluable reputation for making fine, collecti-ble, valuable glassware, a reputation which was being built free of charge! Where's the sense ("cents") in that? Excuse me, ladies, but a former boss called that logic "pinching pennies to blow hell out of dollars".

	Crystal	Desert Gold	Ruby Red	Forest Green	Pink		Crystal	Desert Gold	Forest Green
Bowl, 4 7/8″ Berry	3.00	2.50	9.50	1.50	2.50	Pitcher, 6″ Juice	45.00		92.50
Bowl, 5¼″			15.00			Pitcher, ½ gal. Ice Lip	42.50		165.00
Bowl, 6″ Cereal	12.50	6.00				Plate, 7″ Dessert	6.50	2.50	
Bowl, 6½″ Smooth						Plate, 8″	2.00		
or Scalloped	5.00	6.00	15.00	20.00		Plate, 9″ Dinner	9.00	4.00	35.00
Bowl, 7″ Salad	6.50			30.00		Plate, 9″, Indent			
Bowl, 8″ Smooth						For Punch Cup	3.00		
or Scalloped	6.50		30.00	35.00	7.50	Plate, 12″ Sandwich	7.50	7.50	
Bowl, 8¼″ Oval	5.00					Punch Bowl & Stand	30.00		
Butter Dish, Low	32.50					Punch Cup	3.00		
Butter Dish Bottom	17.50					Saucer	1.50	3.00	4.50
Butter Dish Top	15.00					Sherbet, Footed	6.00		
Cookie Jar and						Sugar and Cover	12.50		*14.50
Cover	30.00	27.50		*16.00		Tumbler, 5 oz. Juice	5.00		2.00
Creamer	4.00			14.50		Tumbler, 9 oz. Water	6.50		2.50
Cup, Tea or Coffee	1.50	3.50		12.50		Tumbler, 9 oz. Footed	13.50	20.00	
Custard Cup	3.50			1.50					
Custard Cup Liner	7.50			1.50					

*No Cover   **Please refer to Foreword for pricing information**

178

SANDWICH INDIANA GLASS COMPANY, 1920's-1980's

Colors:

Crystal	Late 1920's-Today	Pink	Late 1920's-Early 1930's	Teal Blue	1950's
Amber	Late 1920's-1970's	Red	1933-1970's	Lt. Green	1930's

THIS GLASSWARE IS FAST BECOMING VIRTUALLY UNCOLLECTIBLE. READ ON!

If you haven't already read it, please read the last paragraph on the preceding page. I didn't have room on this page for all my opinions.

The big "news" is that Indiana has made for Tiara a butter dish which is extremely close to the old teal color made in the 1950's. It's available as a hostess gift item for selling X number of dollars of glass.

Because of the new Sandwich being made today by Indiana, I'm dropping crystal from my listing. It's become a collectors' pariah! The list is too long to examine each piece to tell the difference between old and new. In many cases, there is little difference since the same molds are being used. Hopefully, somebody at Indiana will wise up and stop making the old colors as I was told they would do after the "pink Avocado" fiasco in 1974. Instead of trying to entice collectors to new wares, they are stuck on trying to destroy the market for the old glassware which has been collectible for years but which may never be again. Perhaps you could start collecting Hocking Sandwich if you like the pattern. Sure, they re-made a cookie jar, but they carefully made it different from the old which showed their awareness of collectors in the field!

For those of you who have collected the crystal Indiana Sandwich or the teal butter dish and have a sizable investment involved, I can only say that time will tell as to the future collectiblity of this pattern. At present, it doesn't look too promising.

The really maddening thing is that all this "new" Sandwich is being touted to prospective buyer as glass that's going to be worth a great deal in the future based on its past history---and the company is steadily destroying those very properties they're using to sell the new glass! Supreme irony!

I can vouch for three items in red Sandwich dating from 1933, i.e. cups, creamers and sugars. May we assume a saucer accompanied the cup? I know this because these specific items are found with inscriptions for the 1933 World's Fair. However, in 1969, Tiara Home Products produced red pitchers, 9 oz. goblets, cups, saucers, wines, wine decanter, 13" serving tray, creamers, sugars and salad and dinner plates. Now, if your dishes glow yellow under a black light or if you KNOW that your Aunt Sophie held her red dishes in her lap while fording the swollen stream in a buggy, then I'd say your red Sandwich pieces are old. Other than that, I know of no way to tell if they are or aren't. NO, I won't even say that all old red glass glows under black light. I know SOME of it does because of a certain type ore they used then. However, I've seen some newer glass glow; but Tiara's 1969 red Sandwich glass does not.

Presently, the only two colors remotely worth having are pink and green; and who knows but what the company will make those tomorrow!

	Pink, Green	Teal Blue	Red		Pink, Green	Teal Blue	Red
Ash Tray Set (Club, Spade, Heart, Diamond Shapes)				Goblet, 9 oz.	15.00		
				Pitcher, 68 oz.	80.00		
$2.50 each	15.00			Plate, 6" Sherbet	2.50	4.50	
Bowl, 4¼" Berry	3.00			Plate, 7" Bread and Butter	3.50		
Bowl, 6"	3.50			Plate, 8" Oval, Indent for			
Bowl, 6", 6 Sides		7.50		Sherbet	5.00	7.50	
Bowl, 8¼"	10.00			Plate, 8 3/8" Luncheon	4.50		
Bowl, 9" Console	15.00			Plate, 10½" Dinner	12.50		
Bowl, 10" Console	18.00			Plate, 13" Sandwich	12.50		
*Butter Dish and Cover,				Sandwich Server, Center			
Domed	157.50	197.50		Handle	27.50		
Butter Dish Bottom	47.50	57.50		Saucer	2.50	3.50	6.00
Butter Dish Top	110.00	140.00		Sherbet, 3¼"	5.00	6.00	
Candlesticks, 3½" Pr.	15.00			Sugar, Large Open	8.50		27.50
Candlesticks, 7" Pr.	37.50			Tumbler, 3 oz. Footed			
Creamer	6.50			Cocktail	15.00		
Cruet, 6½ oz. and Stopper		127.50		Tumbler, 8 oz. Footed			
Cup	4.50	4.50	20.00	Water	12.50		
Creamer and Sugar on Diamond Shaped Tray		27.50		Tumbler, 12 oz. Footed			
				Iced Tea	22.50		
Decanter and Stopper	77.50			Wine, 3", 4 oz.	17.50		

*Beware new Teal

Please refer to Foreword for pricing information

SHARON, "CABBAGE ROSE" FEDERAL GLASS COMPANY, 1935-1939

Colors: Pink, green, amber; some crystal.   *(See Reproduction Section)*

You're looking at one of the most popular patterns in Depression glass; it's also one of the most durable. You'll find pieces scratched from years of usage; but you seldom find one chipped. I was told the salesmen used to put a plate on the floor and stand on it to prove its hardiness! It was manufactured in a time when items were made to last rather than programmed for deterioration.

Due to its popularity, the pattern has been hassled by reproductions of butter dish, cheese dish, shakers, sugar with lid and creamer. However, new is easily told from old; so prices for Sharon have never been jeopardized. See the section at the back of the book for further information on reproductions in Sharon.

There's always been a pricing differential between the green pitchers with and without ice lip. That same distinction is now found in pink and amber pitchers.

Green Sharon commands the highest prices; pink is the most in demand by collectors; and amber is probably the most scarce, but least noticed. Amber footed tumblers are more rarely seen than flat green ones! Thin tumblers in pink are preferred, but due to their scarcity on today's market, collectors are turning to the thick variety.

The cheese and butter dishes are pictured in pink. You'll notice the cheese dish bottom has a ledge of glass OUTSIDE the rim of the top. Otherwise, the bottom is the same as a regular salad plate. (The cheese dish is pictured on the left of the butter). The butter bottom, which was made from a 1½" deep jam dish, has a tiny ledge of glass on the INSIDE of that butter top lid. Its a very shallow ledge. If you tried to scoot the butter across the table by the knob handle, you'd scoot the top off the bottom.

New people confuse the 2" high soup bowl with the 1½" jam dish. Jam dishes are just like the butter bottoms only they don't have the ridge of glass for a butter top to rest against. Pocket measuring tapes are also helpful!

These items have been found in crystal Sharon: a 7½" salad plate, footed tumblers (both pictured in the 5th edition) and a few thousand cake plates. These cake plates are hard to sell to collectors; but present day cake decorating enthusiasts like them!

	Amber	Pink	Green
Bowl, 5" Berry	6.00	7.50	7.50
Bowl, 5" Cream Soup	16.50	30.00	32.50
Bowl, 6" Cereal	10.00	14.50	12.50
Bowl, 7½" Flat Soup, 2" Deep	22.50	27.50	
Bowl, 8½" Large Berry	4.50	16.00	20.00
Bowl, 9½" Oval Vegetable	10.00	16.00	15.00
Bowl, 10½" Fruit	15.00	25.00	22.50
Butter Dish and Cover	40.00	42.50	67.50
Butter Dish Bottom	20.00	20.00	30.00
Butter Dish Top	20.00	22.50	37.50
*Cake Plate, 11½" Footed	16.00	25.00	45.00
Candy Jar and Cover	35.00	40.00	117.50
Cheese Dish and Cover	157.50	600.00	
Creamer, Footed	9.50	12.00	13.50
Cup	8.00	10.00	10.00
Jam Dish, 7½"	25.00	80.00	32.50
Pitcher, 80 oz. with Ice Lip	92.50	105.00	300.00
Pitcher, 80 oz. without Ice Lip	95.00	100.00	320.00
Plate, 6" Bread and Butter	3.00	4.00	4.50
**Plate, 7½" Salad	10.00	14.50	13.50
Plate, 9½" Dinner	9.50	12.00	12.00
Platter, 12½" Oval	11.50	14.50	16.00
Salt and Pepper, Pr.	32.50	37.50	55.00
Saucer	4.00	5.50	5.50
Sherbet, Footed	8.50	10.00	20.00
Sugar	6.50	9.50	10.00
Sugar Lid	16.50	22.50	25.00
Tumbler, 4 1/8", 9 oz. Thick or Thin	18.50	20.00	40.00
Tumbler, 5¼", 12 oz. Thin	22.50	32.50	65.00
Tumbler, 5¼", 12 oz. Thick	22.50	45.00	65.00
**Tumbler, 6½", 15 oz. Footed	47.50	35.00	

*Crystal: $ 5.00
**Crystal: $13.50

SIERRA, "PINWHEEL"   JEANNETTE GLASS COMPANY, 1931-1933

Colors: Green, pink.

This is a surprisingly attractive pattern when you get bunches of pieces together and its still relatively inexpensive. It will take some searching to ferret out some of the more elusive items, however! Sierra is the Spanish word for "saw"; and because of it's "saw-toothed" design, you'll have to check every little serration for chips.

Sierra is "famous" in Depression glass circles for its combination "Adam-Sierra" butter dish. One is pictured in pink. Looking closely, you can see the saw-toothed Sierra pattern molded on the inside of the butter top while the Adam pattern motif is clearly imprinted on the outside of the top! Many collectors still lack this gem!

Notice the cups must have the saw like (uneven) edges before the rim of clear glass. Some people put any paneled cup atop a Sierra saucer.

Pink tumblers and pitchers are easier to find than green; but there are fewer collectors for the pink than the green; thus, demand makes the green higher priced.

	Pink	Green		Pink	Green
Bowl, 5½" Cereal	6.00	7.00	Plate, 9" Dinner	9.50	12.50
Bowl, 8½" Large Berry	10.00	14.50	Platter, 11" Oval	12.50	15.00
Bowl, 9¼" Oval Vegetable	23.50	40.00	Salt and Pepper, Pr.	25.00	27.50
Butter Dish and Cover	45.00	47.50	Saucer	3.50	4.00
Creamer	8.50	12.50	Serving Tray, 2 Handles	8.50	9.50
Cup	6.00	8.50	Sugar	12.00	10.00
Pitcher, 6½", 32 oz.	37.50	62.50	Sugar Cover	10.00	10.00
			Tumbler, 4½", 9 oz. Footed	20.00	27.50

SPIRAL   HOCKING GLASS COMPANY, 1928-1930

Colors: Green, pink.

Learn to ask for this pattern at shows if you collect this. Most dealer leave it behind at their shop. In fact, so many companies made "spiraling" patterns, most dealers tend to lump them all under that heading. Looking on the bright side, that broadens your range of choice!

Generally speaking, Hocking's spirals go to the left or with the clock and Imperial's Twisted Optic spirals go to the right or counterclockwise. However, Imperial's candy jar appears to go left---unless you turn it upside down; and Spiral's center handled server goes right----unless you look through the bottom. (That Spiral server is pictured, by the way, with Twisted Optic. Don't ask; but in simple terms, I goofed)!

The flat sugar and creamer were an early issue. The footed variety came last.

	Pink, Green		Pink, Green
Bowl, 4¾" Berry	4.00	Plate, 8" Luncheon	2.00
Bowl, 7" Mixing	4.50	Preserve and Cover	17.50
Bowl, 8" Large Berry	6.50	Salt and Pepper, Pr.	16.00
Creamer, Flat or Footed	4.00	Sandwich Server, Center Handle	13.50
Cup	3.50	Saucer	1.00
Ice or Butter Tub	13.50	Sherbet	2.50
Pitcher, 7 5/8", 58 oz.	17.50	Sugar, Flat or Footed	4.00
Plate, 6" Sherbet	1.00	Tumbler, 3", 5 oz. Juice	2.50
		Tumbler, 5", 9 oz. Water	3.50

Please refer to Foreword for pricing information

STARLIGHT HAZEL ATLAS GLASS COMPANY, 1938-1940

Colors: Crystal, pink; some white, cobalt.

If you want a challenge, try collecting Starlight sherbet dishes. I've had collector after collector ask me if I'd seen any other than the one pictured!

Cobalt bowls are the only items to turn up so far in that color; and the items pictured in white are all noted thus far.

I like the pink salad bowl with the metal stand holding the utensils! Neat!

	Crystal, White	Cobalt, Pink		Crystal, White	Cobalt, Pink
Bowl, 5½" Cereal	2.50	3.50	Plate, 9" Dinner	3.50	6.00
Bowl, 8½", Closed			Plate, 13" Sandwich	4.00	7.50
Handles	3.00	8.50	Relish Dish	2.50	4.50
Bowl, 11½" Salad	11.50	17.50	Salt and Pepper, Pr.	15.00	
Plate, 6" Bread and			Saucer	1.00	2.00
Butter	2.00	3.00	Sherbet	3.50	
Creamer, Oval	3.00		Sugar, Oval	3.00	
Cup	2.50	3.50			
Plate, 8½" Luncheon	2.50	3.50			

STRAWBERRY and "CHERRYBERRY" U.S. GLASS COMPANY, Early 1930's

Colors: Pink, green, crystal; some iridized.

I have asterisked and priced some items separately below because they are harder to find with the "Cherryberry" motif and therefore, bring more than Strawberry. All other items are of equal value to Strawberry.

If you see the picture and surmise that pitchers and butter dishes are easily found, you're wrong! Further, pitchers come with either Strawberry or what collectors have called "Cherryberry" designs and the "Cherryberry" type are even harder to get! Iridized pitchers, especially with good color, are rare!

Only the tops of the butter carry a design. The bottom is the same plain rayed bottom as Aunt Polly and Floral and Diamond.

The large sugar has no handle and is often found lidless and mistaken for a spooner.

The rarely found 6¼", 2" deep bowl is pictured here in "Cherryberry".

	Crystal, Irridescent	Pink, Green		Crystal, Irridescent	Pink, Green
Bowl, 4" Berry	4.50	6.50	Pickle Dish, 8¼" Oval	7.00	9.00
Bowl, 6¼", 2" Deep	20.00	35.00	**Pitcher, 7¾"	150.00	132.50
Bowl, 6½" Deep Salad	7.50	10.00	Plate, 6" Sherbet	3.50	5.00
Bowl, 7½" Deep Berry	9.50	13.50	Plate, 7½" Salad	6.50	8.50
*Butter Dish and Cover	97.50	125.00	Sherbet	5.50	6.50
Butter Dish Bottom	47.50	52.50	Sugar, Small Open	10.00	12.50
Butter Dish Top	50.00	72.50	Sugar Large	9.00	12.50
Comport, 5¾"	8.50	12.50	Sugar Cover	12.50	20.00
Creamer, Small	8.50	11.00	***Tumbler, 3 5/8", 9 oz.	13.50	20.00
Creamer, 4 5/8" Large	10.50	15.00			
Olive Dish, 5" One Handled	6.50	9.00			

*Cherry Motif — 137.50
**Cherry Motif — 127.50
***Cherry Motif — 18.00

SUNFLOWER JEANNETTE GLASS COMPANY

Colors: Pink, green, some delphite.

Take a look at that delphite creamer used as a pattern shot. Has anyone got the sugar bowl to match? It would be nice to photograph the two pieces together.

The price for the Sunflower cake plate which we used to disdain continues to spiral. It's still the most plentiful piece in the pattern due to its having been given away inside twenty pound sacks of flour during the Depression. I once saw 25 of these at a garage sale for 50¢ each--and only bought ten which I nearly never got rid of in the shop! Live and learn! I believe I could have "afforded" to hold them a few years!

The rarely found trivet is 7″ across and has a slightly raised edge. It is shown below and pictured in the back on the page showing the 2nd edition book cover picture. We often pictured rarely found items in Depression Glass on the covers of the past books. It seemed a shame to "waste" these pictures. So, we included them at the end of the book so you'd still have the opportunity to see some of the really rare items in Depression Glass that we have managed to "capture" on film, at least. I include that lengthy explanation because one gentleman told me he never understood what I meant by "2nd edition cover".

The odd mustard and mayonnaise colored pieces of Sunflower shown are unique to my knowledge. No one had ever found anything else like them until a cup like the mustard colored creamer turned up recently. Ash trays have turned up in delphite.

Pink, Green

	Pink, Green		Pink, Green
*Ash Tray, 5″ Center Design Only	7.00	Saucer	3.00
Cake Plate, 10″, 3 Legs	9.00	Sugar (Opaque $85.00)	8.50
**Creamer (Opaque $85.00)	8.50	Tumbler, 4¾″, 8 oz. Footed	13.50
Cup	7.50	Trivet, 7″, 3 Legs, Turned Up Edge	110.00
Plate, 9″Dinner	10.00		

*Found in ultramarine - $17.50
**Delphite - $50.00

SWANKY SWIGS 1930's-1950's

Swanky Swigs originally came with a Kraft Cheese product. In fact, the last one pictured still has the "Old English Sharp" cheese therein! It was priced 27 cents and was packed in 1954 paper. I'm only scratching the surface on these. If you want to delve deeper, there are lots of interesting articles on them in the *Depression Daze* newspaper, an ad for which is in the back of the book! You can still find these at bargain prices at yard sales!

Top Picture

Top Row	Band No. 1	Red & Black	3 3/8"	1.50 - 2.50
		Red & Blue	3 3/8"	2.00 - 3.00
		Blue	3 3/8"	2.50 - 3.50
	Band No. 2	Red & Black	4¾"	3.00 - 4.00
		Red & Black	3 3/8"	2.00 - 3.00
	Band No. 3	Blue & White	3 3/8"	2.00 - 3.00
	Circle & Dot:	Blue	4¾"	5.00 - 7.50
		Blue	3½"	4.00 - 5.00
		Red, Green	3½"	2.50 - 3.50
		Black	3½"	4.00 - 5.00
		Red	4¾"	5.00 - 7.50
	Dot	Black	4¾"	6.00 - 8.00
		Blue	3½"	4.00 - 5.00
2nd Row	Star:	Blue	4¾"	4.00 - 5.00
		Blue, Red, Green, Black	3½"	2.50 - 3.50
		Cobalt w/White Stars	4¾"	12.00 - 14.00
	Centennials:	W. Va. Cobalt	4¾"	12.50 - 15.00
		Texas Cobalt	4¾"	12.50 - 15.00
		Texas Blue, Black, Green	3½"	7.50 - 9.00
	Checkerboard	Blue, Red	3½"	15.00 - 17.50
3rd Row	Checkerboard	Green	3½"	17.50 - 20.00
	Sailboat	Blue	4½"	10.00 - 15.00
		Blue	3½"	8.00 - 10.00
		Red, Green	4½"	10.00 - 12.50
		Green, Lt. Green	3½"	8.00 - 10.00
	Tulip No. 1	Blue, Red	4½"	5.00 - 6.00
		Blue, Red	3½"	2.50 - 3.50
4th Row	Tulip No. 1	Green	4½"	5.00 - 6.00
		Green, Black	3½"	2.50 - 3.50
		Green w/Label	3½"	4.00 - 5.00
	Tulip No. 2	Red, Green, Black	3½"	12.00 - 15.00
	Carnival	Blue, Red	3½"	2.50 - 3.50
		Green, Yellow	3½"	6.00 - 8.00
	Tulip No. 3	Dk. Blue, Lt. Blue	3¾"	1.00 - 2.00

Second Picture

1st Row	Tulip No. 3	Red, Yellow	3¾"	1.00 - 2.00
	Posey: Tulip	Red	4½"	10.00 - 12.00
		Red	3½"	2.00 - 3.00
		Red	3¼"	6.00 - 8.00
	Posey: Violet, Jonquil, Cornflower No. 1		4½"	10.00 - 12.00
	Posey: Violet, Jonquil, Cornflower No. 1		3½"	2.00 - 3.00
	Cornflower No. 2	Lt. Blue, Dk. Blue	3½"	1.50 - 2.50
2nd Row	Cornflower No. 2	Red, Yellow	3½"	1.50 - 2.50
	Forget-Me-Not	Dk. Blue, Blue, Red, Yellow	3½"	1.00 - 2.00
		Yellow w/Label	3½"	3.00 - 4.00
	Daisy	Red & White; Red, White, & Green	3¾"	1.00 - 1.50
	Bustling Betsy	Blue	3¾"	1.00 - 2.00
		Blue	3¼"	4.00 - 5.00
		Green, Orange	3¾"	1.00 - 2.00
3rd Row	Bustling Betsy	Yellow, Red, Brown	3¾"	1.00 - 2.00
	Antique Pattern:			
	Clock & Coal Scuttle	Brown	3¾"	1.00 - 2.00
	Lamp & Kettle	Blue	3¾"	1.00 - 2.00
	Coffee Grinder & Plate	Green	3¾"	1.00 - 2.00
	Spinning Wheel & Bellows	Red	3¾"	1.00 - 2.00
	Coffee Pot & Trivet	Black	3¾"	1.00 - 2.00
	Churn & Cradle	Orange	3¾"	1.00 - 2.00
4th Row	Kiddie Cup:			
	Squirrel & Deer	Brown	3¾"	1.00 - 2.00
	Bear & Pig	Blue	3¾"	1.00 - 2.00
	Cat & Rabbit	Green	3¾"	1.00 - 2.00
	Bird & Elephant	Red	3¾"	1.00 - 2.00
	Bird & Elephant w/Label		3¾"	3.00 - 4.00
	Duck & Horse	Black	3¾"	1.00 - 2.00
	Dog & Rooster	Orange	3¾"	1.00 - 2.00
	Dog & Rooster w/Cheese			8.00 - 10.00

Please refer to Foreword for pricing information

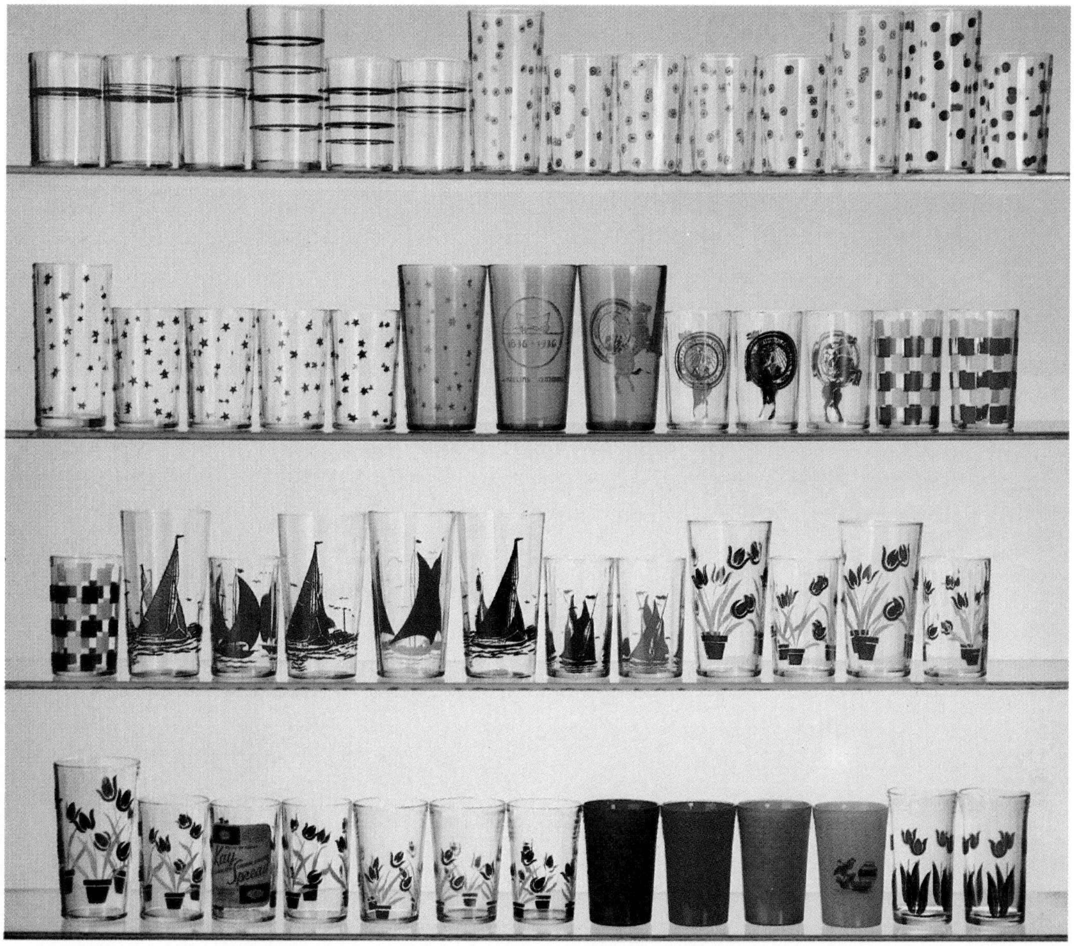

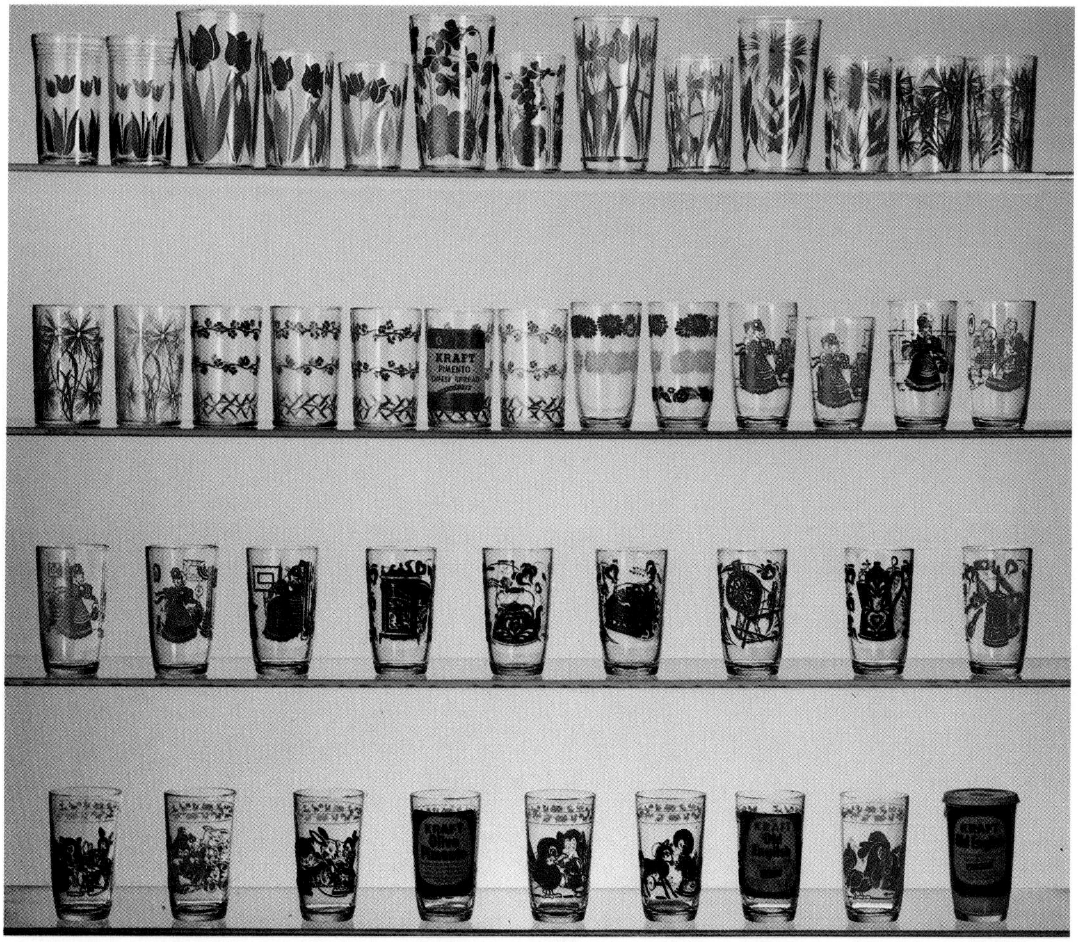
KRAFT
PIMENTO
CHEESE SPREAD

SWIRL, "PETAL SWIRL"   JEANNETTE GLASS COMPANY, 1937-1938

Colors: Ultra-marine, pink, delphite, some amber, ice-blue.

Since the ultra-marine Swirl pitcher was featured here as a pattern shot, two others have also been discovered! A picture is worth a thousand words . . . and that particular pitcher worth quite a bit more!

There aren't as many collectors for pink Swirl as for the ultra-marine color. Therefore, ultra-marine prices often outshine those for pink. However, potential collectors should know that the ultra-marine comes in a greenish and a bluish tint. Matching hues are oft times difficult! The greener pieces seem in shorter supply, but they are also less in demand.

Plates come with both round and fluted edges. Collectors generally prefer the fluted edges.

Coasters will have the concentric rings shown in the center of the ultra-marine plates. Sometimes collectors overlook these. Coasters were also used as an advertisement for General Tires and come encircled with small rubber tires!

Flat iced tea tumblers are hard to find in both colors.

A lot of collectors of Swirl dinnerware have been delighted by the Jennyware kitchen items made by this same company. See the Kitchenware book for pictures.

	Pink	Ultra-marine	Delphite		Pink	Ultra-marine	Delphite
Ash Tray, 5 3/8"	6.00			Pitcher, 48 oz. Footed		750.00	
Bowl, 5¼" Cereal	5.00	7.50	8.50	Plate, 6½" Sherbet	2.00	3.50	3.00
Bowl, 9" Salad	9.50	15.00	16.00	Plate, 7¼"	4.50	7.50	
Bowl, 10" Footed,				Plate, 8" Salad	5.00	9.50	4.50
Closed Handles		22.50		Plate, 9¼" Dinner	6.50	11.00	5.50
Bowl, 10½" Footed				Plate, 10½"			10.00
Console	13.50	18.50		Plate, 12½" Sandwich	7.50	13.50	
Butter Dish	130.00	197.50		Platter, 12" Oval			20.00
Butter Dish Bottom	25.00	40.00		Salt and Pepper, Pr.		27.50	
Butter Dish Top	105.00	157.50		Saucer	1.75	2.50	2.25
Candleholders, Double				Sherbet, Low Footed	5.50	9.50	
Branch Pr.	22.50	24.00		Soup, Tab Handles			
Candleholders, Single				(Lug)	12.50	14.50	
Branch Pr.			77.50	Sugar, Footed	6.50	9.50	7.50
Candy Dish, Open, 3				Tumbler, 4", 9 oz.	7.50	11.50	
Legs	6.00	8.50		Tumbler, 4 5/8", 9 oz.	10.00		
Candy Dish with Cover	55.00	72.50		Tumbler, 4¾", 12 oz.	15.00	35.00	
Coaster, 1" x 3¼"	5.50	6.50		Tumbler, 9 oz. Footed	12.50	20.00	
Creamer, Footed	6.50	9.50	7.50	Vase, 6½" Footed	11.50	15.00	
Cup	4.00	7.50	5.00	Vase, 8½" Footed		17.50	

TEA ROOM INDIANA GLASS COMPANY, 1926-1931

Colors: Pink, green, amber, some crystal.

A marmalade like the flat sugar, but with a notched lid has turned up!

There are some Tea Room collectors who still don't have pieces shown here in their collections. Notice the two handled tray and bowl in pink, the scalloped edge sundae tumbler, the oval vegetable bowl that has been "decorated", and the covered mustard jar with their dippers! I've yet to see a complete green mustard.

As the name implies, Tea Room was intended to be used in the "tea rooms" and "ice cream" parlors of the day. That's why you find so many soda fountain type items in this pattern. Plates, cups and saucers, however, in mint condition are very few and far between.

People who go for this pattern are fanatic in their admiration for it; others can't abide the sight of it. There seems to be no middle ground of acceptability.

New collectors should be aware that there are four different sugar and creamer sets in Tea Room. Two footed types, a 4½" and a 3½". Both are pictured. The 3½"fits on the center handled tray. There is a rectangular type which was pictured in the 5th edition book; and there is the type represented by the green sugar which is shown in front of the amber open sugar. It's covered, has no handles and looks like an enlarged mustard without the slotted top.

Prices for Tea Room still tend to be regional. In the 41 shows and 51,000 miles of travel this past year, highest prices for the pattern were found in Indiana, where it was originally made; New York, where its Art deco style is admired; Florida, where some avid collectors reside; and in Texas--- everything has ALWAYS been BIGGER in TEXAS!

Having examined many pieces found in their original packing, it is my firm belief that many of these items came from the original molds with tiny nicks and cracks in them. Nevertheless, pricing here is for mint glassware. Nicks and chips should lower the prices on pieces. As with Pyramid, you'll have to examine all the little ridges for damage and determine how much imperfection you're prepared to live with for the price being asked. A new wrinkle to watch for with the unscrupulous is clear fingernail polish filling in nicks. Take your bi-focals, if necessary!

	Green	Pink		Green	Pink
Bowl, Finger	22.00	20.00	*Saucer	11.00	11.00
Bowl, 7½" Banana Split	42.50	32.50	Sherbet, Low Footed	16.00	13.50
Bowl, 8½" Celery	22.50	17.50	Sherbet, Low Flared Edge	20.00	18.00
Bowl, 8¾" Deep Salad	47.50	37.50	Sherbet, Tall Footed	25.00	22.00
Bowl, 9½" Oval Vegetable	39.50	35.00	Sugar, 4" (Amber $40.00)	12.50	10.00
Candlestick, Low Pr.	30.00	25.00	Sugar, 4½" Footed	14.00	12.00
Creamer, 4" (Amber $40.00)	12.50	10.00	Sugar, Rectangular	12.50	10.00
Creamer, 4½" Footed	13.50	12.00	Sugar, Flat with Cover	37.50	32.50
Creamer, Rectangular	12.50	10.00	Sundae, Footed, Ruffled Top	27.50	22.50
Creamer and Sugar on Tray,			Tray, Rectangular Sugar &		
3½"	52.50	50.00	Creamer	35.00	30.00
*Cup	22.50	17.50	Tumbler, 8½ oz., Flat	47.50	37.50
Goblet, 9 oz.	52.50	42.50	Tumbler, 6 oz. Footed	17.50	15.00
Ice Bucket	37.50	32.50	Tumbler, 9 oz. Footed		
Lamp, 9" Electric	32.50	30.00	(Amber $45.00)	20.00	16.50
Marmalade, Notched Lid	87.50	77.50	Tumbler, 11 oz. Footed	27.50	22.50
Mustard, Covered	77.50	67.50	Tumbler, 12 oz. Footed	30.00	27.50
Parfait	37.50	32.50	Vase, 6" Ruffled Edge or		
**Pitcher, 64 oz. (Amber $250.00)	77.50	95.00	Straight	35.00	30.00
Plate, 6½" Sherbet	15.00	12.00	Vase, 9" Ruffled Edge or		
*Plate, 8¼" Luncheon	20.00	20.00	Straight	47.50	37.50
Plate, 10½", Two Handled	32.50	29.50	Vase, 11" Ruffled Edge or		
Relish, Divided	16.00	12.50	Straight	62.50	52.50
Salt and Pepper, Pr.	37.50	37.50			

*Prices for absolute mint pieces.
**Crystal — $175.00

THISTLE MACBETH-EVANS, 1929-1930

Colors: Pink, green; some yellow, crystal.

You will, of course, notice that the shapes of this pattern strongly resemble Dogwood. The same basic molds were used for both patterns. However, we're still hoping for pitchers, tumblers, sugars and creamers in Thistle. Dogwood pattern has such lovely ones. I hasten to add that there are perfectly plain pink and green pitchers of the Dogwood SHAPE that would work beautifully with the Thistle pattern. Be advised that it will take time to collect this pattern as these particular fifty year plus dishes are scarce.

Pink is more in demand than the green, possibly because luncheon items (cups, saucers, plates) are easier to find in pink than in green. Serving pieces are hard to find! That large 10¼" bowl pictured is even harder to lay hands on than it's Dogwood counterpart; and it probably won't be cheap when you find it!

I've seen very few grill plates in either pink or green. The grill plates will have the design on the edge rim only, leaving the center portion of the plate perfectly plain.

A cereal bowl, like the one shown, is the only piece to be seen so far in yellow.

I still get letters regarding a heavy pink butter dish with a thistle design on it. This piece is a new version of an older Pattern glass butter dish. It is not Depression glass nor does it belong to this pattern though you could use it with these dishes if you so desire. It's much heavier glass and a different color pink which, to my mind, argue against its blending well with this delicate Thistle pattern. (I am happy to answer letters regarding patterns in this book provided you include a self-addressed, STAMPED envelope. I receive around 400 letters a month and when my postage meter hit $275.00 for unstamped letters, I ceased to feel guilty about not answering them. I got to thinking that if an answer wasn't worth 20 cents to you, why should I waste my time and money? Try to be as brief as possible. Twenty page letters listing the contents of a china cabinet are not fun to wade through after a week long trip to and from a show! I really enjoy most letters, especially the ones from children and people just getting into glass! They're so enthusiastic! One little 15 year old entrepreneur wrote of how he'd bought a 15 cent piece at a yard sale, sold it for a profit, gotten interested enough to really study my book and now had an extra $200.00 in his college fund from his efforts at buying and selling Depression glass! Those kinds of letters are a real treat to get and enjoy! Thanks!)

	Pink	Green		Pink	Green
Bowl, 5½" Cereal	12.00	15.00	Plate, 10¼" Grill	12.50	12.50
Bowl, 10¼" Large Fruit	157.50	100.00	Plate, 13" Heavy Cake	70.00	85.00
Cup, Thin	14.00	17.50	Saucer	7.50	7.50
Plate, 8" Luncheon	8.00	12.50			

"THUMBPRINT", PEAR OPTIC FEDERAL GLASS COMPANY, 1929-1930

Color: Green.

I can't honestly claim that this is a great pattern in Depression glass. It isn't. Were it not for the sugar and creamer and cup and saucer collectors, there would be little activity in the pattern. If you enjoy challenges, its a nice little pattern to have the fun of looking for it; and when you find it, it won't cost much. Too, SETS of dishes are easier to sell! This is often confused with Raindrops pattern. See the explanation there of how the two patterns differ.

	Green		Green
Bowl, 4¾" Berry	2.00	Salt and Pepper, Pr.	17.50
Bowl, 5" Cereal	2.50	Saucer	1.00
Bowl, 8" Large Berry	6.00	Sherbet	4.00
Creamer, Footed	4.50	Sugar, Footed	4.00
Cup	2.50	Tumbler, 4", 5 oz.	3.50
Plate, 6" Sherbet	1.25	Tumbler, 5", 10 oz.	4.00
Plate, 8" Luncheon	2.00	Tumbler, 5½", 12 oz.	4.00
Plate, 9¼" Dinner	4.50	Whiskey, 2¼", 1 oz.	3.00

TWISTED OPTIC IMPERIAL GLASS COMPANY, 1927-1930

Colors: Pink, green, amber; some blue, canary yellow.

A blue sherbet has turned up on an off center sherbet plate, a kind of dessert set. The plate measured 7½" x 9" and was found here in Kentucky. These same pieces have been spotted in the bright canary yellow color. I'm beginning to see an increased stir in activity in Twisted Optic; so don't sweep this under the rug quite yet!

Twisted Optic's center handled server has a Y shaped handle. There's a space in the middle for gripping it. The spirals go left, also, which is generally the wrong direction for this pattern. The server shown belongs to the Spiral pattern. (See Spiral explanation).

	All Colors		All Colors
Bowl, 4¾" Cream Soup	5.50	Plate, 8" Luncheon	2.00
Bowl, 5" Cereal	2.00	Preserve (Same as Candy but with	
Bowl, 7" Salad or Soup	5.50	Slot in Lid)	17.50
Candlesticks, 3" Pr.	10.00	Sandwich Server, Center Handle	12.50
Candy Jar and Cover	15.00	Sandwich Server, Two Handled	5.50
Creamer	4.50	Saucer	1.00
Cup	2.50	Sherbet	4.00
Pitcher, 64 oz.	17.50	Sugar	4.50
Plate, 6" Sherbet	1.50	Tumbler, 4½", 9 oz.	4.50
Plate, 7" Salad	2.00	Tumbler, 5¼", 12 oz.	6.50
Plate, 7½" x 9" Oval with Indent	3.50		

"VICTORY"   DIAMOND GLASS-WARE COMPANY, 1929-1932

Colors: Amber, green; some cobalt blue; black.

Most pieces of this pattern seem to come from the Ohio - Pennsylvania area. Many of the pieces found have gold or painted trims like the console bowl and candlesticks shown in the picture. I have talked to several people who say they have six and eight place settings of this in cobalt blue. A cup and saucer and the blue sandwich server shown as a pattern shot in the 4th edition are the only cobalt blue items I've actually seen.

The most desirable pieces to own include the gravy boat and platter, goblets, soup and cereal bowls. All of these items are rarely seen.

Most flat pieces have ground bottoms rather than molded ones, further attesting to the fact that this was among the better glasswares of that day and probably why there is so little of it found today!

	Pink, Green	Amber, Blue
Bowl, 6½" Cereal	5.50	7.50
Bowl, 8½" Flat Soup	8.50	9.50
Bowl, 9" Oval Vegetable	15.00	25.00
Bowl, 12" Console	15.00	27.50
Candlesticks, 3" Pr.	15.00	25.00
Cheese & Cracker Set, 12" Indented Plate & Compote	17.50	
Comport, 6" Tall, 6¾" Diameter	8.50	10.00
Creamer	7.50	10.00
Cup	5.00	6.00
Goblet, 5", 7 oz.	12.50	17.50
Gravy Boat and Platter	95.00	97.50
Mayonnaise Set: 3½" Tall, 5½" Across, 8½" Indented Plate w/Ladle	27.50	35.00
Plate, 6" Bread and Butter	2.50	3.00
Plate, 7" Salad	3.50	5.50
Plate, 8" Luncheon	4.00	5.00
Plate, 9" Dinner	10.00	11.50
Platter, 12"	15.00	22.50
Sandwich Server, Center Handle	15.00	35.00
Saucer	2.00	4.00
Sherbet, Footed	7.50	10.00
Sugar	7.00	11.50

VITROCK, "FLOWER RIM"   HOCKING GLASS COMPANY, 1934-1937

Colors: White and white w/fired-on colors, usually red or green.

Upon closer examination, the two decaled pieces shown here are Indiana's white custard line, which is what this "Flower Rimmed" pattern is often mistaken for; so, perhaps this was a fortuitous mistake since it will allow comparison. The obvious difference is the SHAPE.

Actually, Hocking sold a whole raft of this white Vitrock ware, particularly kitchenware items. (See *Kitchen Glassware of the Depression Years* for further information on this). Notice the odd shaping of the sugar and creamer. That soup bowl, turned upside down to show the pattern, is a very hard item to find!

	White		White
Bowl, 4" Berry	3.00	Plate, 8¾" Luncheon	2.00
Bowl, 5½" Cream Soup	7.50	Plate, 9" Soup	3.50
Bowl, 6" Fruit	3.00	Plate, 10" Dinner	3.50
Bowl, 7½" Cereal	2.50	Platter, 11½"	12.00
Bowl, 9½" Vegetable	5.00	Saucer	1.00
Creamer, Oval	3.00	Sugar, Oval	3.00
Cup	2.00		
Plate, 7¼" Salad	1.50		

WATERFORD, "WAFFLE" HOCKING GLASS COMPANY, 1938-1944

Colors: Crystal, pink; some yellow, white; 1950's, forest green.

Our Grannie Bear Antique Shop can really sell this pattern! Every set I bring in is gone almost before I get it unpacked! You don't see much of the pink around any more; that's all gone into carefully treasured collections.

Notice the unusual yellow plate shown in the photo at the left and the ash tray which we over turned to show you the design. The interior of that ash tray is sprayed a "Dusty Rose" color, a color found in Oyster and Pearl fired-on bowls and candlesticks.

Other novel items to watch for include some pieces styled like Miss America. They are a crystal creamer and sugar, a pink water goblet complete with three rings encircling the top, and a 3½", 5 oz. juice tumbler in pink. Perhaps I can get these pictured next time.

Difficult pieces to find include cereal bowls, pitchers, and butter dishes in pink. The red trimmed goblets are also rather elusive.

The Post Cereals advertising ash trays, one shown, sell for $4.00-5.00.

A 13½" relish tray was made in Forest Green in the early '50's. The tray sells for about $5.00 by itself. Usually the inserts are missing.

	Crystal	Pink		Crystal	Pink
Ash Tray, 4"	2.50	5.50	Plate, 6" Sherbet	1.50	3.50
Bowl, 4¾" Berry	3.50	6.50	Plate, 7 1/8" Salad	2.00	3.50
Bowl, 5½" Cereal	6.50	12.00	Plate, 9 5/8" Dinner	5.00	10.00
Bowl, 8¼" Large Berry	6.00	12.00	Plate, 10¼" Handled Cake	5.00	9.50
Butter Dish and Cover	20.00	177.50	Plate, 13¾" Sandwich	5.00	8.50
Butter Dish Bottom	5.00	27.50	Relish, 13¾", 5 Part	12.50	
Butter Dish Top	15.00	150.00	Salt and Pepper, 2 Types	7.50	
Coaster, 4"	1.50	4.00	Saucer	1.00	3.50
Creamer, Oval	2.50	7.50	Sherbet, Footed	2.50	6.50
Creamer (Miss America Style)	6.50		Sugar	2.50	6.50
Cup	3.50	9.50	Sugar Cover, Oval	2.50	10.00
Goblets, 5¼", 5 5/8"	9.50		Sugar (Miss America Style)	7.00	
Goblets, 5½" (Miss America Style)	22.50	40.00	Tumbler, 3½", 5 oz. Juice		22.50
Lamp, 4" Spherical Base	22.50		Tumbler, 4 7/8", 10 oz. Footed	6.00	10.00
Pitcher, 42 oz. Tilted Juice	15.00				
Pitcher, 80 oz. Tilted Ice Lip	22.50	97.50			

Please refer to Foreword for pricing information

WINDSOR, "WINDSOR DIAMOND" JEANNETTE GLASS COMPANY, 1936-1946

Colors: Pink, green, crystal; some delphite, amberina red, ice blue.

For the first time, Windsor is shown here in that lovely ice blue color!

Plates, cups and saucers have also shown up to match the amberina red pitcher and tumbler!

Difficult to find in pink are the candlesticks and the 4½", 16 oz. juice pitcher. Neither of these items have been found in green. I did hear of a lady in California who seemed to have candlesticks in her otherwise complete setting of green. Upon her death a dealer purchased her set of Windsor. When he washed the candlesticks, however, some sort of green dye she'd used washed off the candlesticks revealing crystal ones. She'd made her own green ones!

Berry bowls come with both round and pointed edges; the pointed edged ones are the harder to find.

The original comport did not have a beaded edge. The beaded edged one turning up in crystal and with various sprayed on colors is of recent vintage. The comport also originally served as a base for the rather unique punch bowl which was pictured in the 4th edition. The comport was inverted and used as a base upon which the large bowl rested. They were made to fit into one another in this fashion and sold with twelve cups. That explains why there are so many cups without saucers, too!

	Crystal	Pink	Green
*Ash Tray, 5¾"	11.50	30.00	42.50
Bowl, 4¾" Berry	2.50	5.00	6.00
Bowl 5" Pointed Edge		7.50	
Bowl, 5" Cream Soup	4.50	12.50	13.50
Bowl, 5 1/8", 5 3/8" Cereals	3.50	10.00	11.50
Bowl, 7 1/8", Three Legs	4.00	14.00	
Bowl 8" Pointed Edge		16.50	
Bowl, 8", 2 Handled	4.50	10.00	12.50
Bowl, 8½" Large Berry	4.50	10.00	11.00
Bowl, 9½" Oval Vegetable	5.00	10.00	12.50
Bowl, 10½" Salad	5.00		
Bowl, 10½" Pointed Edge		65.00	
Bowl, 12½" Fruit Console	10.00	50.00	
Bowl, 7" x 11¾" Boat Shape	11.00	18.00	20.00
Butter Dish	22.50	37.50	67.50
Cake Plate, 10¾" Footed	5.00	11.50	12.50
Cake Plate, 13½" Thick	5.00	11.50	12.50
Candlesticks, 3" Pr.	12.50	50.00	
Candy Jar and Cover	8.50	20.00	
Coaster, 3¼"	2.50	5.00	
Comport	3.00	7.50	
**Creamer	3.00	7.50	7.50
Creamer (Shaped as "Holiday")	3.00		
Cup	2.50	6.00	7.00
Pitcher, 4½", 16 oz.	17.50	77.50	
Pitcher, 5", 20 oz.	5.00		
Pitcher, 6¾", 52 oz.	11.00	18.50	45.00
Plate, 6" Sherbet	1.50	2.50	3.50
Plate, 7" Salad	3.00	9.50	10.00
**Plate, 9" Dinner	3.50	9.50	9.50
Plate, 10¼" Handled Sandwich	4.00	9.00	10.00
Plate, 13 5/8" Chop	7.50	14.50	15.00
Plate, 15½" Serving	5.00		
Platter, 11½" Oval	4.50	9.50	10.00
Relish Platter, 11½" Divided	5.50		
Salt and Pepper, Pr.	12.50	27.50	35.00
Saucer	1.50	2.50	3.00
Sherbet, Footed	2.50	6.00	7.00
Sugar and Cover	4.50	15.00	17.50
Sugar and Cover (Like "Holiday")	4.00		
Tray, 4" Square	2.50	4.50	6.50
Tray, 4 1/8" x 9"	3.00	6.50	7.50
Tray, 8½" x 9¾", w/Handles	5.00	18.50	19.50
Tray, 8½" x 9¾", No Handles		47.50	
Tumbler, 3¼", 5 oz.	4.00	9.50	10.00
**Tumbler, 4", 9 oz.	4.50	8.50	10.00
Tumbler, 5", 12 oz.	5.50	15.00	20.00
Tumbler, 4" Footed	4.50		
Tumbler, 7¼" Footed	7.50		

*Delphite — 37.50   **Blue — 37.50   **Red — 50.00

Please refer to Foreword for pricing information

Reproductions

NEW "ADAM"   PRIVATELY PRODUCED OUT OF KOREA THROUGH ST. LOUIS IMPORTING COMPANY

The new Adam butter is being offered at $6.50 wholesale. Identification of the new is easy.

Top: Notice the veins in the leaves.
New: Large leaf veins do not join or touch in center of leaf.
Old: Large leaf veins all touch or join center vein on the old.

A further note in the original Adam butter dish the veins of all the leaves at the center of the design are very clear cut and precisely moulded, whereas in the new these center leaf veins are very indistinct - and almost invisible in one leaf of the center design.

Bottom: Place butter dish bottom upside down for observation.
New: Four (4) "Arrowhead-like" points line up in northwest, northeast, southeast, and southwest directions of compass.
Old: Four (4) "Arrowhead-like" points line up in north, east, south and west directions of compass.

There are very bad mold lines and very glossy light pink color on those butter dishes I have examined but these could be improved.

NEW "AVOCADO"   INDIANA GLASS COMPANY Tiara Exclusives Line, 1974 . . .
Colors: Pink, frosted pink, yellow, blue, red amethyst, green?

In 1979 a green Avocado pitcher was supposedly run. It was supposed to be darker than the original green and was to be limited to a hostess gift item. I was supposed to get one for photographing purposes. However, I've never seen said pitcher. Did they make it?

The pink they made was described under the pattern. It tends to be more orange than the original color. The other colors shown pose little threat as these colors were not made originally.

I understand that Tiara sales counselors tell potential clientelle that their newly made glass is collectible because it is made from old molds. I don't share this view. I feel it's like saying that since you were married in your grandmother's wedding dress, you will have the same happy marriage for the fifty-seven years she did. All you can truly say is that you were married in her dress. I think all you can say about the new Avocado is that it was made from the old molds. TIME, SCARCITY and PEOPLE'S WHIM determine collectibility in so far as I'm able to determine it. It's taken nearly fifty years or more for people to turn to collecting Depression Glass--and that's done, in part, because EVERYONE "remembers" it; they had some in their home at one time or another; it has universal appeal. Who is to say what will be collectible in the next hundred years. If we all knew, we could all get rich!

If you like the new Tiara products, then by all means buy them; but don't do so DEPENDING upon their being collectible just because they are made in the image of the old! You have an equal chance, I feel, of going to Las Vegas and DEPENDING upon getting rich at the Black Jack table.

Reproductions (Con't.)

NEW "CAMEO"

Colors: Green (shakers); yellow, green, pink (child's dishes).

Although the photographer I left this shaker with opted to shoot the side without the dancing girl, I trust you can still see how very weak the pattern is on this reproduction of Cameo shaker. Also, you can see how very much glass remains in the bottom of the shaker; and, of course, the new tops all make this very easy to spot at the market. These were to be bought wholesale at around $6.00; but did not sell well.

The children's dishes pose no problem to collectors since they were never made originally. The sugar and creamer are a shade over 1½ inches tall and the butter dish is just 3¾ inches from handle to handle. I'm told miniature cake plate, cups, saucers and plates are planned at a future date. This type of production I have no quarrel with as they aren't planned to "dupe" anyone.

NEW "CHERRY BLOSSOM"

Colors: Pink, green, blue, delphite, cobalt, red, iridized colors.

Several different people have gotten into the act of making reproduction Cherry Blossom. We've even enjoyed some reproductions of reproductions! All the items pictured on the next pages are extremely easy to spot as reproductions (colors never made!) once you know what to look for with the possible exception of the 13″ divided platter pictured at the back. It's too heavy, weighing 2¾ pounds and has a thick, 3/8″ of glass in the bottom; but the design isn't too bad! The edges of the leaves aren't smooth; but neither are they serrated like old leaves.

I could write a book on the differences between old and new scalloped bottom, AOP Cherry pitchers. The easiest way to tell the difference is to turn the pitcher over. My old Cherry pitcher has nine cherries on the bottom. The new one only has seven. Further, the branch crossing the bottom of my old Cherry pitcher LOOKS like a branch. It's knobby and gnarled and has several leaves and cherry stems directly attached to it. The new pitcher just has a bald strip of glass halving the bottom of the pitcher. Further, the old cherry pitchers have a plain glass background for the cherries and leaves in the bottom of the pitcher. In the new pitchers, there's a rough, filled in, straw-like background. You see no plain glass. (My new Cherry pitcher just cracked sitting in a box by my typing stand --- another tendency which I understand is common to the new)!

As for the new tumblers, the easiest way to tell old from new is to look at the ring dividing the patterned portion of the glass from the plain glass lip. The old tumblers have three indented rings dividing the pattern from the plain glass rim. The new has only one. (Turn back and look at the red cherry tumbler pictured with Cherry Blossom pattern). Further, as in the pitcher, the arching encircling the cherry blossoms on the new tumblers is very sharply ridged. On the old tumblers, that arching is so smooth you can barely feel it. Again, the pattern at the bottom of the new tumblers is brief and practically nonexistent in the center curve of the glass bottom. This was sharply defined on most of the old tumblers. You can see how far toward the edge the pattern came on the red cherry tumbler pictured with the pattern. The pattern, what there is, on the new tumblers mostly hugs the center of the foot.

Now for a quick run down of the various items.
2 handled tray - old: 1-7/8″ lbs; 3/16″ glass in bottom; leaves and cherries east/west from north/south handles; leaves have real spine and serrated edges; cherry stems end in triangle of glass.
       - new: 2-1/8 lbs; ¼″ glass in bottom; leaves and cherries north/south with the handles; canal type leaves (but uneven edges); cherry stem ends before cup shaped line.
cake plate - new: color too light pink, leaves have too many parallel veins which give them a "feathery" look; arches at plate edge don't line up with lines on inside of the rim to which the feet are attached.
8½″ bowl - new: crude leaves with smooth edges; veins in parallel lines.
cereal bowl - new: wrong shape, looks like 8½″ bowl, small 2″ center.
       - old: large center, 2½″ inside ring, nearly 3½″ if you count the outer rim before the sides turn up.
plate - new: center shown close up; smooth edged leaves, fish spine type center leaf portion; weighs 1 pound plus; feels thicker at edge with mold offset lines clearly visible. (See next page).
       - old: center leaves look like real leaves with spines, veins, and serrated edges; weighs ¾ pound; clean edges; no mold offset.
cup - new: area in bottom left free of design; canal leaves; smooth, thick top to cup handle (old has triangle grasp point)
saucer - new: off set mold line edge; canal leaf center.

Reproductions (Con't.)

NEW CHERRY BLOSSOM (Con't.)

First of all, notice the cup bottom and the close up of the center design on the reproduction plate. Once you learn to recognize these "fake" leaves, you'll be able to spot 95 percent of the reproduction Cherry Blossom. These new leaves look like orderly docking stations at the local marina with a straight canal going down the center. Old Cherry Blossom dishes have real looking leaves, complete with main stem, delicate veins branching from that stem, and serrated edges. Notice the smooth edges of the reproduction leaves.

The Cherry child's dishes were first made in 1973.

First to appear was a child's cherry cup with a slightly lop-sided handle and having the cherries hanging upside down when the cup was held in the right hand. (This defiance of gravity was due to the inversion of the design when the mold, taken from an original cup, was inverted to create the outside of the "new" cup). After I reported this error, it was quickly corrected by re-inverting the inverted mold. These later cups were thus improved in design but slightly off color. The saucers tended to have slightly off center designs, too. Next came the "child's butter dish" which was never made by Jeannette. It was essentially the child's cup without a handle turned upside down over the saucer and having a little glob of glass added as a knob for lifting purposes. You could get this item in pink, green, light blue, cobalt, gray-green, and iridescent carnival colors. A blue one is pictured on the preceding page.

Pictured are the colors made so far in the butter dishes and shakers begun in 1977. Some shakers were dated '77 on the bottom and were marketed at the ridiculous price of $27.95, a whopping profit margin! Shortly afterward, the non dated variety appeared. How can you tell new shakers from old--- should you get the one in a million chance to do so?

First, look at the tops. New tops COULD indicate new shakers. Next, notice the protruding ledges beneath the tops. They are squared off juts rather than the nicely rounded scallops on the old (which are pictured under Cherry Blossom pattern). The design on the newer shakers is often weak in spots. Finally, notice how far up inside the shakers the solid glass (next to the foot) remains. The newer shakers have almost half again as much glass in that area. They appear to be ¼ full of glass before you ever add the salt!

Butter dishes are naturally more deceptive in pink and green since that blue was not an original color. The major flaw in the new butter is that there is ONE band encircling the bottom edge of the butter top; there are TWO bands very close together along the skirt of the old top. Using your tactile sense, the new top has a sharply defined design up inside; the old was glazed and is smooth to touch. The knob on the new is more sharply defined than the smoothly formed knob on the old butter top.

Reproductions (Con't.)

NEW "MAYFAIR"

Colors: Pink, green, blue, cobalt (shot glasses), 1977 onward.
          Pink, green (cookie jars), 1982.

Only the pink shot glass need cause any concern to collectors because the glass wasn't made in those other colors originally. At first glance, the color of the newer shots is often too light pink or too orange. Dead give away are the stems of the flower design, however. In the old that stem branched to form an "A" shape; in the new, you have a single stem. Further, in the new design, the leaf is hollow with the veins molded in. In the old, the leaf is molded in and the veining is left hollow. In the center of the flower on the old, dots (another) cluster entirely to one side and are rather distinct. Nothing like that occurs in the new design.

As for the cookie jars, at cursory glance, the base of the cookie has a very indistinct design. It will feel smooth to the touch its so faint. In the old cookie jars, there's a distinct pattern which feels like raised embossing to the touch. Next, turn the bottom upside down. The new bottom is perfectly smooth. The old bottom contains a 1 ¾" mold circle rim that is raised enough to catch your fingernail in it. There are other distinctions as well; but that is the quickest way to tell old from new.

In the Mayfair cookie lid, the new design (parallel to the straight side of the lid) at the edge curves gracefully toward the center "V" shape (rather like bird wings in flight); in the old, that edge is flat, straight line going into the "V" (like airplane wings sticking straight out from the side of the plane as you face it head on).

The green color of the cookie, as you can see from the picture, is not the pretty, yellow/green color of true green Mayfair. It also doesn't "glow" under black light as the old green does.

So, you see, none of these reproductions give us any trouble; they're all easily spotted by those us now "in the know"!

NEW "MISS AMERICA"

Colors: Crystal, green, pink, ice blue, red amberina.

The new butter dish in "Miss America" design is probably the best of the newer products; yet there are three distinct differences to be found between the original butter top and the newly made one. Since the value of the butter dish lies in the top, it seems more profitable to examine it.

In the new butter dishes pictured, notice that the panels reaching the edge of the butter bottom tend to have a pronounced curving, skirt-like edge. In the original dish, there is much less curving at the edge of these panels.

Second, pick up the top of the new dish and feel up inside it. If the butter top knob is filled with glass so that it is convex (curved outward), the dish is new; the old inside knob area is concave (curved inward).

Finally, from the underside, look through the top toward the knob. In the original butter dish you would see a perfectly formed multi-sided star; in the newer version, you see distorted rays with no visible points.

Shakers have been made in green, pink and crystal. The shakers will have new tops; but since some old shakers have been given new tops, that isn't conclusive at all. Unscrew the lid. Old shakers have a very neatly formed ridge of glass on which to screw the lid. It overlaps a little and has neatly rounded off ends. Old shakers stand 3 3/8" tall without the lid. New ones stand 3¼" tall. Old shakers have almost a forefinger's depth inside (female finger) or a fraction shy of 2½ inches. New shakers have an inside depth of 2", about the second digit bend of a female's finger. (I'm doing finger depths since most of you will have those with you at the flea market, rather than a tape measure). In men, the old shaker's depth covers my knuckle; the new shaker leaves my knuckle exposed. New shakers simply have more glass on the inside of the shaker---something you can spot from twelve feet away! The hobs are more rounded on the newer shaker, particularly near the stem and seams; in the old shaker these areas remained pointedly sharp!

New Miss America tumblers have ½" of glass in the bottom, has a smooth edge on the bottom of the glass with no mold rim and show only two distinct mold marks on the sides of the glass. Old tumblers have only ¼" of glass in the bottom, have a distinct mold line rimming the bottom of the tumbler and have four distinct mold marks up the sides of the tumbler. The new green tumbler doesn't "glow" under black light as did the old.

New Miss America pitchers are all perfectly smooth rimmed at the top edge above the handle. All old pitchers that I have seen have a "hump" in the top rim of the glass above the handle area, rather like a camel's hump. The very bottom diamonds next to the foot in the new pitchers "squash" into elongated diamonds. In the old pitchers, these get noticeably smaller, but they retain their diamond shape.

Reproductions (Con't.)

NEW SANDWICH (Indiana) INDIANA GLASS COMPANY Tiara Exclusive Line, 1969 . . .

Colors: Amber, blue, red, crystal.

The smoky blue and amber shown here are representative of Tiara's line of Sandwich which is presently available. (See Sandwich pattern for older amber color).

The bad news is that the crystal has been made now and there are only minute differences in this new and the old. I will list the pieces made in crystal and you can make yourself aware of these re-issues if you collect the crystal Sandwich.

Ash Tray Set
Basket, Handles, 10½"
Bowl, 4" Berry
Bowl, 8"
Butter Dish & Cover
Candlesticks, 8½"
Cup, 9 oz.
Cup (Fits Indent in 6 oz. Oval Sandwich Plate)
Decanter & Stopper, 10"
Goblet, 5¼", 8 oz.
Pitcher, 8" Tall, 68 oz. Fluted Rim
Plate, 10" Dinner

Plate, 8" Salad
Plate, 8½" x 6¾" Oval Sandwich
Sandwich Tray, Handled
Saucer, 6"
Sherbets
Tray, 10" (Underliner for Wine
   Decanter & Goblets)
Tumbler, 6½" High, 12 oz.

I discussed the red color made in 1969 under the Sandwich heading, Page 180.

See last two paragraphs of text under New Avocado.

NEW "SHARON" Privately Produced 1976 . . .

Colors: Blue, dark green, light green, pink, burnt umber.

A blue Sharon butter turned up in 1976 and turned my phone line to a liquid fire! The color is Mayfair blue---a fluke and dead giveaway as far as real Sharon is concerned.

When found in similar colors to the old, pink and green, you can immediately tell that the new version has more glass in the top where it changes from pattern to clear glass, a thick, defined ring of glass as opposed to a thin, barely defined ring of glass in the old. The knob of the new dish tends to stick up more. In the old butter dish there's barely room to fit your finger to grasp the knob. The new butter dish has a sharply defined ridge of glass in the bottom around which the top sits. The old butter has such a slight rim that the top easily scoots off the bottom.

In 1977 a "cheese dish" appeared having the same top as the butter and having all the flaws inherent in that top which were discussed in detail above. However, the bottom of this dish was all wrong. It's about half way between a flat plate and a butter dish bottom, bowl shaped; and it is over thick, giving it an awkward appearance. The real cheese bottom was a salad plate with a rim for holding the top. These "round bottom cheese dishes" are but a parody of the old and are easily spotted. We removed the top from one in the picture so you could see its heaviness and its bowl shape.

The butter/cheese dishes wholesale to dealers for around $6.00.

Reproductions (Con't.)

NEW "SHARON" (Con't.)

The newest reproduction in Sharon is a too light pink creamer and sugar with lid. They are pictured with their "Made in Taiwan" label. These sell for around $15.00 for the pair and are also easy to spot as reproductions. I'll just mention the most obvious differences. Turn the creamer so you are looking directly at the spout. In the old creamer the mold line runs dead center of that spout; in the new, the mold line runs decidedly to the left of center spout.

On the sugar, the leaves and roses are "off"but not enough to DESCRIBE it to new collectors. Therefore, look at the center design, both sides, at the stars located at the very bottom of the motif. A thin leaf stem should run directly from that center star upward on BOTH sides. In this new sugar, the stem only runs from one; it stops way short of the star on one side. OR look inside the sugar bowl at where the handle attaches to the bottom of the bowl. In the new bowl, this attachment looks like a perfect circle; in the old, its an upside down "v" shaped tear drop.

As for the sugar lid, the knob of the new lid is perfectly smooth as you grasp its edges. The old knob has a mold seam running mid circumference. You could tell these two lids apart blind folded!

While there is a hair's difference between the height, mouth opening diameter, and inside depth of the old Sharon shakers and those newly produced, I won't attempt to upset you with those sixteenth and thirty seconds of a degree of difference. Suffice it to say that in physical shape, they are very close. However, as concerns design, they're miles apart. The old shakers have true appearing roses. The flowers really LOOK like roses. On the new shakers, they look like poorly drawn circles with wobbly concentric rings. The leaves are not as clearly defined on the new shakers as the old. However, forgetting all that, in the old shakers, the first design you see below the lid is a ROSE BUD. It's angled like a rocket shooting off into outer space with three leaves at the base of the bud (where the rocket fuel would burn out). In the new shakers, this "bud" has become four paddles of a windmill. It's the difference between this 🌿 and this. 🌿

The shakers wholesale for around $6.50 a pair.

217

First Edition Cover

Amethyst   Right Center: Royal Lace Sherbet

Blue   Center Front: Princess Cup
                          Right Rear: Mayfair Pitcher

Green   Center Middle: Cherry Shakers
                          Left Rear: Mayfair Pitcher

Pink   Left Front: Cameo Wine
                          Right Front: Cameo Water Tumbler
                          Right Front: Cameo Creamer
                          Center Middle: Mayfair Footed Bowl

Yellow   Center Rear: Mayfair Pitcher

Second Edition Cover

Amber	Left Center: Madrid Gravy Boat and Platter
	Left Rear: Parrot Footed and Flat Iced Teas
Amethyst	Left Foreground: Iris Demi-Tasse Cup and Saucer
Blue	Right Foreground: Iris Demi-Tasse Cup and Saucer
	Center: Floral Sherbet
	Right Rear: Princess Cookie Jar and Florentine Pitcher
Custard	Left Center: Sunflower Sugar
Green	Left Front: Sunflower Trivet
	Left Center: Number 612, 9 and 12 oz. Flat Tumblers
	Center: Cherry Opaque Bowl
	Left Rear: Floral Juice Pitcher and Mayfair Cookie Jar
	Right Rear: Princess Footed Pitcher and Tumbler: Mayfair Liqueur
Iridescent	Right Foreground: Iris Demi-Tasse Cup and Saucer
Mustard	Right Center: Sunflower Creamer
Orange	Right Center: Cherry Opaque Bowl (Reddish with yellow rim)
Pink	Center Foreground: Cameo Ice Tub
	Left Foreground: Adam-Sierra Butter Dish
	Center: Cameo Shakers
	Rear Center: Waterford Lamp by Westmoreland (pattern not included) in book, but shown to differentiate from Miss America and English Hobnail)
Red	Left Foreground: Iris Demi-Tasse Cup and Saucer
	Center: Miss America Goblet
Yellow	Center: Cherry Vegetable Bowl
	Right Center: Dogwood Cereal Bowl; Adam 8″ Plate, Cup and Saucer
	Left Rear: Mayfair Juice Pitcher
	Right Rear: Mayfair Shakers

Third Edition Cover

Amber	Center: Moondrops Etched Butter
	Right Front: Victory Gravy Boat and Platter
	Left Middle: Cherry Blossom Child's Cup and Saucer; Florentine No. 2 Footed Tumbler
Blue	Left Front: Windsor Delphite Ash Tray
	Left Center: Heritage Berry Bowl
	Left Rear: English Hobnail Handled Bowl
	Right Center: Floral Delphite Tumbler
	Right Rear: Rock Crystal Berry on Silver Pedestal
Green	Left Center: Rock Crystal Shaker
	Left Rear: American Pioneer Lamp
	Right Center Front: Heritage Berry Bowl
	Right Center: American Sweetheart Shaker
	Right Rear: Floral Ice Tub
Iridescent	Center: Louisa Carnival Rose Bowl
Pink	Left Rear: Floral Ice Tub
	Right Middle: American Pioneer Covered Jug
Red	Left Middle: Windsor Tumbler
	Center: Cherry Blossom Bowl
	Center Rear: Rock Crystal Fruit Bowl
Yellow	Right Rear: Pyramid Pitcher

Fourth Edition Cover Description

Amber

Center Front: Radiance Butter Dish
Center Middle: English Hobnail Pitcher
Center Back: Tea Room Pitcher

Blue, Light
　　Cobalt

Center Left: Fire King Dinnerware Juice Pitcher
Center Right: Radiance Handled Decanter

Crystal

Center Back: Tea Room Pitcher

Green

Center Front: Mayfair Butter Dish
Left Front: Floral Eight Sided Vase
Left Center: Floral Dresser Set
Right Center: Mayfair Juice Pitcher
Left Rear: Rock Crystal 64 oz. Pitcher

Pink

Left Front: Mayfair Footed Shaker, 1 oz. Liqueur & Round Cup and
Saucer
Left Rear: Colonial Bead Top Pitcher
Right Rear: Princess Footed Pitcher

Red

Center Middle: English Hobnail Pitcher

Yellow

Right Front: Mayfair Sugar and Lid
Right Front: Cameo Butter Dish and Lid
Right Rear: Footed Pitcher

Publications I recommend

DEPRESSION GLASS DAZE

THE ORIGINAL NATIONAL DEPRESSION GLASS NEWSPAPER

Depression Glass Daze, the Original, National monthly newspaper dedicated to the buying, selling & collecting of colored glassware of the 20's and 30's. We average 60 pages each month filled with feature articles by top notch columnists, readers "finds", club happenings, show news, a china corner, a current listing of new glass issues to beware of and a multitude of ads!! You can find it in the DAZE! Keep up with what's happening in the dee gee world with a subscription to the DAZE. Buy, sell or trade from the convenience of your easy chair.

Name_____ Street_____

City_____ State_____ Zip_____

☐ 1 year-$14.50   ☐ Check enclosed   ☐ Please bill me
☐ MasterCard   ☐ VISA (Foreign subscribers - please add $1.00 per year)

Exp. date_____ Card No._____

Signature_____

Orders to D.G.D., Box 57GF, Otisville, MI 48463 - Please allow 30 days

A colorful magazine devoted to keeping glass collectors informed about all kinds of glass - antique to contemporary collectibles. Filled with articles, pictures, price reports, ads, research information and more! 10 "BIG" issues yearly.

Name_____ Street_____

City_____ State_____ Zip_____

☐ New   ☐ 1 year-$12.50   ☐ Single Copy $2.00
☐ Renewal   ☐ 1 Yr. Canada or Foreign $15.00 (U.S. Funds please)

Orders to P.O. Box 542, Marietta, OH 45750

223